THE LIFE OF
WILLIAM MAKEPEACE
THACKERAY

IN TWO VOLUMES

VOL. II

From a sketch by Richard Doyle in the British Museum.

Pellissier & Allen. Ph. Sc.

THE LIFE OF WILLIAM MAKEPEACE THACKERAY

BY

LEWIS MELVILLE

WITH PORTRAITS AND ILLUSTRATIONS

IN TWO VOLUMES

VOL. II

HERBERT S. STONE AND COMPANY
CHICAGO AND NEW YORK
MDCCCXCIX

TABLE OF CONTENTS

VOLUME II

LIST OF ILLUSTRATIONS

VOLUME II

CHAPTER XVII

THE NEWCOMES—THE FOUR GEORGES

CHAPTER XVII

THE NEWCOMES—THE FOUR GEORGES

AFTER his return from America, Thackeray only stayed three weeks in London, while he was transferring his household goods from Young Street to 36, Onslow Square, next door to his friend Baron Marochetti, the sculptor. Then with his children he went abroad. To Paris first, then in July to Baden-Baden, and in the same month to Newchatel, whence he wrote to Mr. Reed, whose friendship he had won in America: "The European continent swarms with your people [Americans]. They are not all as polished as Chesterfield. . . . I saw five of them at Basle the other night with their knives down their throats. It was awful. My daughter saw it, and I was obliged to say, 'My dear, your great-great-grandmother, one of the finest ladies of the old school I ever saw, always applied cold steel to her wittles.' It's no *crime* to eat with a knife, which is all very well, but I wish five of 'em at a time wouldn't."*

They wintered at Rome, where they met Mrs. Kemble, Mrs. Sartoris, and Mr. Browning and his wife, who wrote to Miss Mitford, "If anybody wants small talk by

*Thackeray must surely have been thinking of this scene when, many years later, he wrote in a *Roundabout Paper:* "I don't know whether you have ever . . . seen, as I have, a whole tablefull of people performing the same trick [swallowing their knives], but if you look at their eyes when they do it, I assure you there is a roll in them which is dreadful."

handfuls, or glittering dust swept out of salons, here's Mr. Thackeray."

Before he left Washington for the South, his *Lectures on the English Humourists* were announced by Messrs. Harper in the list of their forthcoming publications.* A gentleman, who was conversing with him, asked if the volume would be published before he had finished his tour. "Bless you, no," the great man replied. "Do you think I'd rip open my goose?" But when that reason no longer existed [1853] they were published with notes by James Hannay, simultaneously in England and America, but without illustrations, though Thackeray had actually sketched Steele and Dr. Johnson and Boswell before the idea was abandoned.†

Thackeray's next great book, which ranks with *Barry Lyndon*, *Vanity Fair*, *Pendennis*, and *Esmond*, was *The Newcomes: Memoirs of a Most Respectable Family* (*Edited by Arthur Pendennis, Esq.*). The first number—for this was published in monthly parts—appeared in October, 1853, the last in August, 1855.‡ Much of this novel was written while he was abroad, travelling in Germany, Switzerland, and Italy, or staying at the

*In connection with the publication of this volume, Thackeray called on Mr. Harper, who introduced one of his little daughters to him. Thackeray patted her head gravely and then remarked kindly, "So this is a Pirate's daughter." Mr. Harper told him that the list of successful authors was just then headed by George Payne Rainsford James, a fact that greatly astonished the visitor.

†A later edition of the *Humourists* has been illustrated by Mr. F. Barnard; of the *Four Georges* by Mr. Frank Dicksee, R.A.; and of *Esmond* by the late Mr. Du Maurier.

‡Thackeray wrote a letter to the editor of The *Times*, which appeared in the paper, November 23, headed *Mr. Washington*, in answer to some strictures of the New York correspondent of The *Times* respecting a passage in the first number of *The Newcomes*, which had given offence in the United States. See Appendix.

The MS. of *The Newcomes* is preserved at Godalming, and is partly in Thackeray's hand, and partly in the hand of his eldest daughter and Mr. Eyre Crowe.

MR. THACKERAY'S NEW MONTHLY WORK.

THE NEWCOMES

EDITED BY

ARTHUR PENDENNIS ESQre

ILLUSTRATED by RICHARD DOYLE.

LONDON: BRADBURY AND EVANS, 11, BOUVERIE STREET.
1854

No. 6. MARCH. Price 1s

Château de Brecquerecque at Boulogne-sur-Mer. While in Boulogne he was attended by Dr. Corkesley, the well-known English physician of that town, who was so engrossed by *The Newcomes* that he absent-mindedly addressed his patient as "Mr. Honeyman" throughout the whole of the first interview, to Thackeray's intense amusement.

In the next year Thackeray made a last attempt to get a position under Government, this time in the Diplomatic service. "The Secretaryship of our Legation at Washington was vacant the other day, and I instantly asked for it," he said in a letter to Mr. Reed, dated November 8, 1854; "but in the very kindest letter Lord Clarendon showed how the petition was impossible. First, the place was given away. Next, it would be unfair to appoint out of the service. But the first was an excellent reason—not a doubt of it. So if ever I come, as I hope and trust to do this time next year, it must be in my own coat, and not the Queen's."*

He was ill again during the latter part of the year. "I am just out of bed with the eleventh severe fit of spasms which I have had this year," he wrote to Mr. Reed; and in the following summer, while staying at Rome, he caught the fever from the effects of which he never entirely recovered. It was just before this illness that he began to write that glorious nonsense *The Rose and the Ring; or, the History of Prince Giglio and Prince Bulbo. A Fireside Pantomime for Great and Small Children.* "One year at Rome," so runs a note by Mrs.

*"As for me," Thackeray wrote in 1855 to Miss Perry, "I have pestered you with my account of dollars and cents, and it is quite clear neither kings nor laws can do anything so well for me as these jaws and this pen—please God they may be allowed to wag a little longer."

Ritchie in *The Orphan of Pimlico*, "when we were living in an old palace over a pastrycook's shop, we used sometimes to ask little Pen Browning and the neighbouring children in to tea and tarts, and once (it was about Twelfth Night time) we tried in vain to find some Twelfth Night pictures to give them. When we told our father, he began to draw the king and queen for us, and the prince and princess. This was the beginning of *The Rose and the Ring*. One little maiden was very ill in those days with some horrid fever. My father, who used often to go and see her, went on with the pictures to amuse her as she lay on her sick bed. I can remember the child starting up eagerly, and tossing back her thick black hair, and some hand stretching out with the pages. Then he fell ill, and we left Rome."

After his recovery, he returned to London to prepare the second course of lectures, which, unlike the *Humourists*, was to be delivered first in America. On September 6, 1855, he wrote to George Hodder: "I want a little work done in the way of arranging papers, copying at the B. M., etc.—if you are free and will come here on Tuesday morning next, I can employ your services, and put some money in your way." This arrangement and copying was in connection with the lectures on *The Four Georges*, which superseded an earlier scheme for as many discourses on men of the world.*

Thackeray was one of the few men of genius who could dictate their work, and the commencement of this habit may probably be traced as far as 1849, when, after his illness, he was too weak to sit long at a desk, and was compelled to employ an amanuensis. At the house

*" He spoke of his intended lectures on the House of Hanover, and said he sometimes pondered the question whether every soul of these people he had to speak of was not d——d in the end."—SIR CHARLES GAVAN DUFFY.

in Onslow Square he usually wrote in his bedroom, for his study, a small room on the ground-floor, was exposed to the noises from the street. Mr. Hodder has recorded how Thackeray was sometimes in doubt as to whether he should commence operations sitting or standing or walking about or lying down; how often he would light a cigar, and after pacing the room for a few minutes, would put the unsmoked remnant on the mantelpiece, as if he had gathered fresh inspiration from the "gentle odours" of the "sublime tobacco"; and how, when he made a humorous point, which caused Mr. Hodder to laugh, his own countenance would be quite unmoved.

The literary labour on the lectures was completed during September, and Thackeray, with Mr. Hodder as his secretary and companion, made arrangements to depart on October 13. On October 11, a grand banquet, with sixty covers, was given at the London Tavern to wish him God-speed.* Dickens presided, and proposed the toast of the evening, and Thackeray endeavoured to deliver a carefully prepared oration. Some complimentary verses, by "A friend of the O'Mulligan," were recited. The last verse runs:

"I'm tould there's a banquet performing somewhere,
That a warm-hearted party assemble to hail him,
And a world-honoured penman is taking the chair.
I'd like to be present—I'm fond of such orgies:
And since he's about to be crossing the surges
To tell all the Yankees about the Four Georges,
'Fore George, there's a sentiment I would declare.
I'd say, 'Fill a glass to the sworn foe of Quackeray;
May his ship be helped westward by Ariel and Puck;
Here's health, fame, and gold, to our guest, William Thackeray,
And, in token, we gave him this horseshoe for luck.'"

*In the bill of fare there was turtle soup *à la* "Hobson Newcome," and *à la* "*bon voyage*"; there were omelettes *à la* "Becky Sharp"; and a salmi *à la* Fotheringay.

A few hours later came the dreaded parting from his children. Mr. Hodder, who had a business appointment with Thackeray for the morning of the 18th, witnessed the farewell scene. "When I arrived," he has since written, "I found him in his study, and his two daughters in the dining-room, all in a very tearful condition; and I do not think I am far wrong in saying that if ever man's strength was overpowered by woman's weakness, it was so upon this occasion, for Mr. Thackeray could not look at his daughters without betraying a moisture in his eyes, which he in vain strove to conceal." The business was transacted, and Mr. Hodder continues: "Then came the hour of parting! A cab was at the door, the luggage had all been properly disposed of, and the servants stood in the hall to notify by their looks how much they regretted their master's departure. 'This is the moment I have dreaded,' said Thackeray, as he entered the dining-room to embrace his daughters; and, when he hastily descended the steps of the door, he knew they would be at the window to

'Cast one longing, lingering look behind.'

'Good-bye,' he murmured, in a suppressed voice, as I followed him to the cab; 'keep close behind me, and let me try to jump in unseen.' The instant the door of the vehicle was closed upon him, he threw himself back in a corner, and buried his face in his hands."*

*He never forgot the agony of this parting, and many years later referred to it in his writings: "Worse still, man, you have just parted from the dear ones with bursting heart; . . . and, lonely man, just torn from your children . . . their little tokens of affection, yet in your pocket . . . pacing the deck at evening in the midst of the roaring ocean, you can remember how you were told supper was ready, and how you went down to the cabin, and had brandy and water and biscuit. You remember the taste of them. Yes; for ever. You took them while you and your Grief were sitting together, and your Grief clutched you round the soul."

For the second time Thackeray was bound Westward Ho! There is not very much to remark about this trip, except that it was even more successful than the earlier one. Longfellow went to one of the lectures, and "found a crowded audience, and had to take a back seat, where he could hear only about a half of a very agreeable lecture on the times of the first George"; and the poet and the poet-novelist supped together on the same evening. From Savannah, Thackeray wrote to Miss Perry: "I have brought a snug little purse from snug little Augusta, though I had a rival—a Wild Man, lecturing in the very same hall. I tell you it is not a dignified *métier*, that which I pursue."

On his return to Philadelphia, a young bookseller offered him a fairly large sum to repeat his lectures on *The English Humourists*. He was very loth to do so, but eventually yielded, partly owing to the urging of friends, and partly, no doubt, induced to do so by the liberal pecuniary offer. The experiment was, however, ill-advised, and met with very little success. It was too late in the season for one thing; besides, the lectures had been printed, and every one was familiar with them. The audiences were small, and the young man was losing heavily. All Thackeray's friends were disappointed; only he himself took it good-humouredly. "I don't mind the empty benches, but I cannot bear to see that sad, pale-faced young man as I come out, who is losing money on my account," he said to Mr. Reed, through whose agency the young bookseller had remitted the money due to him. Mr. Reed received no acknowledgment of the remittance, and he was not a little annoyed at this, especially when he read in a newspaper that Thackeray had sailed for home. The day after he had gone, when there could be no refusal, he received a certificate of deposit in a New York bank for an amount quite sufficient to make up the loss incurred in connection with the lectures enclosed in the following letter:—

"*24th April*.

"MY DEAR REED,—When you get this . . . Remember-ember me to ki-ki-kind friends . . . a sudden resolution. . . . to-morrow in the *Baltic!* Good-bye, my dear, kind friend, and all kind friends in Philadelphia. I didn't think of going away when I left home this morning, but it's the best way.

"I think it right to send back twenty-five per cent to poor H——. Will you kindly give him the enclosed; and depend upon it I shall go and see Mrs. Boot" [Reed's aged grandmother, then residing in England] "when I get to London, and tell her all about you. My heart is uncommonly heavy; and I am

"Yours gratefully and affectionately,

"W. M. T."

It was during this visit that Thackeray made the acquaintance of the well-known actor, Lester Wallack. Mr. Wallack, in his *Memoirs*, has given a picture of the novelist:—

"I thought him, with his great height, his spectacles, which gave him a very pedantic air, and his chin carried in the air, the most pompous, supercilious person I had ever met," he has written; "but I lived to alter that opinion, and in a very short time. . . . Thackeray then lived with a very great and dear friend of mine and my father's, and they had rooms together in Houston Street. I had a house next but one to them, and this is how I became so intimate with Thackeray. . . .

Thackeray, I suppose, took a fancy to me; at any rate it was understood every night, when I came home from acting, that if I saw a light in a certain window I was to go in. . . . When I did find them in, we never parted until half-past two or three in the morning. Then was the time to see Thackeray at his best, because then he was like a boy. He did not attempt to be the genius of the party. . . . Such an unsophisticated, gentle creature as he was. . . . On one occasion there was to be a dinner-party of four. Thackeray said it might probably be the last time he should meet us convivially during this visit, so we agreed to dine together with him. . . . After waiting a long time for Thackeray, at last there came a ring at the bell, and the waiter brought up a large parcel, and a note from him to say that a letter he had received compelled him to pack up as quickly as possible and start for England by the first steamer; and he added, 'By the time you receive this, dear William, I shall be almost out of the harbour. Let me wish you a pleasant evening with the Wallacks, and let me ask you to accept this little gift, as a remembrance of the many, many pleasant days and nights we have passed together!' The gift was a beautiful silver vase. I never saw Thackeray again; but our short and intimate association is one of the most delightful reminiscences of my life."

Thackeray, running away from his friends for fear of having to say good-bye, sailed in the *Baltic* on Saturday, April 20. The following letter, with the names suppressed, appeared in the *Academia* (No. 8, February 19, 1868). It is, I believe, reprinted from the columns of the *New York Nation*.

"On Board, Last Day, *May* 7, 1856.

"My dear old ——, I tell you that writing is just as dismal and disgusting as saying good-bye. I hate it, and but for a sense of duty I wouldn't write at all—confound me if I would. But you know after a fellow has been so uncommonly hospitable and kind and that sort of thing, a fellow ought, you see, to write and tell a fellow that a fellow's very much obliged and—in a word you understand. So you made me happy when I was with you, you made me sorry to come away, and you make me happy now when I think what a kind, generous W.D.R. you are. You have—back in the Bower of Virtue—you'll fill that jug when you one day drink my health, won't you? and when you come to Europe you'll come to me, etc., and my girls mind, and we'll see if there is not some good claret at 36, Onslow Square. . . . We have had a dreary, rough passage—yesterday the hardest blow of all. I have been ill with one of my old intermittent attacks, after which my mouth broke out with an unusually brilliant erudition, and I am going to Liverpool with a beard eight days long. It is not becoming in its present stage. I have not been seasick, but haven't been well a single day. Wine is ojus to me, segars create loathing—couldn't I write something funnier and more cheerful? Perhaps I may when we are fairly in Liverpool—perhaps we may be there to-night, perhaps not till to-morrow morning, for it blew a hurricane in our face last night, and the odds are we shall not have water enough to pass the bar.

"Home (*viz.* 36, Onslow Square,
"Brompton, London), *May* 9.

"We did pass the bar, and didn't I have a good dinner at the Adelphi, and wasn't I glad to get back to town yesterday, and wasn't there a great dinner at the Garrick club (the annual Shakespeare dinner, which ought to have come off on the 23rd ult., but was put off on account of the naval review), and didn't I make a Yankee speech, and oh lor'—haven't I got a headache this morning? I'm ashamed to ask for a sober-water, that's the fact. And so here's the old house, the old room, the old teapot by my bedside—the old trees nodding in at my window: it looks as if I'd never been away, and that it's all a dream I have been making. Well, in my dream I dreamt there was an uncommonly good fellow, by name W. D. R., and I dreamed that he treated me with all sorts of kindness, and I sent him and C.P.B. and D.D. (and what's his name downstairs?) my heartiest regards, and when my young women come home I shall tell them what a good deal of kindness their papa had across the water—so good-bye, my dear—and believe me always gratefully yours,

"W. M. THACKERAY.

"P. S.—Tell Tim W. that we hadn't a single actor at the Shakespeare dinner, and that F.F. and C.D. send their best remembrances to him. How did that Sunday dinner go off? Was it as bad as the dreary Friday?"

Soon after his arrival in London,* Thackeray made arrangements, through the agency of Mr. Hodder, to deliver the lectures on *The Four Georges* a certain num-

*"Yesterday I met Thackeray, who is just returned from the United States. He thinks there is every probability of the quarrel leading to war, for there is a very hostile spirit, constantly increasing throughout the States, and an evident desire to quarrel with us. He says he has never met with a single man who is not persuaded that they are entirely in the right and we in the wrong, and they are equally persuaded if war ensues they will give us a great thrashing: they don't care for the consequences; their riches are immense, and two hundred thousand men would appear in arms at a moment's notice."—GREVILLE'S *Memoirs*, June 1, 1856.

ber of times in London and the provinces for the sum of fifty guineas a time, which sum, however, was to include travelling and other incidental expenses. Mr. Beale himself had suggested the terms, which Thackeray accepted without showing any special elation, or letting the impresario see that he thought the offer anything exceptional, though as soon as the latter had left he remarked: "Fifty guineas a night! Why, I shouldn't have received half that sum for an article in *Fraser* a few years ago." He was always careful never to lower the market-price of his works, and, though exceptionally generous, after the success of *Vanity Fair* had placed him in the very front rank of men-of-letters, he invariably set the full value upon his literary labours. "Always ask enough," he said; "they can but drop you down a bit if they don't like it."

After the London lectures had been delivered, he went with Mr. Hodder, who acted throughout as agent for Messrs. Cramer & Beale, to Exeter, Plymouth, Clifton, Birmingham, and Oxford, at which city he was very well received by the undergraduate audience, and was so delighted at the enthusiasm of the young men that he exclaimed: "There's an audience for you! Gad, I'd lecture to those young fellows for nothing;" and he received many of them in his private room, where he thanked them for the sympathy and encouragement they had given him.*

*"I breakfasted this morning with Fowler, of Lincoln, to meet Thackeray (the author), who delivered his lecture on George III. in Oxford last night. I was much pleased with what I saw of him; his manner is simple and unaffected: he shows no anxiety to shine in conversation, though full of fun and anecdote when drawn out. He seemed delighted with the reception he had met with last night—the undergraduates seem to have behaved with most unusual moderation."—REV. C. L. DODGSON, *The Journal of Lewis Carroll.*

Norwich was the last place in England where the lectures were to be given, and here he was seized with one of the violent attacks to which he was subject, which delayed his journey northwards. Once in Scotland, however, he was lionised, and though Professor Aytoun advised him to "Let the Georges alone, and stick to the Jeameses," the lectures were well attended—in Edinburgh by actually three per cent of the whole population, which, gratifying as it was, only caused Thackeray to utter the wish, "Ah! if I could but get three per cent of London."

In connection with these lectures, many charges of disloyalty were brought against the author, and while they were being delivered in America, many newspapers and people asserted that he would never dare to read them in England. When, nothing daunted, he made arrangements for their delivery, a certain class or school of persons waxed exceeding wroth. Amongst these the place of honour must most certainly be given to a rector (whose father had been presented with a valuable living by George IV.), who was so enraged that he wrote: "An elderly, infidel buffoon of the name of Thackeray has been lecturing in town on the subject of the Four Georges, etc., etc."

These charges of disloyalty, absurd as they were, annoyed Thackeray very much indeed. He felt deeply the stigma of "traitor," with which he was branded by those to whom tradition is a part of religion, and who felt themselves as keenly injured by what they regarded as the slights paid to the memory of the Georges as if the satire had been directed against themselves.

"What is this about the *Saturday Review?*" he wrote from America to Miss Perry. "After giving Vernon

Harcourt *2s. 6d.* to send me the first five numbers, and only getting No. 1, it is too bad they should assault me—and for what? My lecture is rather extra loyal whenever the Queen is mentioned — and the most applauded passages in them I shall have the honour of delivering to-night in the lecture on George II., where the speaker says, 'In laughing at those old-world follies and ceremonies, shall we not acknowledge the change of to-day? As the mistress of St. James's passes me now, I salute the sovereign, wise, moderate, exemplary of life, the good mother, the good wife, the accomplished lady, the enlightened friend of Art, the tender sympathiser in her people's glories and sorrows.' I can't say more, can I? And as for George III., I leave off just with the people on the crying point."*

When he was delivering the lectures at Edinburgh in 1857, he thought it necessary, at a public dinner given in his honour, when replying to the toast, to repeat his defence.

"I had thought," he said, "that in these lectures I had spoken in terms, not of disrespect or unkindness, but in feelings and in language not un-English, of her Majesty the Queen; and whenever I have had to mention her name, whether it was upon the banks of the Clyde or upon those of the Mississippi, whether it was in New England or in Old England, whether it was in some great hall in London to the artisans of the suburbs of the metropolis, or to the politer audiences at the western end—whenever I had to mention her name, it was received with shouts of applause, and with the most

*"I heard one of Thackeray's lectures, the one on George III., and thought it better than good—fine and touching. To what is it that people are objecting? At any rate, they crowd and pay."—MRS. BROWNING to Miss Mitford, January 7, 1856.

Kensington. 12 September.

Dear Sir

Immediately after my lectures I went abroad and beg your pardon, for having forgotten in the hurry of my departure to return the MSS wh. you were good enough to lend me. I am sorry that reading the Bramin's letters to his Bramine did not increase my respect for the Reverend Laurence Sterne.

(XCII.)

In his printed letters there is one addressed to Lady P: full of love and despair for my lady, & announcing that he had got a ticket for Miss +++ benefit that night wh. he must use if deprived of the superior delight of seeing Lady P. I looked in the Dramatic ~~Record~~ quere (I think is the name of the book) to find what ~~young~~ lady took a benefit on a

Tuesday and found ~~her~~ the names of 2, 1 at Covent Garden & one at Drury Lane ~~that we~~ on on [the same] Tuesday evening and no other Miss's benefit on a Tuesday during the season. ~~The~~ Miss Poyntz I think is one of the names, but I'm 5 miles from the book as I write to you, and forget the lady's name & the day.

However on the day Sterne was writing to Lady P. and going to Miss —'s benefit he is dying in ~~and~~ his Journal to the Brahmine can't eat, has the Doctor, and is in a dreadful way. He wasn't dying but lying I'm afraid — God help him — a falser and wickeder man it's difficult to read of — Do you know ~~Swin~~

the accompanying pamphlet. (My friend Mr. Cooper gave me this copy, wh. he had previously sent to the Reform Club, and has since given the Club another copy) — there is more of Yorick's love-making in these letters, with blasphemy to flavor the compositions, and indications of a scornful unbelief. Of course any man is welcome to believe as he likes for me except a parson: and I can't help looking upon Swift & Sterne as a couple of traitors and renegades, as one does upon Bonneval or poor Bem the other day, with a scornful pity for them in spite of all their genius and greatness.

With many thanks for your loan believe me dear Sir

very faithfully yours

W M Thackeray.

hearty cheers. And why was this? It was not on account of the speaker; it was on account of the truth; it was because the English and the Americans—the people of New Orleans a year ago, the people of Aberdeen a week ago—all received and acknowledged with due allegiance the great claims to honour which that lady has, who worthily holds that great and awful situation which our Queen occupies. It is my loyalty that is called in question, and it is my loyalty I am trying to plead to you. Suppose, for example, in America—in Philadelphia or in New York—I had spoken of George IV. in terms of praise or affected reverence, do you suppose they would have hailed his name with cheers or have heard it with anything like respect? They would have laughed in my face if I had so spoken of him. They know what I know and you know, and what numbers of squeamish loyalists who affect to cry out against my lectures know, that that man's life was not a good life—that that king was not such a king as we ought to love or regard or honour. And I believe, for my part, that in speaking the truth as we hold it, of a bad sovereign, we are paying no disrespect at all to a good one. Far from it. On the contrary, we degrade our own honour and the Sovereign's by unduly and unjustly praising him: and the mere slaverer and flatterer is one who comes forward, as it were, with flash notes, and pays with false coin his tribute to Cæsar. I don't disguise from you that I feel somehow or other on my trial here for loyalty, for honest English feeling."

It is unnecesary to devote any space to the objections that were raised against the lectures—Mr. Trollope has stated them at full length—for I cannot see why it should be deemed even bad taste, much less disloyalty, to discuss the failings of four sovereigns who had been dead respectively for a hundred and twenty-five, ninety-five, thirty-five, and twenty-five years. Surely it is perfectly legitimate to criticise the acts and life of a public character, however highly placed, who has been dead for a quarter of a century, without violating any of the canons of decency or taste; and progress would indeed be slow if it were necessary to wait more than a century and a quarter after the death of a man before we might discuss his doings and argue the question of his morality.

At Hull, Thackeray met Mr. Charles Cooper (now editor of *The Scotsman*), from whose *Autobiography* I take the following rather amusing incident. Mr. Cooper attended the first lecture, and wrote a long account of it for the paper he then represented. The novelist sent a note to the office, asking the gentleman who had reported the lecture to call upon him; and Mr. Cooper, certain that his report was accurate, very proud of the invitation, and expecting praise, called. To his dismay, however, Thackeray began severely,—

"Do you know, sir, you have done your best to deprive me of my living. . . . I make my living by delivering those lectures. If they are reported, no one will come to hear them, and I shall not be wanted. . . . There are people who will be satisfied with your reports, and I shall be deprived of my just gains as a worker. . . . Confound it, sir, that is what I complain of [the excellence of the report]. If the report had not been good, I should not have cared. The public would have seen that it was rubbish that I could not have written." Then he changed the subject. "Now, young sir, what do you think of the lecture?"

"I thought it very clever," Mr. Cooper answered;

"but I thought you had used a great deal of cleverness in trying to hide a kindly heart under cover of a cheap cynicism. . . . Please remember it is the criticism of a very young man. Perhaps it is impertinent. . . . It struck me that the cynicism was what any clever man who chose to give his mind to it could produce, and therefore I spoke of it as 'cheap cynicism.' "

"Thank you," Thackeray said warmly. "Perhaps you are right. But no one has ever said such a thing to me before. Don't imagine I'm offended. *Ex oribus parvilorum;* you know the rest."

"I did," Mr. Cooper adds, "and I felt a little mortified. But the kindness of the tone soon removed all that feeling. I was a babe to him, and I had been a venturesome babe. . . . It made me much more modest in future in expressing opinions as to any man's literary work."

The lecture tour was concluded, and the last number of *The Newcomes* had appeared in August [1855]. He was doing nothing, for he had ceased to contribute to the magazines. Indeed, since 1852, excepting the *Fraser* article and the contributions to *Punch*, his minor writings consisted only of *Lucy's Birthday*, written in the album of an American lady, and afterwards reprinted in the *Keepsake* for 1854; *The Idler*, published in the *Idler Magazine of Fiction;* and the charming and pathetic verses entitled *The Pen and the Album*, which may have been suggested by a gift from an American acquaintance, as the following letter may show:

"GIRARD HOUSE, *January* 23, 1853.
[PHILADELPHIA]

"MY DEAR MR. BIDDLE,—This note is written with your gold pen, which suits me to a nicety, and which I shall always value as a token of the good will and friendliness of the kind giver. I believe I have never written for popularity, but God forbid I should be indifferent to such marks of esteem and confidence as now and then fall to my share, when scholars and good men are pleased with my works. I am thankful to have shaken your kind hand, and to carry away your good opinion. Please God, the gold pen shall tell no lies while it lives with me. As for the splendid case, I shall put it into my children's museum. I know how pleased and proud they will be at such tokens of friendship shown to their father.

"Believe me always, my dear Sir,

"Your faithful and obliged

"W. M. THACKERAY.*

"TO CLEMENT C. BIDDLE, ESQ.,
"SPRUCE STREET."

He had at this time collected his earlier writings, and they were now republished in four volumes by Messrs. Bradbury & Evans, under the title of *Miscellanies*, and no doubt contain what he considered the best of his *minor* writings, though that last expression can scarcely apply to *Barry Lyndon*.

*Haud Immemor.

CHAPTER XVIII

THE OXFORD ELECTION

CHAPTER XVIII

THE OXFORD ELECTION

THACKERAY, for some time past, had been looking for a constituency that would elect him as its Parliamentary representative, and when Mr. Neate (Professor of Political Economy), the member for the city of Oxford, was unseated in June 1857, for what Thackeray called "a twopennyworth of bribery which he never committed," he allowed himself to be nominated. He stood, of course, in the Liberal interest. His Tory, or rather Peelite opponent, was a strong man—no less dangerous an enemy than Edward Cardwell, a brilliant Oxford man, formerly with Gladstone and Lowe, one of the great lights of the Oxford Union; afterwards [1859] Secretary for Ireland, and later [1864] Secretary for the Colonies in Lord Palmerston's second Liberal administration; while under Gladstone he went to the War Office, and was ultimately raised to the Peerage.

Thackeray's address to the electors, dated from the Mitre, July 9, 1857, was a model of lucidity, and expressed very clearly his political opinion:—

"Gentlemen, I should be unworthy of the great kindness and cordiality with which you have received me to-night were I to hesitate to put your friendship to the test and ask you to confirm it at the poll . . . I would use my best endeavours, not merely to popularise the Government of this country. With no feeling but that of good will towards these leading aristocratic families who are administering the chief offices of the State, I believe it could be benefited by the skill and talents of persons less aristocratic, and that the country thinks so likewise. I think that to secure the due freedom of representation, and to defend the poor voter from the chance of intimidation, the ballot is the best safeguard we know of, and would vote most hopefully for that measure. I would have the suffrage amended in nature as well as in numbers, and hope to see many educated classes represented who have now no voice in elections. . . . The usefulness of a member of Parliament is best tested at home; and should you think fit to elect me as your representative, I promise to use my utmost endeavour to increase and advance the social happiness, the knowledge, and the power of the people."*

The canvassing went on apace, and Thackeray did all he could to win the seat. He even sent a droll note to Dickens, urging him to "Come down and make a speech, and tell them who I am, for I doubt whether more than two of the electors have ever heard of me, and I think there be as many as six or eight who have heard of you." But I do not think Dickens went.

As was only to be expected from two such men as Thackeray and Cardwell, the contest was conducted with much courtesy and generosity. When Lord Monck went down to address the electors for the Conservative candidate, he spoke in high terms of Thackeray; and the

*"Had a curious conversation with Thackeray at the Cosmopolitan about a French invasion, *à-propos* of the fiery Colonels, with regard to whom there was a great deal of talk at this time. He said, alluding to his recent candidature at Oxford, 'The chief reason why I wished to be in Parliament was that I might stand up once a year and tell my countrymen what will happen when the French invade us.'"—SIR M. E. GRANT DUFF'S *Diary*, April 4, 1858.

latter, when on the hustings, chided his supporters for hissing when the name of his opponent was mentioned. A characteristic anecdote was told in the papers by a friend of Thackeray, who was staying with him at the hotel. One day during the election he was looking out of a window, when he saw a crowd hustling and hooting some of Mr. Cardwell's supporters. Thackeray started up with an oath, and rushed down to the street, notwithstanding the efforts of some old electioneerers who wished to hold him back. He was next seen towering above the crowd, dealing about him right and left, in defence of his opponent's partisans, and in defiance of his own friends.*

The first day of the election Thackeray made a really good speech, part of which is well worth reproducing for its biographical interest:—

"As I came down to this place," he said, "I saw on each side of me placards announcing that there was no manner of doubt that on Tuesday the friends of the Right Hon. Edward Cardwell would elect him to a seat in Parliament. I also saw other placards announcing, in similar terms, a confidence that there was no doubt that I should be elected to a seat in Parliament for the city of Oxford. Now, as both sides are perfectly confident of success—as I, for my part, feel perfectly confident, and as my opponents entertain the same favourable opinion in regard to themselves—surely both sides may meet

*It is interesting to compare this reality with an extract from *The Newcomes:* "When Sir Barnes and his staff were hustled in the market-place, and most outrageously shoved, jeered, and jolted, the Colonel from the King's Arms organised a rapid sally, which he himself headed with his bamboo-cane, cut out Sir Brian and his followers from the hands of the mob, and addressed these ruffians in a noble speech, of which the bamboo-cane, Englishmen, shame, fair play, were the most emphatic expressions."

here in perfect good humour. I hear that not long since, in the memory of many now alive, this independent city was patronized by a great university, and that a great duke, who lived not very far from here, at the time of election used to put on his boots and ride down and order the freemen of Oxford to elect a member for him. Any man who has wandered through your beautiful city as I have done within these last few days, cannot but be struck with the difference between the ancient splendour, the academic grandeur, that prevailed in this place—the processions of dons, doctors, and proctors—and your new city, which is not picturesque or beautiful at all, but which contains a number of streets, peopled by thousands of hard-working, honest, rough-handed men. These men have grown up of late years, and have asserted their determination to have a representative of their own. Such a representative they found three months ago, and such a representative they returned to Parliament in the person of my friend, Mr. Neate. But such a representative was turned out of that Parliament by a sentence which I cannot call unjust, because he himself is too magnanimous and generous to say so, but which I will call iniquitous. He was found guilty of a twopennyworth of bribery which he never committed; and a Parliament which has swallowed so many camels, strained at that little gnat, and my friend, your representative, the very best man you could find to represent you, was turned back, and you were left without a man. I cannot hope—I never thought to equal him; I only come forward at a moment when I felt it necessary that some one professing his principles and possessing your confidence, should be ready to step into the gap which he had made. I know that the place was very eagerly sought for by other folks on the other side, entertaining other opinions. Perhaps you don't know that last week there was a Tory baronet down here, walking about in the shade, as umbrageous almost as that under which my opponent, Mr. Cardwell, has sheltered himself. Of course, you know there came down a ministerial nominee—Lord Monck; but you do not know that Mr. Hayter, who is what is called the Whipper-in for the ministerial party, came down here also on Saturday week, in a dark and mysterious manner, and that some conversation took place, the nature of which I cannot pretend to know anything about, because I have no spies, however people may be lurking at the doors of our Committee-room. But the result of all was that Lord Monck disappeared, and Mr. Hayter vanished into darkness and became a myth; and we were informed that a powerful requisition from the city of Oxford had invited Mr. Cardwell. Mind, Mr. Cardwell has given no note in reply—no mark, no sign. We do not know, even now, whether he accepted that polite invitation; we do not know it even to this day, except that his godfathers have been here, and have said so. After the manner in which the electors of Oxford have received me, could I possibly have gone back simply because we are told that Mr. Cardwell had received an invitation, which we did not know whether he had accepted or not? I feel it, therefore, to be my humble duty to stand in the place where I found myself. I do not know that I would have ventured to oppose Mr. Cardwell under other circumstances. I am fully aware of his talents. I know his ability as a statesman, and no man can say that I have, during the whole of my canvass, uttered a word at all unfriendly or disrespectful towards that gentleman.

I should have hesitated, on any other occasion, in opposing him, but I cannot hesitate now, because I know that we have the better cause, and that we mean to make that better cause triumphant.

"I say that any man who belongs to the Peelite party is not the man who ought to be put forward by any constituency at the eve of a great and momentous English war. As to my own opinions on public questions, you may have heard them pretty freely expressed on many occasions. I only hope, if you elect me to Parliament, I shall be able to obviate the little difficulty which has been placarded against me—that I could not speak. I own I cannot speak very well, but I shall learn. I cannot spin out glib sentences by the yard, as some people can; but if I have got anything in my mind, if I feel strongly on any question, I have, I believe, got brains enough to express it. When you send a man to the House of Commons, you do not want him to be always talking; he goes there to conduct the business of the country; he has to prepare himself on the question on which he proposes to speak before six hundred and fifty-six members, who would be bored if every man were to deliver his opinion. He must feel and understand what he is going to say; and I have not the least doubt that I shall be able to say what I feel and think, if you will give me the chance of saying it. If any one in the House of Commons talked all he thought upon everything, good God! what a Babel it would be! you would not get on at all. On the first night I came among you, many questions were put to me by a friend, who capped them all by saying, 'Now, Mr. Thackeray, are you for the honour of England?' I said that that was rather a wild and a wide question to put, but to the best of my belief, I was for the honour of England, and would work for it to the best of my power. About the ballot we are all agreed. If I was for the ballot before I came down here, I am more for the ballot now. As to triennial Parliaments, if the constituents desire them, I am for them." (A voice: "Will you have the ballot?") "No, we are too manly, too plucky, too honest, and we will beat them without it; but another day, when we have a better representation, we will have the ballot. If you elect me, I shall not go to the House of Commons hostile to the present ministry, but determined to keep them to their work, and to prevent them from shrinking from any of the promises they have made. I think them, in a war crisis, eminently the best men to carry on the councils of the country, and to contend against the Tories and Peelites, who have very nearly paralyzed their arms."

However, in spite of all his endeavours, the great novelist was unsuccessful, and on July 21, when the result was announced by the Mayor, the numbers stood: Cardwell, 1,085, Thackeray, 1,018. When we consider the great hold such a man as Edward Cardwell had on Oxford, the result is indeed remarkable, as showing what a good fight the famous novelist made. "Give me leave to speak . . . green and yellow my friends also," Thackeray said in his speech after the declaration of the poll. "Let me tell you a little story, but a true one. Some years ago, when boxing was more common in this country than it is at the present time, two celebrated champions met to fight a battle on Moulsey Heath. Their names were Gully and Gregson. They fought the most tremendous battle that had been known for many long years, and Gregson got the worst of it. As he was lying on his bed some time afterwards, blinded and his eyes shut up, he asked a friend to give him something to drink. A person in the room handed him some drink, and grasped him by the hand. 'Whose hand is this?' asked Gregson. ' 'Tis Jack Gully's,' was the reply. Now Gregson was the man who was beaten, and Gully was the conqueror, and he was the first man to shake him by the hand, to show him that he had no animosity against him. This should be the conduct of all loyal Englishmen, to fight a good fight, and to hold no animosity against the opposite side. With this feeling I go away from Oxford. With this feeling I shall have redeemed one of the promises I made you yesterday; the other I cannot, by any possibility, answer, because, somehow or other, our side has come out a little below the other side. I wish to shake Mr. Cardwell by the hand, and to congratulate him on being the representative of this great city. I say it is a victory you ought to be proud of; it is a battle which you ought to be proud of who have taken part in it; you have done your duty nobly and fought most gallantly. I am a man who was unknown to most of you, who only came before you with the recommendation of my noble and excellent friend, Mr. Neate, but I have met with many friends. You have fought the battle gallantly against great influences—against an immense strength—which have been brought against you, and in favour of that honoured and respected man, Mr. Cardwell. Stop! don't hiss. When Lord Monck came down here and addressed the electors, he was good enough to say a kind word in favour of me. Now, that being the case, don't let me be outdone in courtesy and generosity, but allow me to say a few words of the respect and cordiality which I entertain for Mr. Cardwell. As for the party battle which divides you, I am, gentlemen, a stranger, for I never heard the name of certain tradesmen of this city till I came among you. Perhaps I thought my name was better known than it is. You, the electors of Oxford, know whether I have acted honestly towards you; and you on the other side will say whether I ever solicited a vote when I knew that vote was promised to my opponent; or whether I have not always said, 'Sir, keep your word; here is my hand on it: let us part good friends.' With my opponents I part so. With others, my friends, I part with feelings still more friendly, not only for the fidelity you have shown towards me, but for your noble attachment to the gallant and tried whom you did know, and who I hope will be your representative at some future time. Don't cry out bribery: if you know of it, prove it; but as I am innocent of bribery myself, I do not choose to fancy that other men are not equally loyal and honest. It matters very little whether I am in the House of Commons or not, to prate a little more; but you have shown a great spirit, a great resolution, and great independence; and I trust at some future day, when you know me better than you do now, you will be able to carry your cause to a more successful issue. Before I came to Oxford, I knew that there was a certain question that would go against me, and which I would not blink to be made a duke or a marquis to-morrow. In March last, when I was at dinner at Edinburgh, some friends of mine asked me to stand for the representation of their city. My answer was this: 'That I was for having the people amused after they had done their worship of a Sunday.' I knew that I was speaking to a people who, of all others, were the most open to scruples on that point, but I did my duty as an honest man, and stated what my opinion was. I have done my duty honestly to this city. And I believe that this is the reason why I am placed in a minority; but I am contented to bow to that decision. I told you that I was for allowing a man to have harmless pleasures when he had done his worship on Sundays. I expected to have a hiss, but they have taken a more dangerous shape—the shape of slander. Those gentlemen who will take the trouble to read my books—and I should be glad to have as many of you for subscribers as will come forward—will be able to say whether there is anything in them that should not be read by any one's children, or by my own, or by any Christian man. I say, on this ground I will retire, and take my place with my pen and ink at my desk, and leave to Mr. Cardwell a business which I am sure he understands better than I do."

Of course to-day every one is delighted at Thackeray's defeat, for if ever a man's defeat were a gain for the world, the Oxford election must occupy a prominent place in such annals.

Whether he would have made an admirable politician is difficult to say with any certainty, but the probability is that he would have achieved no remarkable success in that *rôle*. His extremely candid friend, Trollope, appears to be positive that Thackeray, in the House of Commons, would have been a disastrous failure. His health was bad, his habits were still irregular, and, though there is no doubt he would have done his duty, it would soon have become irksome to him. He was not a man to have obeyed the orders of his party's whip unhesitatingly. He was the very last person in the

No. 2.] [DECEMBER.] [Price 1s.

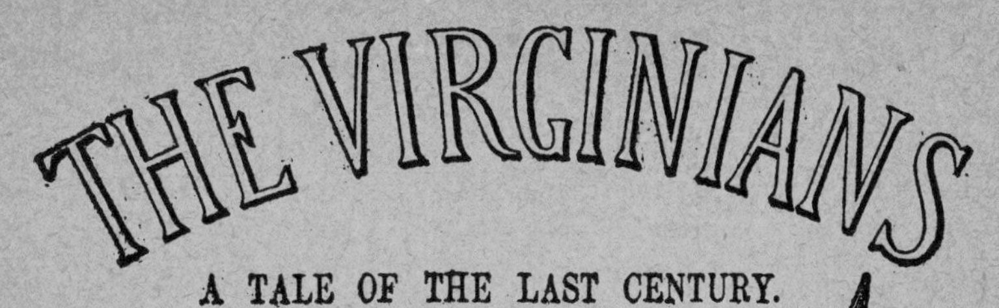

THE VIRGINIANS

A TALE OF THE LAST CENTURY.

BY W. M. THACKERAY.

Author of "Esmond,"
"Vanity Fair,"
"The Newcomes,"
&c. &c.

LONDON:
BRADBURY AND EVANS, 11, BOUVERIE STREET.
1857

world to have believed his friends to be always right, and his opponents always wrong; and he would, I feel confident, have voted against his party whenever he thought it was in error. He was far too philosophical to have ever developed into a leader of the House, for he could not help seeing that there were always at least two sides to every question; he would not have invariably possessed the feeling of certainty, which is so necessary for success in the House of Commons, that *his* view must be the correct one. His eye for the ridiculous and the *outré*, and his keen sense of humbug, would have made the House almost unbearable to him. He would have been a "trimmer," and by his defeat, the Secretary to the Treasury escaped much worry and annoyance; while on the other hand there is no doubt that Mr. Cardwell was a born statesman, and did good work in all the offices that he filled.

Anyhow, with regard to his defeat—alike whether he had else been a good, bad, or indifferent politician—we can only say, as Carlyle said to his wife after the lady, of whom Blanche Amory is the prototype, had finished her visit and left, "Oh! my dear, we cannot be sufficiently thankful."

During his second visit to America, in course of a conversation with Mr. Cooke* about Virginia, and the character of the country and the people, he mentioned a literary scheme that was then occupying his mind. "I shall write a novel with the scene laid here . . ." he said. "I shall not write it for two years. It will take me at least two years to collect my material and become

*Mr. Cooke asked Thackeray if he intended to give his impressions of America to the public. "I shall record," said Thackeray, "I shall record my opinions on the Americans in the book I don't intend to write."

acquainted with the subject. I cannot write upon a subject I know nothing of . . . I shall give it the title of *The Two Virginians*. . . . I shall lay the scene in Virginia. There will be two brothers who will be prominent characters; one will take the English side in the war, and the other the American; and they will both be in love with the same girl." And now, his political hopes disappointed, for a time at least, he went back to his desk; and in November, 1857, appeared the first number of *The Virginians*.

CHAPTER XIX

MR. THACKERAY, MR. YATES, AND THE GARRICK CLUB—THACKERAY AND DICKENS

CHAPTER XIX

MR. THACKERAY, MR. YATES, AND THE GARRICK CLUB—THACKERAY AND DICKENS

AND now I have to mention an incident in which, I think, Thackeray behaved in a manner quite unlike himself—rather harshly, and, I fear, incorrectly, too.

Thackeray and Edmund Yates were both members of the Garrick Club. They were both literary men, though the younger man had not yet "arrived"; and they seem to have been on terms of friendship, to judge from the following letter:—

"*Michaelmas Day*, 1845.

"MY DEAR YATES,—Am I to condole with, or congratulate you, on the announcement" [of twins] "in to-day's paper? May every year increase your happiness, and good fortune attend your increase. I know I am writing in an affected manner, as you are pleased to desire my autograph. I assure the friend for whom it is destined that I am quite incapable of being funny on a sudden, easily abashed, of a modest, retiring disposition, forty-four years old, and

"Yours truly, my dear Yates,
"W. M. THACKERAY.

"P. S.—The Thackeray of the signature, I do not think, is near so elegant as my ordinary Thackerays are;

in fact, my attention was drawn off just as I was turning it.

"E. YATES, Esq. (*Private and confidential.*)"

Less than three years later, Yates was appointed editor of *Town Talk*, a new venture of Maxwell, the publisher; and having written a pen-and-ink sketch of Dickens, which was a great success, he followed on with a portrait of Thackeray. This is what he wrote:—

"MR. W. M. THACKERAY.

"HIS APPEARANCE.

"Mr. Thackeray is forty-six years old, though, from the silvery whiteness of his hair, he appears somewhat older. He is very tall, standing upwards of six feet two inches, and as he walks erect, his height makes him conspicuous in every assembly. His face is bloodless and not particularly expressive, but remarkable for the fracture of the bridge of his nose, the result of an accident in youth. He wears a small gray whisker, but otherwise is clean shaven. No one meeting him could fail to recognise in him a gentleman; his bearing is cold and uninviting, his style of conversation either openly cynical or affectedly good-natured and benevolent; his *bonhomie* is forced, his wit biting, his pride easily touched; but his appearance is invariably that of the cool, suave, well-bred gentleman who, whatever may be rankling within, suffers no surface display of his emotion.

"HIS CAREER.

"For many years Mr. Thackeray, though a prolific writer, and holding constant literary employment, was unknown by name to the great bulk of the public. To *Fraser's Magazine* he was a regular contributor, and very shortly after the commencement of *Punch* he joined Mr. Mark Lemon's staff. In the *Punch* pages appeared many of his wisest, most thoughtful, and wittiest essays; *Mr. Brown's Letters to his Nephew* on love, marriage, friendship, choice of a club, etc., contain an amount of worldly wisdom which, independently of the amusement to be obtained from them, renders them really valuable reading to young men beginning life. The *Book of Snobs*, equally perfect in its way, also originally appeared in *Punch*. Here, too, were published his buffooneries, his *Ballads of Policeman X*, his *Jeames's Diary*, and some other scraps, the mere form of which consisted in outrages on orthography, and of which he is now deservedly ashamed. It was with the publication of the third or fourth number of *Vanity Fair* that Mr. Thackeray began to dawn upon the reading public as a great genius. This great work—which, with perhaps the exception of *The Newcomes*, is the most perfect literary dissection of the human heart, done with the cleverest and most unsparing hand—had been offered to, and rejected by, several of the first publishers in London. But the public saw and recognised its value; the great guns of literature, the *Quarterly* and the *Edinburgh*, boomed forth their praises, the light *tirailleurs* in the monthly and weekly press re-echoed the *feux-de-joie*, and the novelist's success was made. *Pendennis* followed, and was equally valued by the literary world, but scarcely so popular with the public. Then came *Esmond*, which fell almost still-born from the press; and then *The Newcomes*, perhaps the best of all. *The Virginians*, now publishing, though admirably written, lacks interest of plot, and is proportionately unsuccessful.

"HIS SUCCESS,

commencing with *Vanity Fair*, culminated with his *Lectures on the English Humourists of the Eighteenth Century*, which were attended by all the court and fashion of London. The prices were extravagant, the lecturer's adulation of birth and position was extravagant, the success was extravagant. No one succeeds better than Mr. Thackeray in cutting his coat according to his cloth. Here he flattered the aristocracy; but when he crossed the Atlantic George Washington became the idol of his worship, the *Four Georges* the object of his bitterest attacks. These last-named lectures have been dead failures in England, though as literary compositions they are most excellent. Our own opinion is that his success is on the wane. His writings were never understood or appreciated, even by the middle classes; the aristocracy have been alienated by his American onslaught on their body; and the educated and refined are not sufficiently numerous to constitute an audience. Moreover, there is a want of heart in all he writes, which is not to be balanced by the most brilliant sarcasm and the most perfect knowledge of the workings of the human heart."

Not unnaturally, Thackeray was very indignant and angry. He hated "personal" journalism. Read what, in a *Roundabout Paper* (*On Screens in Dining-rooms*), he wrote about a New York reporter who had published a curiously inaccurate account of a dinner given by Mr. Smith to the contributors of the *Cornhill Magazine*.

"Attack our books, Mr. Correspondent, and welcome. They are fair subjects for just censure or praise. . . . But Mr. Nameless behind the . . . screen uninvited, peering at the company and the meals, catching up scraps of the jokes, and noting down the guests' behaviour and conversation—what a figure his is! *Allons*, Mr. Nameless! put up your note-book, walk out of the hall, and leave gentlemen alone who would be private and wish you no harm."

But in Yates's case the offence was unpardonable. It was (or so it seemed to Thackeray) a gratuitous insult from a *fellow-clubman* to whom he had held out the hand of friendship. There was no call for such an article, and in the midst of his wrath he wrote to the author.

From the tone of Thackeray's letter it is evident how bitterly he resented this so-called "personal" portrait; and in strong terms he pointed out to Yates that to make journalistic use of private conversations in the club, "where, before you were born, I believe, I and other gentlemen have been in the habit of talking, without any idea that our conversation would supply paragraphs for professional vendors of 'Literary Talk,' " was indefensible. It is not necessary to dwell on the unpleasant incident too long, or to give Thackeray's angry letter in full.

The letter was severe, but it was, in some measure, deserved; and in writing it, the veteran was only avenging himself for the insults offered him by the young man of seven-and-twenty.

Yates, however, was no coward. He immediately wrote a reply, in which, while urging that he had not meant all that Thackeray had read in his article, he reminded him of similar misdemeanors committed against fellow-clubmen in *his* youth—against Dr. Lardner and Sir Edward Bulwer Lytton as *Doctor Athanasius Lardner* and *Mistaw Edwad Lytton Bulwig* in the *Yellowplush Papers;* against Mr. Stephen Price, Mr. Wyndham Smith, and Captain Granby Calcroft, in the *Book of*

Snobs; and, above all, in later days, against Mr. Andrew Arcedeckne as *Foker* in *Pendennis*. Had this letter been sent, it is almost certain that Thackeray would have let the matter drop. It is impossible to see what else he could have done. But, most unfortunately, Yates showed the letter to Dickens, who, thinking it too flippant, drafted another, which was neither dignified nor wise for a man who, after all, was the offender.

At the time it was believed (and the belief has not yet been refuted) that Dickens conducted the affair in a spirit distinctly hostile to Thackeray.

Anyway, Thackeray took the strange step of sending the correspondence to the committee of the Garrick Club, with the following letter:—

"36, ONSLOW SQUARE, *June* 19, 1858.

"GENTLEMEN,—The accompanying letters have passed between me and Mr. Edmund Yates, another member of the Garrick Club.

"Rather than have any further personal controversy with him, I have thought it best to submit our correspondence to you, with a copy of the newspaper which has been the cause of our difference.

"I think I may fairly appeal to the committee of the Garrick Club to decide whether the complaints I have against Mr. Yates are not well founded, and whether the practice of publishing such articles as that which I enclose will not be fatal to the comfort of the Club, and is not intolerable in a society of gentlemen.

"Your obedient servant,
"WILLIAM THACKERAY."

Yates protested that the committee was incompetent to enter into the matter, since there was no mention of the Club in the article; but the objection was overruled, on the ground that "the practice of publishing such articles, being reflections by one member of the Club against another, would be fatal to the comfort of the Club, and intolerable in a society of gentlemen"; and it was decided that the offender should apologise to Thackeray or retire from the Club, else the matter would have to be submitted at a specially summoned General Meeting.

Yates, after consulting Dickens, John Forster, W. Wills, and Albert Smith, determined to appeal to the General Meeting. This was summoned for July 10, and while neither Thackeray nor Yates was present, the latter sent a letter to be read, in which he expressed his willingness to apologise "for any unpleasant feeling that I may have awakened in the Club by the publication of the unfortunate article"; but he added that he considered Thackeray had placed it out of his power to apologise to him.

In spite of all the efforts of Dickens and Wilkie Collins, backed by Robert Bell, Samuel Lover, Palgrave Simpson, Sir James Ferguson, and others, the resolution to support the committee was carried by seventy against forty-six. Yates was allowed until July 20 to apologise, and then, no communication being received from him, the Secretary of the Club wrote to inform him that the committee had erased his name from the list of members.

Some months later Dickens wrote to Thackeray, offering his services as a mediator. Thackeray, however, did not accept the offer, as will be seen from the following letter. Indeed, at the time, I believe Thackeray was disinclined to accept anything at the hands of Dickens. He positively refers to Yates as "your friend," and informs Dickens that the matter is now entirely out of his hands, and placed in those of the Club Committee.

"36, ONSLOW SQUARE, 26*th Nov.*, 1858.

"DEAR DICKENS,—I grieve to gather from your letter that you were Mr. Yates's adviser in the dispute between me and him. His letter was the cause of my appeal to the Garrick Club for protection from insults against which I had no other remedy.

"I placed my grievance before the Committee of the Club as the only place where I have been accustomed to meet Mr. Yates. They gave their opinion of his conduct, and of the reparation which lay in his power. Not satisfied with his sentence, Mr. Yates called for a General Meeting, and, the meeting which he had called having declared against him, he declines the jurisdiction which he had asked for, and says he will have recourse to lawyers.

"You say that Mr. Edwin James is strongly of opinion that the conduct of the Club is illegal. On this point I can offer no sort of judgment, nor can I conceive that the Club will be frightened by the opinion of any lawyer, out of their own sense of the justice and honour which ought to obtain among gentlemen.

"Ever since I submitted my case to the Club, I have had, and can have no part in the dispute. It is for them to judge if any reconcilement is possible with your friend. I subjoin the copy of a letter which I wrote to the Committee, and refer you to them for the issue.

"Yours, etc.,

"W. M. THACKERAY.

"C. DICKENS, ESQ."

(ENCLOSURE.)

"ONSLOW SQUARE, *Nov.* 26, 1858.

"GENTLEMEN,—I have this day received a communication from Mr. Charles Dickens relative to the dispute which has been so long pending, in which he says,—

" 'Can any conference be held between me, as representing Mr. Yates, and any appointed friend of yours, as representing you, in the hope and purpose of some quiet accommodation of this deplorable matter, which will satisfy the feelings of all parties?'

"I have written to Mr. Dickens to say that since the commencement of the business, I have placed myself entirely in the hands of the Committee of the Garrick, and am still, as ever, prepared to abide by any decision at which they may arrive on the subject. I conceive I cannot, if I would, make the dispute once more personal, or remove it out of the court to which I submitted it for arbitration.

"If you can devise any peaceful means for ending it, no one will be better pleased than

"Your obliged, faithful servant,

"W. M. THACKERAY.

"THE COMMITTEE OF THE GARRICK CLUB."

Unfortunately, the feud did not end at once. Thackeray, it was said, made veiled allusions to the journalist in *The Virginians*. Yates, too, fed the flame by sarcastic references to his opponent in the *Lounger* column of the *Illustrated Times*, until, in the issue of January 29, 1859, he brought about a crisis by writing a spiteful travesty of *Bouillabaisse*, of which the following stanzas quoted show the animus of the author:—

"I show the vices which besmirch you,
The slime with which you're covered o'er,
Strip off each rag from female virtue,
And drag to light each festering sore.

"All men alive are rogues and villains,
All women drabs, all children cursed;
I tell them this, and draw their shillin's;
They highest pay when treated worst.

"I sneer at every human feeling
Which truth suggests, or good men praise;
Then, tongue within my cheek concealing,
Write myself 'Cynic'—for it pays."

Mr. Vizetelly, the editor of the *Illustrated Times*, had stood by Yates, in spite of pressure from friends of Thackeray, and had declared that as long as the great novelist continued his uncomplimentary allusions to his contributor, so long should his contributor have the opportunity of replying in the columns of his paper; and he pointed out how manifestly unfair it would be to close the only ground open to him to respond to the attacks. But the verses brought matters to a head. Half a dozen of the most valued members of Mr. Vizetelly's staff threatened to resign in a body unless the offending versifier were dismissed. However, owing, no doubt, to the editor's tact, this extreme measure was averted; and Yates continued to write his column week by week, but without further references to Thackeray, who, in his turn, never again alluded to the journalist in his novels.

Edmund Yates soon saw the silliness and bad taste of the offending article, and, when the *Cornhill Magazine* was established, sent to the editor, without remark, a poem, which he hoped would be regarded as an olive branch. It was, however, returned by a secretary, with the curt remark that he was "desired by Mr. Thackeray to return the enclosed." Yates, however, nobly revenged himself years later, when, on Thackeray's death, he wrote the beautiful obituary notice that is quoted elsewhere in this volume. It was always his impression that, after the first, Thackeray was more angry with Dickens than with him, and that the affair, much to his detriment, was made a trial of strength between the two novelists. Mr. Jeaffreson supports this opinion, by declaring that Thackeray said to him, "You must not think, young un, that I am quarrelling with Mr. Yates. *I am hitting the man behind him.*"

This unfortunate quarrel has led to much speculation as to whether any real friendship had existed between the great rivals—for as rivals they will be considered to the end of the chapter. They are the Fielding & Smollett of our century, and the mention of one invariably suggests the other. Perhaps it is not to be wondered at if Smollett is occasionally annoyed because Fielding is the first thought.

Thackeray, we know, never lost an opportunity of paying graceful tribute to Dickens in his books or in his lectures; and his private correspondence is full of remarks testifying to his appreciation of his rival's work.

While *Pendennis* was appearing, he advised a friend to get *David Copperfield*. "By jingo, it's beautiful; it beats the yellow chap of this month hollow;" "How beautiful it is; how charmingly fresh and simple! In those admirable touches of tender humour—and I shall call humour, Bob, a mixture of love and wit—who can equal this great genius? There are little words and phrases in his books which are like personal benefits to the reader;"—are two remarks of his on the book, which he regarded as the author's masterpiece. When he read the number of *Dombey* containing the death of Paul, he put it in his pocket, went out, and flung it down before Mark Lemon at the *Punch* office, exclaiming excitedly, "There's no writing against this; one hasn't an atom of chance. It's stupendous." And this, too, when *Vanity Fair* was in course of publication. But, in spite of Thackeray's praise, and Lord Jeffrey's "There has been nothing in literature like the actual dying of that sweet Paul," this death-bed scene is now regarded as the "kind of thing that appears in Sunday-school books about the virtuous little boy that died." At this very time, when Thackeray was complaining that it was useless trying to run before Dickens or by his side, since he couldn't touch him, or even get near him, he was writing, in *Vanity Fair*, the Waterloo chapters, that end with the description of a death: "No more firing was heard at Brussels—the pursuit rolled miles away. The darkness came down on the field and city, and Amelia was praying for George, who was lying on his face, dead, with a bullet through his heart."

But Thackeray was too keen a critic to let himself unduly depreciate even his own writings.

"Have you read Dickens? Oh! it is charming! brave Dickens!" he wrote to Mrs. Brookfield. "It has some of his very prettiest touches, those inimitable touches, which make such a great man of him; and the reading of the book has done another author a great deal of good. In the first place, it pleases the other author to see that Dickens, who has long left off alluding to the author's works, has been copying the O.A., and greatly simplifying his style, and overcoming the use of fine words. By this the public will be the gainer, and *David Copperfield* will be improved by taking a lesson from *Vanity Fair*. Secondly, it has put me on my mettle, for ah! madame, all the mettle was out of me, and I have been dreadfully and curiously cast down this month past. I say, secondly, it has put me on my mettle, and made me feel that I must do something, that I have fame, and name, and family to support."

Thackeray admitted that Dickens was not a deep thinker, but, he said, "he has a clear and bright-eyed intelligence, which is better than philosophy. I think he is equal to Fielding and Smollett—at any rate, to Smollett. He is not such a scholar as Fielding was." Perhaps it was for this last reason that Dickens underrated Thackeray, whose literary culture was far wider. He was not a discerning critic, and read little and thought less of his rival's later work.

"He" [Dickens] "can't forgive me for my success with *Vanity Fair*—as if there were not room in the world for both of us." And another time: "Dickens is making ten thousand a year. He is very angry at me for saying so; but I *will* say it, for it is true. He doesn't like me. He knows that my books are a protest against him—that if the one set are true, the other must be false. But *Pickwick* is an exception; it is a capital book. It is like a glass of good English ale."

I do not think in his heart, Thackeray had much doubt as to which set of books was right; neither do I think, if jealousy existed between the two men, it was on his side. A man with fewer jealousies and animosities has rarely lived. Yet I think he admired the *author* rather than the *man*. "Genial? Yes," he once said of him; "but frank"—a twinkle came over the spectacles—"well, frank as an oyster."

It is strange, remembering the number of mutual friends, that they saw so little of each other. They occasionally met at public dinners; but there are few records of social intercourse beyond a party in 1847 or 1848, that Thackeray was persuaded to give by the Dickens family, and a children's ball at Tavistock House some six years later, to which Thackeray came in the evening to fetch his daughters. But there was so little intimacy that when Dickens's correspondence was published, only one letter that had passed between the two men could be discovered; though subsequently another, in which Dickens returned thanks for a charming allusion to his work in the "Charity and Humour" discourse, was found by Mrs. Ritchie, and inserted in a supplementary volume.*

Thackeray, staying with his children, and Dickens met and visited each other during an autumn in the early fifties at Boulogne. Here, one day, when Marcus Stone was walking with Dickens, Louis Napoleon and the Prince Consort passed. Mr. Stone naturally raised his hat, but not so Dickens, who had known the Emperor well during his exile, for they were both frequenters of Gore House, then occupied by the Countess of Blessington.† But Dickens, Mr. Stone has explained, was a

*This is the passage referred to in the letter:—

"All children ought to love him" [Dickens]; "I know two that do, and read his books ten times for once they peruse the dismal preachments of their father. I know one who, when she is happy, reads *Nicholas Nickleby;* when she is unhappy, reads *Nicholas Nickleby;* when she is tired, reads *Nicholas Nickleby;* when she is in bed, reads *Nicholas Nickleby;* when she has nothing to do, reads *Nicholas Nickleby;* and when she has finished the book, reads *Nicholas Nickleby* again. This candid young critic, at ten years of age, said, 'I like Mr. Dickens's books better than your books, papa,' and frequently expressed her desire that the latter author should write a book like one of Mr. Dickens's books. Who can?"

†The French valet of the Countess wrote to her from Gore House after the sale in 1849: "M. Thackeray est venu aussi; il avait les larmes aux yeux en partant. C'est peut-être la seule personne que j'ai vu réellement affectée à votre départ."

After the death of Lady Blessington, the annual which she had man of such strong political opinions, and disapproved so vehemently of the *coup d'état* that he passed as if he had not seen them. Thackeray, on the other hand, when walking one day in Hyde Park with Carlyle and Sir Charles Gavan Duffy, met an Italian image boy, who had a bust of Louis Napoleon among the figures he carried on his head. Thackeray took off his hat and saluted it, half—but only half—mockingly, and murmured something about a man who understood his business, and mastered the art of government. Yet even if he had objected to the *coup d'état* as heartily as Dickens, I do not think he would have passed without salutation the Emperor of the country in which he was a guest, and the husband of his own Queen. It will be remembered how, when a friend called on him on Sunday, December 15, 1861, with the *Observer* in his hand, he spied the black border of the paper, and instantly started up. "The Prince Consort is dead?" he cried; and the visitor intimated assent. "Ah!" said Thackeray, dropping into his chair, "*poor dear gentlewoman!*"

With regard to Dickens and Thackeray in Boulogne, I am indebted to Mrs. Patchett Martin for some recollections of her father, Dr. J. M. Cookesley, who was then in practice as an English physician of that town. Dr. Cookesley was himself a man of strong literary bent, a near relative of the Devonshire Dr. Cookesley, who detected the genius of the boy William Gifford, at the

established, the *Keepsake*, was brought out by her niece, Miss Marguerite Power, who, for old friendship's sake, was supported by several of the old Gore House set, including Thackeray.

It was for Lady Blessington, when she sent him an album-print of a boy and girl fishing, with a request he would make some verses for it, that he wrote *Piscator and Piscatrix*. "I liked the idea, and set about it at once," he told Mr. Locker Lampson. "I was two entire days at it—and was so occupied with it, so engrossed by it, that I did not shave during the whole time."

cobbler's stall, and paid for his education, eventually sending him to Oxford.* The Boulogne doctor was a man who had seen somewhat of the world, and had passed through stirring adventures when, as a medical student, he went out as a volunteer to Portugal to fight for Donna Maria.

Dr. Cookesley, who attended Thackeray professionally, formed a strong personal liking for him, while he appears to have regarded Dickens as wanting in gentlemanly consideration for the feelings of others. Thackeray, he declared, was neither cynic nor pessimist, but a naturally generous-minded kind-hearted man, whom he frequently dubbed "the gentle giant"; while Dickens, for all his pathos and sentimentality in print, was an infinitely harder, more commercially-minded, and selfish, character.

It must be remembered, however, that the good English doctor of Boulogne, from being an ardent Liberal and reformer, had become a strong partisan of Louis Napoleon and his beautiful Empress. He doubtless knew of Dickens's behaviour with regard to the Emperor and the Prince Consort, which he would have denounced in no measured terms as an exhibition of outrageous vulgarity. Also it must be admitted that Dr. Cookesley knew little or nothing of Dickens personally. Still, his tribute to the personal worth and kindliness of the author of *Vanity Fair* is well deserving of consideration.

Thackeray has been too often harshly judged, simply because his writings display such unrivalled knowledge of the snobs and rascals of the world. We are all too ready to identify authors with their imaginary creations; but

* See *Life of John Murray*, the publisher.

to take a mean view of Thackeray because he could so thoroughly understand and depict a Becky Sharp is as though we were to denounce Shakespeare as a treacherous dissimulator because in Iago he has portrayed that type of character with marvellous fidelity.

CHAPTER XX

EDITOR OF *THE CORNHILL MAGAZINE*

CHAPTER XX

EDITOR OF *THE CORNHILL MAGAZINE*

IN preceding chapters I have shown Thackeray's career in all its various stages—as an amateur writing parodies; as proprietor, editor, and contributor, to the luckless *National Standard;* as part owner and Paris correspondent to the equally unfortunate *Constitutional and Public Ledger;* as an artist; as a writer of magazine articles; as the principal writer on the staff of *Punch;* as the great novelist; and, finally, as the popular lecturer. It only now remains to show him in one other light—as the editor of a successful magazine.

Thackeray, more than once, had hinted his wish to establish a magazine, as Dickens had done with so much success; and it is most probable that he would have carried out this idea, had not Mr. George Smith (of Messrs. Smith & Elder), who was also anxious to bring out a monthly periodical, obtained his co-operation as editor of the venture by means of the offer of an enormous salary.*

In those days the price of periodical literature was very high, and the shilling monthly was almost unknown, though there had been issued a shilling booklet, edited by Edmund Yates, called *The Train*, its rival, *The Idler*, supported by James Hannay, and some production at

*Thackeray had suggested to Mr. Smith a small daily print after the style of the *Tatler*, to be called *Fair Play*.

the same price of Douglas Jerrold's. Now, however, the Macmillans were bringing out a new shilling magazine, under the editorship of Professor Masson, the first number of which was to appear in November, 1859; and Mr. Smith decided to produce his periodical at the same price and about the same time. *Temple Bar* is a year younger.

There was some discussion as to what the new paper should be called. It was suggested that the name should be *Thackeray's Magazine;* but finally, as Thackeray wrote to George Henry Lewes, in a letter dated November 1, 1859—afterwards reprinted in the first number of the *Cornhill Magazine* as an editorial introduction—"Our storehouse being in Cornhill" [Messrs. Smith & Elder's offices were then "over against St. Peter's Church in Cornhill"] "we name and date our Magazine from its place of publication." "We might have assumed a title much more startling," Thackeray went on, in his characteristic style; "for example, *The Thames on Fire* was a name suggested; and, placarded in red letters about the city and country, it would no doubt have excited some curiosity. But on going to London Bridge, the expectant rustic would have found the stream rolling on in its accustomed course, and would have turned away angry at being hoaxed."

When *The Virginians* was finished* in September,

*While the last number of *The Virginians* did not appear until October, the book had been finished about the end of August; and there must still be some gentlemen alive who can remember the exact day on which the last pages were written; for it chanced, as Mr. Fields has told us, that Thackeray had invited a large party of friends to dine with him at Greenwich. They were all to meet in a private room at some hotel, and Thackeray himself would be there at six o'clock to the minute. The guests were all assembled, and six o'clock came, but no Thackeray appeared. Half an hour passed—still no Thackeray. At seven o'clock it was stated that the dinner was spoilt, and the party was seriously thinking of returning to town. A few minutes later, however, there was a merry shout in the entry, and

Thackeray threw himself heart and soul into his editorial work, though to do so he had to cut short a much-needed holiday, and to postpone—for ever, as it unfortunately happened—a pleasure trip to America. "My dear Mr. Longfellow," he had to write in November, "has Hiawatha ever a spare shaft in his quiver which he can shoot across the Atlantic? How proud I should be if I could have a contribution or two from you for our *Cornhill Magazine*. I should like still better to be driving to Cambridge in the snow, and expecting a supper there. Two or three months ago I actually thought such a scheme was about to come off. I intended to shut up my desk for a year—not write a line—and go on my travels. But the gods willed otherwise.

"I am pressed into the service of this magazine, and engaged to write ever so much more for the next three years. Then, if I last so long, I shall be free of books and publishers, and hope to see friends to whose acquaintance I look back with—I can't tell you how much gratitude and kind feeling."

The Magazine—like the *Pall Mall Gazette* in *Pendennis*—was to be written by scholars and gentlemen, and new blood was eagerly sought; but very little success was met with in this way, as Thackeray himself admitted at a dinner given to the staff in December, 1859, by

Thackeray bounded into the room. "He had not changed his morning dress, and ink was still visible upon his fingers. Clapping his hands and pirouetting briskly on one leg, he cried out, 'Thank Heaven, the last sheet of *The Virginians* has just gone to the printer.' He made no apology for his late appearance, introduced nobody, shook hands with everybody, and begged us all to be seated as quickly as possible. His excellent delight at completing his book swept away every other feeling, and we all shared his pleasure—albeit the dinner was overdone throughout."

On September 7, Thackeray wrote to George Smith from Folkestone, "I am surprised I have finished *The Virginians* so well. Oh! what a load off my mind!"

Mr. George Smith, at his house in Gloucester Place, Hyde Park. "I see," said Thackeray, "I see there are only a certain number of regular cabs upon the stand, and whether they are bad or good, rickety or otherwise, we must make the best of them."

Still, things might easily have been worse, for Anthony Trollope, Robert Bell, G. A. Sala, E. F. Dallas, *Jacob Omnium*, James Hannay, John Oxenford, G. H. Lewes, General Burgoyne, Frederick Greenwood, and John Hollingshead, with Sykes, who designed the cover, and Millais for artists formed the original staff; while amongst occasional contributors during Thackeray's editorship were Tennyson, Monckton Milnes, Lever, Dr. W. H. Russell, Herman Merivale, Mrs. Gaskell, Mrs. Browning, F. Locker-Lampson, the late Lord Lytton, Mrs. Beecher Stowe, Adelaide Procter, Matthew Arnold, Ruskin, Fitzjames Stephen, and Miss Thackeray (now Mrs. Ritchie).

Anthony Trollope has insisted, with really quite unnecessary vehemence, that "a man so susceptible, so prone to work by fits and starts, so unmethodical, could not have been a good editor." It is difficult to speak with certainty of the character of a man, but it is comparatively easy to discuss the quality of an editor, since he leaves his records for all the world to examine.

Let us look at the contents of the first number of the *Cornhill Magazine*. First comes Anthony Trollope's *Framley Parsonage*. This is followed by a paper on *The Chinese and Outer Barbarians*, by Sir John Bowring, and G. H. Lewes's *Studies in Animal Life*. Then there is an *Inauguration Ode, dedicated to the Author of Vanity Fair*, by "Father Prout" [Rev. F. Mahony]; and after this, *A Man of Letters of the Last Generation*, by Thornton Hunt; *The Search for Sir John Franklin*, by Sir Allen Young, one of the officers of the *Fox;* and *The First Morning of* 1860, by Mrs. Archer Clive. *Lovel the Widower*, is commenced; and the whole winds up with the first of the *Roundabout Papers—On a Lazy Little Boy*.

This surely was not such a bad shilling's worth for those days, or, for the matter of that, for these days either; and as regards later numbers, the names of the contributors that Thackeray had gathered together amply vouch for the continuance of this excellence.

Surely the tree is judged by its fruit, and the editor must be judged by his paper; and because Thackeray himself has said that he found his chair painful, owing to his great soft-heartedness and sensitiveness, it is absurd to label him "bad editor," though it is not difficult to admit that he may have been unmethodical as an editor, since we know of his want of method (à la Trollope) as a writer. But even then, as Mr. Marzials says, admirable work is often turned out by the unmethodical; and, after all, if Thackeray were only half as good an editor as he was a novelist, the *Cornhill Magazine* would have been without a rival.

From the very first there was no doubt of the hearty reception of the new periodical by the public. It would have had a very large sale simply from the fact that it was a novelty, and that a hundred and twenty-eight pages, a map, and two full-page illustrations—for in those early days the *Cornhill* was illustrated—could be purchased for a shilling. But when, in addition to all else, it was known to be edited by the great Thackeray, and that he himself was to be a contributor, the sale was simply enormous, absolutely unheard of in the days when the reading public was only a small percentage of the number to which it now—thirty-nine years later—amounts. Of the first number, which appeared in January (1860), no less than a hundred and ten thousand copies were sold; of the second number, over a hundred thousand; and some months after, when it may be supposed that the circulation had reached its level, the sale still averaged about eighty to eighty-five thousand.*

Thackeray, himself, had fled ignominiously to Paris before the Magazine appeared. He had been literally overwhelmed with manuscripts, not only at the office—which was all very well—but actually at "the editor's private residence, to which, in spite of prayers, entreaties, commands, and threats, authors, and ladies especially," would send their communications. Even against this he held up manfully; but when the intending contributors began to *call* on him in Onslow Square, he packed up his portmanteau and ran away. "The darlings demanded that I should rewrite, if I could not understand their nonsense, and put their halting lines into proper form. I was so appalled when they set upon me with their 'ipics' and their 'ipecacas' that you might have knocked me down with a feather, sir. It was insupportable, and I fled away into France," he told Fields, the American publisher, who has further confided to the public ear how, when he called on Thackeray at his hotel in the

*The following notice, on the familiar orange-slip, was inserted in the issue for April 1862:—

"The extent of the circulation of *The Cornhill Magazine* mainly concerns those who advertise in it; and Messrs. Smith, Elder & Co. think it right to give advertisers their unqualified assurance that the average sale of each number of the Magazine was 84,427, at the time of making up the accounts at the end of last year; and that the smallest number of copies sold, up to that period, of any single number of *The Cornhill Magazine* was 67,019; while of some of the numbers more than 100,000 copies were sold."

Rue de la Paix, he found him almost delirious with joy at the news from London of the immense sale of the Magazine, and full of enthusiasm for George Smith. "London is not big enough to contain me now, and I am obliged to add Paris to my residence! Great heavens," said he, throwing up his long arms, "where will this tremendous circulation stop? Who knows but that I shall have to add Vienna and Rome to my whereabouts? If the worst comes to the worst, New York also may fall into my clutches, and only the Rocky Mountains may be able to stop my progress."

"Those days in Paris were simply tremendous," says Fields. "We dined at all possible and impossible places together. We walked round and round the glittering courts of the Palais Royal, . . . and all my efforts were necessary to restrain him from rushing in and ordering a pocketful of diamonds and 'other trifles,' as he called them; 'for,' said he, 'how can I spend the princely income which Smith allows me for editing the *Cornhill* unless I begin instantly somewhere?' If he saw a group of three or four persons talking together in an excited way . . . he would whisper to me, with immense gesticulation, 'There, there, you see the news has reached Paris, and perhaps the number has gone up since my last accounts from London.' His spirits during these few days were colossal, and he told me he found it impossible to sleep for counting subscribers."

He also expressed his delight in the *Roundabout Paper, On Some Late Great Victories*. "The Victories," he wrote, "which I wish especially to commemorate in this paper are the six great, complete, prodigious, and undeniable victories, achieved by the corps which the editor of the *Cornhill Magazine* has the honour to command. . . . Up the Hill of Ludgate, around the Pauline Square, by the side of Chepe, until it reaches our own hill of Corn, the procession passes. The Imperator is bowing to the people. . . . I fancy the Imperator standing on the steps of the Temple (erected by Titus) on the Mons Frumentarius, and addressing the citizens. 'Quirites!' he says, 'in our campaign of six months we have been engaged six times, and in each action have taken near upon *a hundred thousand prisoners*. Go to! What are other magazines compared to our magazine?' (Sound trumpets!) 'What banner is there like that of Cornhill? You philosopher yonder!' (He shakes under his mantle.) 'Do you know what it is to have a hundred and ten thousand readers? a hundred thousand readers? a hundred thousand *buyers?*' (Cries of 'No!' 'Pooh!' 'Yes, upon my honour!' 'O come!' and murmurs of applause and derision.) 'I say more than a hundred thousand purchasers—and I believe *as much as a million readers?*' (Immense sensation.) 'To these have we said an unkind word? We have enemies; have we hit them an unkind blow? Have we sought to pursue party aims, to forward private jobs, to advance selfish schemes? The only persons to whom, wittingly, we have given pain are some who have volunteered for our corps—and of these volunteers we have had *thousands*.' (Murmurs and grumbles.) 'What commander, citizens, could place all these men—could make officers of all these men?' (cries of 'No—no!' and laughter), 'could say, "I accept this recruit, though he is too short for our standard, because he is poor, and has a mother at home who wants bread?" could enrol this other, who is too weakly to bear arms, because he says, "Look, sir, I shall be stronger anon"?

The leader of such an army as ours must select his men, not because they are good and virtuous, but because they are strong and capable. To these our ranks are ever open; and in addition to the warriors who surround me'—(the generals look proudly conscious)—'I tell you, citizens, I am in treaty with other great and most tremendous champions, who will march by the side of our veterans to the achievement of fresh victories. Now, blow trumpets! Bang, ye gongs! and drummers, drub the thundering skins! Generals and chiefs, we go to sacrifice to the gods.' "

It is pleasant to dwell for a moment on this hearty, healthy joy and excitement. We are all of us *blasé* and *désillusionné* at twenty now, and here is a picture of a man of forty-nine as jolly and as happy at the success of his venture as a school-boy on the first days of his holidays.

Whilst reading such a tale of Thackeray, how naturally the reflection rises to our mind, "What a proud, morose cynic the man was, to be sure!"

But Thackeray was far more delighted with his daughter's first contribution to the *Cornhill*.* One day

*On May 4, 1860, Thackeray wrote in great good spirits to Sir H. Davidson: "How dy do, my dear old Davus? Read the *Cornhill Magazine* for May; the article *Little Scholars* is by my dear old fat Annie. She sends you her love, so does Minnie. We're going out to drive. We've got two horses in our carriage now. The Magazine goes on increasing, and how much do you think my next twelve months' earnings and receipts will be if I work? £10,000. Cocka-doodle-oodloodle. We are going to spend four thousand in building a new house on Palace Green, Kensington. We have our health. We have brought Granny and G. P. to live at Brompton Crescent, close to us, and we are, my dear old Davus's

"Faithful W. M. T., A. T., and H. M. T."

This letter is quoted from Mr. Francis St. John Thackeray's article in *Temple Bar*, July, 1893.

Mr. Taine, in his *Notes on England*, mentions that "Thackeray the novelist has made £160 in twenty-four hours through the medium in London he told Fields that he had just been reading his little girl's first paper—*Little Scholars*. "When I read it," he said, "I blubbered like a child; it was so good, so simple, so honest; and my little girl wrote it, every word of it."* Of course it was good, simple, and honest—it could hardly have been otherwise when we remember whose child she was; but none the less it is pleasing to think of the father's quiet joy—this time, depend upon it, it was *not* uproarious or exulting—and to feel that it was one of the happiest incidents in a life so marred by great unhappiness, and by much toil and trouble. And I can see into the great man's heart, as, after reading *Little Scholars* for the first time, he lays down the paper with eyes dimmed by those tears of great joy; and I know that it was full of reverence and gratitude as silently he offered up a deep, heartfelt prayer of thanksgiving to the God whom he loved with so pure a love, and served with so willing a heart. It must make us sad to think that he was not with her, who has inherited so much of his own marvellous charm, to feel still more happy, and to smile approval upon the authoress of *The Story of Elizabeth*, of *Old Kensington*, and of the fascinating *Chapters from Some Unpublished Memoirs*, in which last, on almost every page, can be seen how greatly and fondly she admired and loved the famous man who to her was simply "Father."

As an editor, Thackeray was very particular—"old-fashioned" I am afraid my younger readers will call it—

of two lectures—one delivered in Brighton, the other in London; from the magazine to which he contributed his novels he received £2,000 a year, and £10 a page in addition; this magazine has a hundred thousand subscribers; he estimated his own yearly earnings at £4,800.

*"I assure you," Thackeray said to Dean Hole, "that Annie can write ten times more cleverly than I." The Dean, however, tacitly declined to be assured.

as to the morality and tone of the stories he accepted for *Cornhill.* Thus he declined Mrs. Browning's poem, *Lord Walter's Wife,* as well as a story by Trollope, purely because he thought the subjects unfitted for family reading. *Virginibus puerisque* he pleaded in mitigation of his offence; and very frank and honest was his kind letter to Mrs. Browning, returning her poem, and very beautiful and appreciative her reply.

It had been understood that in the first number of the *Cornhill Magazine* Thackeray should commence another of his great novels; but *The Virginians* had only been finished two or three months before, and, having the full weight of editorial responsibility and work upon him besides, he did not feel able to do himself justice. So Anthony Trollope was commissioned to produce a novel with at least one clergyman in a prominent place—the result was the charming *Framley Parsonage.*

It is not difficult to guess at what Thackeray's contribution would have been. For some time past paragraphs had been appearing in different papers stating that "the author of *Esmond* and the *Essays on the Humourists,* who had hitherto delighted in the times of elaborate flowing wigs, and swords, and coats with huge lapels, had suddenly betaken himself to those misty days of savage names and scanty clothing." This rumour had a certain substratum of truth. Evidently the news contained in the following extract from a letter written in May, 1858, by Thackeray to Motley had leaked out. "I intend to write a novel of the time of Henry V.," he wrote, "which will be my *capo d'opera,* in which the ancestors of my present characters, Warringtons, Pendennises, and the rest, shall be introduced. It will be a most magnificent performance, and nobody will read it." It is almost needless to say that this intention was never carried out.

In January, 1860, Thackeray had been asked to continue Macaulay's history, and this offer, as far as I can understand, he neither refused nor accepted. "Queen Anne has long been my ambition," he wrote to Dr. Skelton, "but she will take many a long year's labour, and I can't ask any other writer to delay on my account. At the beginning of the year I had prepared an announcement stating that I was engaged on that history; but kept it back, as it was necessary that I should pursue my old trade of novelist for some time yet to come. Meanwhile her image stands before St. Paul's, for all the world to look at; and who knows but some one else may be beforehand with both of us, and sketch her off while we are only laying the palette."

Thackeray had, however, stocked his library with the necessary material for the work. "Here," he said to Bayard Taylor, the last time they were together, "here, I am going to write my greatest work—a *History of the Reign of Queen Anne*. There are my materials"—pointing to a collection of volumes in various bindings, which occupied a separate place on the shelves. "Probably" [I shall begin it] "as soon as I am done with *Philip;* but I am not sure I may not have to write another novel first. But the history will mature all the better for the delay. I want to *absorb* the authorities gradually, so that when I come to write, I shall be filled with the subject, and can sit down to a continuous narrative, without jumping up every moment to consult somebody. The History has been a pet project of mine for some years past. I'm slowly working up to the level of it, and know that when I once begin I shall do it well."

No doubt he would have done it well, and it can only conjure up regrets to think of what we have lost—to think of the pictures of society he would have drawn, of the manners and customs of the day he would have portrayed, the descriptions of Grub Street and of the coffee-houses he would have given. But Fate seemed determined he should not have *all* the laurels. A novelist than whom none are greater and few his equal; a poet, in his own line excelled by none; a writer of *the* finest burlesque in the language; an art critic of no mean capacity; a draughtsman and caricaturist, almost the equal of Doyle; an essayist who ranks with Addison and Montaigne;—it was denied him the opportunity of shining as an historian. The unexpected journey to the East necessitated the abandonment of the *Life of Talleyrand;* and another and a more untimely journey to a far more distant land deprived the world of the *History of the Reign of Queen Anne.* Yet when it is remembered what he did achieve, much as his early death is to be deplored, it is difficult to be very angry with Fate.

During the first year of the *Cornhill,* he contributed to the pages of the magazine *Lovel the Widower*—a novel founded on *The Wolves and the Lamb; The Last Sketch,* an appreciation of Charlotte Brontë, prefixed to *Emma,* a fragment; *Nil Nisi Bonum,* a graceful tribute to the memories of Washington Irving and Macaulay; and *Vanitas Vanitatum,* a poem (some verses of which he had years before written in a lady's album) that embodies his philosophy, and is in part quoted elsewhere. The lectures on *The Four Georges* were also printed for the first time in the *Cornhill. The Adventures of Philip,* with illustrations, mostly by Frederick Walker, ran through the magazine monthly from January, 1861, until August, 1862, when it was immediately published by Messrs. Smith & Elder, who had already taken advantage of Thackeray's popularity to issue in book form both *Lovel the Widower* and *The Four Georges.*

I have, until now, left all mention of those inimitable little essays that only Thackeray could write—the delightful *Roundabout Papers*, that commenced in the January, 1860, number, and, with here and there an interval, continued until November, 1863.* These papers are thirty-two in all, if *The Last Sketch* and the indignant *Strange to Say on Club Paper* be included.† He is autobiographical, impersonal, fanciful, discussive, angry or reproachful, exulting, sorrowful, sometimes even sad, yet throughout preaching the gospel of Love and deploring *Vanitas Vanitatum.*

He is egotistical—"a plague on his I's!" Well—"My dear fellow, if you read *Montaigne's Essays*, you must own that he might call any one by the name of any other; and that an essay on the Moon or an essay on Green Cheese would be as appropriate a title as one of his on Coaches, on the Art of Discoursing, on Experience, or what you will. Besides, if I *have* a subject (and I *have*), I claim to approach it in a roundabout manner. . . .

"My Pegasus won't fly so as to let me survey the field below me. He has no wings; he is blind of one eye certainly; he is restive, stubborn, slow; crops a hedge when he ought to be galloping, or gallops when

*During this year (1861) Thackeray contributed *A Leaf Out of a Sketch-Book* to *The Victoria Regina*, a volume of original contributions in poetry and prose, edited by Adelaide Procter.

†The MS. of the *Roundabout Papers* is in the library of Harvard College, and the librarian has written an interesting article about it in *Scribner's Magazine* for September, 1893.

he ought to be quiet. He will never show off when I want him. Sometimes he goes at a pace which surprises me. Sometimes, when I most wish him to make the running, the brute turns restive. I am obliged to let him take his own time. . . .

"That right line 'I' is the very shortest, simplest, and most straightforward means of communication between us, and stands for what it is worth, and no more. Sometimes authors say, 'The present writer has often remarked'; or, 'The undersigned has observed'; or, 'Mr. Roundabout presents his compliments to the gentle reader, and begs to state, etc.'; but 'I' is better and straighter than all these grimaces of modesty; and although these are Roundabout Papers, and may wander goodness knows whither, I shall ask leave to maintain the upright and simple perpendicular."

He is equally interesting when he discourses of the *Cornhill Magazine*, or of domestic servants, or of the New York journalism of the day, or of Christmas and pantomimes, or of the stealing of pears from the trees in his garden, or of workhouses, or avarice, or of his boyhood, or of the marriage of the Prince and Princess of Wales, or of the thorns in an editorial chair, or of pictures seen during his "week's holiday," or of the famous "Desseins" (where he makes Sterne, Monk Eustace of St. Peter's, and Beau Brummel, converse), or of brave soldiers; but he is at his best when he may write of great *littérateurs* (whether contemporary or not), of Dumas (his favourite author, mentioned with admiration and reverence a dozen times), of Scott, of Madame D'Arblay, of Washington Irving, and of Macaulay.

The Christmas number [1863] contained the customary orange-coloured flyleaf, which announced that "a new serial story by W. M. Thackeray'' would be commenced early in the new year. This referred to *Denis Duval*, to which Thackeray had devoted much time and trouble, for it is said he intended that it should be the last novel he would write, and, as such, should be the grand *chef d'œuvre* of his life. The novel, or rather the fragment of the novel that had been written, and some of the notes that Thackeray had collected, were published posthumously in the magazine from March to July, 1864; and when it appeared, the carpers and sneerers who had cried out that the great novelist was exhausted, was played out, that his best work was done, and that, for the sake of his reputation, he had better write no more, were silenced once for all; for there is little in the whole of our literature—nothing at all, even in Thackeray's works—that is more perfect than the description in *Denis Duval* of Madame de Saverne's sorrows, and madness, and death.

Though Thackeray continued to contribute to the *Cornhill* until his death, he had long since resigned the editorship; and of this he gave notice in a valedictory address (to contributors and correspondents), dated March 18, and published in the number for April, 1862:—

''Ladies and Gentlemen (who *will* continue, in spite of the standing notice below, to send papers to the Editor's private residence), perhaps you will direct the postman to some other house when you learn that the Editor of the *Cornhill* no longer lives in mine. . . .

''The Editor no more, I hope long to remain a contributor to my friend's Magazine. I believe my own special readers will agree that my books will not suffer when their author is released from the daily task of reading, accepting, refusing, losing, and finding the work of other people. To say No has often cost me a morning's peace and a day's work. I tremble *recenti metu*. Oh! those hours of madness, spent in searching for Louisa's lost lines to her dead Piping Bulfinch, or Nhoj Senoj's mislaid Essay. I tell them for the last time that the (late) Editor will not be responsible for rejected communications, and herewith send off the chair, and the great *Cornhill Magazine* Tin Box, with its load of care.

"While the present tale of *Philip* is passing through the press, I am preparing another, on which I have worked at intervals for many years past, which I hope to introduce in the ensuing year; and I have stipulated for the liberty of continuing the little essays which have amused the public and the writer, and which I propose to continue from time to time to the pages of the *Cornhill Magazine*.

"W. M. THACKERAY."

Thus, after April, Thackeray was no longer Editor of the *Cornhill*, and Leslie Stephen—who, in after years was to marry his younger daughter—reigned in his stead.

The reason usually given as the cause of Thackeray's resignation is that he found the work too painful to go on with, and I certainly believe this had much to do with it. "How can I go into society with comfort?" he asked a friend. "I dined the other day at ——'s, and at the table were four gentlemen whose masterpieces of literature I had been compelled to decline with thanks." And in *Thorns in the Cushion* he told of the "thorn-letters" he received. He even quoted one, and, commenting on it, said, "Here is the case put with true female logic: 'I am poor; I am good; I am ill; I work hard; I have a sick mother and hungry brothers and sisters dependent on me. You can help us if you will.' And then I look at the paper with the thousandth part of a faint hope that it may be suitable, and I find it won't do; and I knew it wouldn't do; and why is this poor lady to appeal to my pity, and bring her little ones kneeling to my bedside, and calling for bread which I can give them if I choose?''

Well, the poem was useless; it was entirely without merit or value, and could never appear in the *Cornhill*, or, for the matter of that, in any other magazine. Yet I dare swear that the manuscript in question—and who knows how many others also—was never returned to its authoress, who, instead, received a brief and formal note. I can see the dear, great man writing it in secret, and hurriedly thrusting the letter into a drawer at the sound of approaching footsteps, stating that the editor of the *Cornhill Magazine* had much pleasure in accepting the little verses, and enclosing a cheque, quite out of proportion to the length, let alone the merits, of the poem. And if that cheque could be shown we should notice that, by some error, it was drawn on Mr. Thackeray's own banking-account, and not on that of Messrs. Smith & Elder, the proprietors of the magazine. And then, too, the poem would never appear in the periodical. Still more strange, and most astonishing of all, when Mr. Leslie Stephen would examine the manuscripts accepted, and not yet printed by his predecessor, there would be no trace of the poem, and no record of it in the books of the firm—but then, all the world knows how unmethodical Thackeray was.

Then the authors of rejected manuscripts spent much of their valuable time in writing insulting letters to

Thackeray, and the members of the *corps de ballet* at the Theatre Royal, Donnybrook, held a quite animated, albeit entirely one-sided correspondence with him, *à propos* of an incident in *Lovel the Widower*, and altogether it is not difficult to understand the multitude of petty annoyances that caused him to exclaim: "Ah, me! we wound where we never intended to strike; we create anger where we never meant harm; and these thoughts are the thorns in our cushion. Out of mere malignity, I suppose, there is no man who would like to make enemies. But here in this editorial business you can't do otherwise, and a queer, sad, strange, bitter thought it is that must ever cross the mind of many a public man. Do what I will, be innocent or spiteful, be generous or cruel, there are A and B and C and D who will hate me to the end of the chapter—to the chapter's end—to the finis of the page—when hate and envy, fortune and disappointment, shall be over."

Occasionally he would return a contribution with some sound, even if unpalatable, advice. "I scarcely know what to say to you, save what I have already told you," he wrote to a persistent aspirant. "However, I can only entreat you to abandon your literary aspirations. You would never write your way, at present, at any rate; your composition is very bad and my profession, in truth, is not fitted for a man possessed of bad health. Pray seek some light employment. Do not grind the wind."*

He told Mr. James Payn how a young fellow had sent him a long story, for which he demanded particular attention from "the greatest of novelists," upon the ground that he had a sick sister entirely dependent upon

*Reprinted in the *Literary World*, February 22, 1884.

him for support, and how, touched by the appeal, he wrote his correspondent a long letter of advice, enclosing also some pecuniary assistance. "I feel for your position," he said, "and appreciate your motive for exertion; but I must tell you at once that you will never do anything in literature. Your contribution is worthless in every way, and it is the truest kindness, both to her for whom you are working, and to yourself, to tell you so straight. Turn your mind at once to some other industry"—and how this produced a reply couched in the most offensive terms conceivable, and ended by telling "the greatest of novelists" that, although he had attained by good luck the top of the tree, he would one day find himself where he deserved to be, at the bottom of it. "For my part," said Thackeray (upon Mr. Payn showing some preliminary symptoms of suffocation), "I see little to laugh at. What a stupid, ungrateful beast the man must be! And if ever I waste another half-hour writing to a creature of that sort, call me a horse, or worse!"*

*James Payn: *Some Literary Recollections.*

CHAPTER XXI

DEATH

CHAPTER XXI

DEATH

IT was not editorial worries alone that induced Thackeray to resign the editorship of the *Cornhill;* and there was a reason in the background even of more importance than the desire to put all his energies into the writing of *Denis Duval.* This *real* reason I believe to have been his failing health. It is true he was only fifty-one, but he had had many severe illnesses (while at the Charterhouse, when writing *Pendennis,* at Rome, and elsewhere), and these had wrought much injury to his constitution, even apart from the internal disease that produced those terrible spasms of pain to which he was subject; in addition to these, late hours and lack of necessary exercise, coupled with tremendous continuous brain work, had now made it absolutely imperative that he take care of himself. His method of working even was injurious to his health. "I can conceive nothing more harassing in the literary way," Motley wrote in June, 1858, to his wife, "than his [Thackeray's] way of living from hand to mouth. I mean in regard to the way he furnishes food to the printer's devil. Here he is just finishing the number that must appear in a few days. Of course, whether ill or well, stupid or fertile, he must produce the same amount of fun, pathos, or sentiment. His gun must be regularly loaded and discharged at command. I should think it would wear his life out." And it *did* wear his life out; and Dickens told Mr. Fields that when he looked at Thackeray lying in his coffin, he wondered that the figure he had known in life as of such noble presence could seem so shrunken and wasted. His hands were quite thin, like those of an old man of eighty.

About this time, too, Thackeray told his cousin, Mr. Francis St. John Thackeray, "I have taken too many crops out of my brain." He was undoubtedly overworked, and disinclined to write. "I would like to rest my head in some quiet corner," he said to Miss Perry one day, when his number for the *Cornhill* was nearly due. "I had a nice scene this morning, but 'tis all gone, and I cannot call to mind a bit of it now." "I never take up the pen without an effort. I work only from necessity," he told another friend, and Mrs. Ritchie says that only the hours which he spent upon his drawing-blocks and sketch-books brought no fatigue and weariness; they were of endless interest and amusement to him, and rested him when he was tired.

It was about the year 1860 that he wrote to an old Charterhouse friend: "Now we are half a century old, and the kind hand which wrote the name in the books, in that fine, well-remembered writing is laid under the grass which will cover us old gentlemen too ere long, after our little life's journey is over. And the carriage is going down hill, isn't it? Mine is, after having had some pleasant travelling, after being well-nigh upset, after being patched up again, after being robbed by footpads, etc., etc. The terminus can't be far off—a few years more or less. I wouldn't care to travel over the ground again, though I have had some pleasant days and dear companions."

Thackeray knew that the end was near,* and he told his friend, Mr. Synge, when that gentleman was leaving England for some years: "I want to tell you that I shall never see you again. I feel that I am doomed. I know that this will grieve you; but look in that book and you will find something that I am sure will please and comfort you." The "something" was a prayer in which "he prayed that he might never write a word inconsistent with the love of God, or the love of man: that he might never propagate his own prejudices or pander to those of others: that he might always speak the truth with his pen, and that he might never be actuated by a love of greed. And I particularly remember," Mr. Synge has written, "that the prayer wound up with the words, 'For the sake of Jesus Christ our Lord.' "†

It is only my fancy, of course, but I shall always believe that when Thackeray wrote in *On Lett's Diary*, of Dr. London and Dr. Edinburgh he was unconsciously thinking of himself, and that, like the former, knowing that the end was approaching, "he made up his accounts with man and heaven. . . . And he said not a word to his family at home; but lived among them cheerful and tender, and calm and loving; though he knew that the night was near when he should see them and work no more. . . . And he died; and his family never knew until he was gone that he had long been aware of the inevitable doom."‡

* "I asked him if he had ever received the best medical advice. Certainly he had, was his reply; 'but what is the use of advice if you don't follow it?' he continued. 'They tell me not to drink, and I *do* drink. They tell me not to smoke, and I *do* smoke. They tell me not to eat, and I *do* eat. In short, I do everything I am desired not to do, and therefore, what am I to expect!' "—Mr. Hodder's *Memoirs*.

† Quoted from Mr. Merivale's *Life of Thackeray*.

‡ "Now, the dear girls are provided for. The great anxiety is taken from my life, and I can breathe freely for the little time that is left for me to be with them," Thackeray said to Mr. Bayard Taylor, after the second visit to America.

In the same way, nothing can disturb my conviction that, thinking of the end of his life, Thackeray endeavoured to make his peace with the world when he wrote: "In former days, I too have militated, sometimes, as I now think, unjustly; but always, I know, without personal rancour. Which of us has not idle words to recall, flippant jokes to regret? Have you never committed an imprudence? Have you never had a dispute and found out you were wrong? So much the worse for you. Woe be to the man *qui croit toujours avoir raison*. . . . As I write . . . I think about one or two little affairs of my own. . . . Never mind, old Squaretoes: never mind, Madame Pomposa! Here is a hand. Let us be friends, as we once were, and have no more of this rancour."

In 1859 Thackeray had taken a long lease of a rather dilapidated house on the west side of Kensington Palace Gardens, with the intention of repairing and improving it before he lived there. Eventually, however, he pulled down the whole building, and reared upon its site a fine mansion—he himself drew up the plans—of red brick, with stone facings in the style of Queen Anne—a style singularly appropriate for the dwelling-place of the author of *Esmond* and *The English Humourists*. Thackeray moved to Palace Green early in February, 1862, and a few weeks later gave a house-warming. "The cards of invitation," Mr. John Irvine has recorded, "were for 'W. Empty House' (denoting at once its unfurnished condition and the initials of its owner); and the bill proclaimed the fare of our host's play of *The Wolves and the Lamb* to be followed by a farce entitled *A Desperate Game*, by J. Maddison Morton, the author of *Box & Cox*, who, curiously enough, ended his days as a Charterhouse Codd. I see in the play-bill that Mr. Thackeray is announced as *Mr. Bonnington*, but in fact he only appeared upon the stage just before the fall of the curtain, to say, 'Bless you, my children.' ''

Installed in his new house, working for the *Cornhill*, and preparing *Denis Duval*, the time passed tranquilly, without any event of public interest, until November, 1862, when Thackeray once more had a serious illness. It was of the time while he was still convalescent that Archdeacon Sinclair has related the following characteristic tale, which illustrates Thackeray's character better than many pages of description. ''At the height of the cotton famine,'' the Archdeacon says, in the *Sketches of Old Times and Distant Places*, ''I resolved to hold a public meeting in Kensington, to raise contributions in aid of the Lancaster Fund. Among the speakers who occurred to me was my neighbour, W. M. Thackeray, whose name I knew would be a powerful attraction. I called upon him, but . . . he was unwell and had not come downstairs. I sent up my card, and he soon made his appearance. When I told him my errand was to request *a speech*, he at once declined, not being well enough, as he said, even to attend the meeting. I urged that he had several days to recover in. But for him to move a resolution at a public meeting was out of the question. . . . 'You forget,' he added, 'that my vocation is not to be a speaker, but a writer.' In reply I explained that I did not wish for a long harangue, that I had an abundance of orators ready to come forward, and that in Kensington the great difficulty was to collect an audience. 'But,' I added, 'if you will only let me print your name in my handbills, I shall be sure of a large attendance, and I can depend on my orators to call forth contributions.' Thackeray was amused at this unexpected turn, and, in the kindest manner, said, 'Though I am far from well, you may depend upon me. If I am alive I shall be with you.' I immediately issued handbills, announcing that among other speakers W. M. Thackeray would address the meeting. A crowd assembled. Great applause followed as he rose. As soon as silence was restored he began with perfect self-possession and delivered, with much emphasis, a few weighty and well-considered sentences. They were received with enthusiasm, and I was afterwards congratulated repeatedly on my success in calling forth for the first, and, as unhappily it proved, the last time, the rhetorical powers of the great novelist." The Archdeacon has omitted to state that at the meeting which was held, on December 1, at the Vestry Hall, Kensington, Thackeray headed the subscription list with a donation of fifty pounds.

In the following May, Cruikshank was exhibiting his works, and the exhibition was little better than a failure until (anxious to do his old friend a kindness, and render what help he could) "kind Thackeray came with his grave face, and looked through the little gallery, and went off to write one of his charming essays" which appeared in the *Times* of May 15. Later in the year a National Shakespeare Committee, with Hepworth Dixon, the editor of the *Athenæum*, as honorary secretary, was formed to celebrate the tercentenary of Shakespeare's birth. The Prince was to be invited to become chairman, and Lytton, Tennyson, and Dickens were elected Vice-Presidents, and it was proposed that Thackeray should be appointed to join them; but Dixon, who bore him a grudge, induced the committee to reject the motion, with the result that the whole body was assailed in all directions as soon as this proceeding became known. In the midst of the squabble Thackeray died, and soon after the affair toppled over like a pack of cards.*

On December 12 Thackeray kept his last Founder's Day at Greyfriars (when his old schoolfellow and friend, Leech, was one of the stewards), "looking very weak, and anticipating resource to a small surgical operation," and four days later he was dining cheerfully at the Garrick Club, "pretending," one of the company has narrated, "to incite one very old friend to give a party of an excessively gay description, in order, as he said, that we might fancy ourselves all young again."

On the next day, Thursday, December 17, Thackeray, with his eldest daughter, dined at Dr. Merriman's, who, with Dr. Elliotson, had watched him through his dangerous illness in 1849. "As he entered," Dr. Merriman wrote in the *St. Mary Abbotts Parish Magazine*, "I saw he was not well, and with his usual kindness he said, 'I would only have turned out to come to you as an old friend.' I remember saying, 'Oh! but you, like every Englishman, will be better for your dinner. Do you know Jean Ingelow?' 'No—the woman in all London whom I am most anxious to know,' was the reply. 'Do you know the quondam Miss Croker?' 'No, but she is not here,' he replied. They were *both* present, and I had the great pleasure of introducing him to them. He soon revived under this mental pleasure. Ere we reached the dining-room he was himself again, and, falling in with an old Carthusian, Sir George Barrow, all

*" Full particulars of this affair are to be read in a pamphlet published in 1864, entitled *The National Shakespeare Committee and Mr. Thackeray*.

went as pleasantly as possible. . . . My friend stayed late, his daughter going on to some other party, and I strolled up Young Street with him; we halted by 'No. 13,' when he alluded to old times and happy days there; he told me *Vanity Fair* was his greatest work, and *The Cane-bottomed Chair* his favourite ballad; and we parted at the top of 'Our Street,' never to meet again alive in this world."

Carlyle saw Thackeray on December 19 or 20, and he wrote afterwards to Lord Houghton: "Poor Thackeray! I saw him not ten days ago. I was riding in the dusk, heavy of heart, along by the Serpentine and Hyde Park, when some human brother from a chariot, with a young lady in it, threw me a shower of salutations. I looked up—it was Thackeray with his daughter: the last time I was to see him in this world. He had many fine qualities; no guile or malice against any mortal; a big mass of a soul, but not strong in proportion; a beautiful vein of genius lay struggling about in him. Nobody in our day wrote, I should say, with such perfection of style. I predict of his books very much as you do. Poor Thackeray! Adieu! Adieu!"

Trollope saw him about the same time. "I saw him," he wrote, "for the last time about ten days before his death, and sat with him for half an hour talking about himself. I never knew him pleasanter, or more at ease as to his bodily ailments"; and Dickens was one of the last persons, outside his family, to see him alive. The two famous novelists had not spoken for some years—since the Yates affair—and they met on the steps of the Athenæum Club a few days before Christmas. They passed each other, and then Thackeray turned back, and with outstretched hand went up to Dickens and said he could no longer bear to be on any but the old terms of friendship; and the men shook hands heartily, and once again were friends. "He told me," Dickens has recorded, "he told me he had been in bed three days—that, after these attacks, he was troubled with cold shiverings 'which quite took the work out of him'—and that he had it in his mind to try a new remedy, which he described. He was very cheerful, and looked very bright." Sir Theodore Martin, who had witnessed the reconciliation, afterwards remarked: "The next time I saw Dickens he was looking down into the grave of his great rival in Kensal Green. How he must have rejoiced, I thought, that they had so shaken hands!"

On Tuesday, December 21, he attended the funeral of Lady Rodd, a relative, and afterwards went to the Garrick Club; on Wednesday he was out several times, and was seen in Palace Gardens reading a book. At last the sad day came, after which "the tears shall be wiped from all eyes, and there shall be neither sorrow nor pain." "On December 24," says Dr. Merriman, "I was summoned about 8 a. m. to Palace Gardens, to find him lying dead in his bed! Life had been extinct for some hours; effusion had taken place into his powerful and great brain, and he had passed away in the night to the better country, where there is no night."*

How pleasant to remember the last words, which Thackeray saw and revised in print, of the unfinished novel *Denis Duval:* "And my heart throbbed with an exquisite bliss."

* Strangely enough Thackeray's step-father had died (also from sudden stoppage of the heart's action) on December 23 in the preceding year, and his mother followed him to the grave after exactly a year's interval.

Mr. Justin McCarthy has said that he was invited to dine with Thackeray on the day of his sudden death.

Matthew Arnold was greatly shocked by Thackeray's sudden death, but in his letter to his mother recording the sad event cannot refrain from that spirit of critical depreciation which is the prevailing tone of the entire two volumes of his recently published *Letters*, wherever they deal with his English contemporaries.

"While writing these last words I have heard the startling news of the sudden death of Thackeray. He was found dead in his bed this morning. If you have not seen it in the newspaper before you read this, you will all be greatly startled and shocked as I am. I have heard no particulars. I cannot say that I thoroughly liked him, though we were on friendly terms; and he is not, to my thinking, a great writer. Still, this sudden cessation of an existence so lately before one's eyes, so vigorous and full of life, and so considerable a power in the country, is very sobering, if, indeed, after the shock of a fortnight ago, one still needs sobering."*

Edmund Yates has told of the great shock the news gave him, as for ever destroying the hope he had entertained that the breach between him and the great novelist might eventually have been healed. "For many months," he continued, "any bitterness which I may have entertained against him had died out, and when I treated of his loss in print, I was able conscientiously to claim my share of the great and general grief!" And nobly did Mr. Yates make his public *amende honorable* in the following passage, which may well be quoted here as a truthful obituary notice, written by one who had known him.

"On Christmas Eve in the twilight, at the times when the clubs are filled with men who have dropped in

* *Letters of Matthew Arnold*, vol. i., page 213.

on their homeward way to hear the latest news or to exchange pleasant jests or seasonable greetings, a rumour ran through London that Thackeray was dead. I myself heard it on the club steps from the friend who had just returned from telegraphing the intelligence to an Irish newspaper, and at first doubted, as did all, the authenticity of the information. One had seen him but two days before, another had dined in his company but two nights previously; but it was true! Thackeray was dead; and the purest English prose-writer of the nineteenth century, and the novelist with a greater knowledge of the human heart, as it really is, than any other—with the exception perhaps of Shakespeare and Balzac—was suddenly struck down in the midst of us. In the midst of us! No long illness, no lingering decay, no gradual suspension of power; almost pen in hand, like Kempenfeldt, he went down.* 'Well,' said the *Examiner*, 'whatever little feuds may have gathered about Mr. Thackeray's public life lay lightly on the surface of the minds that chanced to be in contest with him. They could be thrown off in a moment—at the first shock of the news that he was dead.'

"It seemed impossible to realise the fact. No other celebrity, be he writer, artist, actor, seemed so thoroughly a portion of London. That 'good grey head which all men knew' was as easy of recognition as his to whom the term applied, the Duke of Wellington. Scarcely a day passed without his being seen in the Pall

*To how many men must the following lines have been recalled when they heard of Thackeray's death on Christmas Eve:—

"I lay the weary pen aside,
And wish you health, and love, and mirth,
As fits the solemn Christmas birth,
As fits the holy Christmas birth,
Be this, good friends, our carol still,—
Be peace on earth, be peace on earth,
To men of gentle will!"

Mall districts, and a Londoner, showing country cousins the wonders of the Metropolis, generally knew how to arrange for them to have a sight of the great English writer.

"The *Examiner* was right, God knows! the shock had thrown off all but regretful feelings, and an impossibility to comprehend the magnitude of the sudden loss.

"We talked of him—of how, more than any other author, he had written about what is said of men immediately after their death—of how he had written of the death-chamber, 'They shall come in here for the last time to you, my friend in motley.' We read that marvellous sermon which the week-day preacher delivered to entranced thousands over old John Sedley's dead body, and 'sadly fell our Christmas Eve.' One would have thought that the *Times* could have spared more space than a bare three-quarters of a column for the record of such a man's life and death. One would have thought that Westminster Abbey would have opened her doors for the earthly remains of one whose name will echo to the end of time. And, as I write, the thought occurs to me that the same man was, perhaps, the last to wish for either of these distinctions."

Of his funeral on December 30 it is unnecessary to speak.* The Middle Temple, of which he was a mem-

*About fifteen hundred persons were assembled at the cemetery, including many who were only acquainted with Thackeray through his books, and many names that are famous in literature and art—Browning, Dickens, Trollope, Mark Lemon, G. H. Lewes, Sir Theodore Martin, Dr. W. H. Russell, *Jacob Omnium*, Rev. Dr. Rudge (Master of the Charterhouse), Millais, Cruikshank, Leech, Shirley Brooks, Charles Matthews, Redgrave, Tenniel, Doyle, Du Maurier, Louis Blanc, George Smith, F. Greenwood, Edmund Yates, Horace Mayhew, Baron Marochetti (whose bust of Thackeray is placed in Westminster Abbey), and many others. Carlyle was prevented from attending, by illness in his family. Thackeray's two daughters were present in the chapel, and also looked into the grave.

ber, asked to be allowed to bury him in the Temple, where Goldsmith lies; but the offer was declined, and his mortal remains were laid at rest in the cemetery at Kensal Green, under a plain stone, bearing the simple but sufficient record:—

WILLIAM MAKEPEACE THACKERAY
BORN *July* 18, 1811.
DIED *December* 24, 1863.

CHAPTER XXII

THACKERAY AND HIS FRIENDS

CHAPTER XXII

THACKERAY AND HIS FRIENDS

WHEN, a little before the end, one of his daughters asked Thackeray which of his friends he had loved the best, he replied, "Why, dear old Fitz,* of course, and Brookfield."

His friendship with Edward Fitzgerald, dating from their Cambridge days, and probably cemented by their trip to Paris in 1829, never *really* wavered during their lives. In the earlier years they wrote very frequently to each other, and Fitzgerald was able to fill a volume with the drawings he received from this correspondence, for it was Thackeray's custom to illustrate his letters to his intimates. Besides, he illustrated his friend's *Undine* in about fourteen little coloured drawings, with which the possessor was so pleased that, after reading the *Spectator*, he wrote to John Allen, asking if he did not think it would make a nice book to publish all the papers about Sir Roger de Coverley alone, with illustrations by Thackeray.

Fitzgerald used often to stay in Great Coram Street (Jorum Street, Thackeray called it) and in Young Street. The novelist loved to have him in the house, for he was a delightful companion; the only drawback

*It is a singular fact that Tennyson also regarded "dear old Fitz" —after the death of Arthur Hallam—as his "best-loved friend," though, like Thackeray, he saw but little of the Recluse of Woodbridge in later life.

being that they talked so much of books and poems that neither did much work.

The poet's diary contains many entries, and his letters many references, concerning his great literary brother. He tells how, in 1832, Thackeray came to see him before returning to Devonshire: "He came very opportunely to divert my Blue Devils, notwithstanding we do not see very much of each other; and he has now so many friends (especially the Bullers) that he has no such wish for my society. He is as full of good-humour and kindness as ever." Yet they continued to correspond when Thackeray was abroad, and met frequently after his return until after 1848, or 1849, when they saw less of each other.

"I am going to his" [Spedding's] "rooms this very evening: and there I believe Thackeray, Venables, etc., are to be," Fitzgerald wrote on April 17, 1850. "I hope there is not a large assembly, for I get shyer and shyer, even of those I know." It is in this letter that he said, "Thackeray is in such a great world that I am afraid of him; he gets tired of me, and we are content to regard each other at a distance." But I do not believe Thackeray got tired of him. "I am glad *you* like it," the novelist wrote to him of *Vanity Fair*.

Perhaps the explanation of the less frequent letters and meetings is to be found as much in Fitzgerald's shyness as in anything else.

But there never was any real coldness between them, and the memory of their younger days never faded. When Fitzgerald heard that Thackeray was about to cross the Atlantic to deliver the lectures, he at once exclaimed: "And so dear old Thackeray is really going to America. I must fire him a letter of farewell." And he did write to him, and told him of a provision he had made in his will. "You see," he said, "you can owe me no thanks for giving what I can no longer use when I go down to the pit. . . ." Thackeray's letter of farewell to his "dearest old friend," in which he asked the poet to be his literary executor, and, if anything happened, to look after his wife and children, has already been quoted in an earlier chapter; and when, in 1854, Fitzgerald went to town, he hoped to catch a sight of "old Thackeray, who, Doone wrote me word, came suddenly on him in Pall Mall the other day; while all the while people supposed *The Newcomes* was being indited at Rome or Naples." "Oddly enough," he wrote to Mr. E. B. Cowell on January 26, 1857, "as I finished the last sentence, Thackeray was announced; he came in, looking gray, grand, and good-humoured; and I held up this letter, and told him whom it was written to, and he sends his love! He goes lecturing all over England, has fifty pounds for each lecture, and says he is ashamed of the fortune he is making. But he deserves it."

A few days after, he went to hear his friend discourse on George III. "Very agreeable to me, though I did not think highly of the lecture."

This must have been one of the last meetings of the two men. But the long interval did not deaden their feelings, and the news of his friend's death came as a great shock to Fitzgerald. "Really, a great figure has sunk under earth," he said to George Crabbe; and in a letter, dated January 7, 1864, asking Samuel Laurence for particulars of his two portraits of Thackeray, he wrote: "I am surprised almost to find how much I am thinking of him, so little as I had seen him for the last ten years—not once for the last five. I have been told—by you, for one—that he was spoiled. I am glad, therefore, that I have scarce seen him since he was 'old Thackeray.' I keep reading his *Newcomes* of nights, and, as it were, hear him saying so much in it; and it seems to me as if he might be coming up my stairs, and about to come (singing) into my room, as in old Charlotte Street, etc., thirty years ago."

He had naturally followed Thackeray's career with great interest, and read everything he wrote, as the many criticisms in his letters testify. "Don't you think Thackeray's *Mrs. Perkyn's Ball* very good? I think the empty faces of the dance-room were never done better," he asked Carlyle, when the Christmas book appeared. "Thackeray, to be sure, can write good ballads, half-serious," he told Frederick Tennyson; and as late as 1876 he wanted to put "Ho, pretty page" to an old Cambridge tune which Thackeray and he had often sung together. "The words, you know, are so delightful (stanzas one, two, and the last), and the old tune of 'Troll, Troll the bonny brown bowl' so pretty and (with some addition) so appropriate, I think, that I fancied others besides friends might like to have them together. But if you don't approve, the whole thing shall be quashed," he wrote to Mrs. Ritchie. The *Roundabout Papers* he thought the pleasantest pages in the *Cornhill Magazine*. "A night or two ago I was reading old Thackeray's *Roundabouts*," he wrote to Sir Frederick Pollock in 1871, "and (sign of a good book) heard him talking to me. I wonder at his being so fretted by what was said of him, as some of these Papers show that he was: very unlike his old self, surely. Perhaps ill-health (which Johnson said made every one a scoundrel) had something to do with this. I don't mean that W. M. T. went this length, but in this one respect he was not so good as he used to be." To Samuel Laurence, some four years later, he wrote: "As to Thackeray's" [books], "they are terrible; I really look at them on the shelf, and am half afraid to touch them. He, you know, could go deeper into the Springs of Common Action than these ladies" [Miss Austen and George Eliot]; "wonderful he is, but not delightful, which one thirsts for as one gets old and dry." And finally, comparing the literary merits of Disraeli with Thackeray, he wrote to a lady in America: "The book" [Lothair] "is like a pleasant magic lantern; when it is over, I shall forget it, and shall want to return to what I do not forget: some of Thackeray's monumental figures of *pauvre et triste Humanité*, as old Napoleon calls it; Humanity in its depths, not in its superficial appearances."*

To the Rev. William Brookfield and his wife so many references have been made in these volumes that it is scarcely necessary to say anything further concerning them. They were his life-long friends. Writing to them from Paris, in a letter describing the dinners he had eaten, the theatres he had visited, the sights he had seen, and the people he had met, he concluded: "With all this racket and gaiety, . . . do you understand a gentleman feels very lonely? I swear I had sooner have a paper and gin-and-water *soirée* with somebody than the best President's orgeat." "I tell you and William most things," he wrote on another day. Their house was always open to him; their regard for him was carried to his children; and Mrs. Brookfield, on the last day of her life, quoted to Mrs. Ritchie a passage from

*See *The Letters of Edward Fitzgerald.*

the great novelist's works, in which he said of great men, "They speak of common life more largely and generously than common men do; they regard the world with a manlier countenance. . . . Learn to admire rightly; try to frequent the company of your betters in books and life." If any one has not yet seen the letters that Thackeray wrote to these friends, let them, without delay, obtain the volume, and read it through, from beginning to end. It contains the most delightful side-lights imaginable upon the writer's character.

Alfred Tennyson and Thackeray formed a complete mutual admiration society *à deux*. The poet wrote of the novelist as a "lovable man"; and he, in his turn, addressed his letters to "My dear old Alfred." The friendship, which commenced at the University, was only broken by Thackeray's death. A characteristic incident must be told here. One night, when Tennyson and Thackeray had been praising Miss Barrett's poems, the former said he loved Catullus for his perfection in form and for his tenderness. "I do not rate him highly," the latter objected. "I could do better myself." The next morning, remembering what he had said, Thackeray was horrified, and wrote to Tennyson at once: "When I have dined, sometimes I believe myself to be equal to the greatest painters and poets. That delusion goes off; and then I know what a small fiddle mine is, and what small tunes I play upon it."*

Thackeray, ill in bed, read *The Idylls of the King* with

*Mr. James Payn, in the *Illustrated London News*, described an amusing scene between Thackeray and an ancient scholar of the old school. He maintained that all that was really valuable in English literature was owed to Pindar. "But, my good sir," pleaded the novelist, "you don't mean to say that Pindar wrote *Vanity Fair?*" "Yes, I do," he said, "in the highest and noblest sense; and if it is a good book, Pindar wrote *Vanity Fair*."

much admiration. "Oh! I must write to him now for this pleasure, this delight, this splendour of happiness which I have been enjoying," he said in a note to the poet, who declared that this tribute gave him "more pleasure than all the journals and monthlies and quarterlies which have come across me, not so much for your being the Great Novelist, I hope, as from your being my very good friend."

When Tennyson's *Grandmother* appeared in *Once a Week*, Thackeray was greatly struck by it. "I wish I could have got that poem for my *Cornhill*," he said to Mr. Locker-Lampson; "I would have paid fifty pounds for it; but I would have given five hundred pounds to have been able to write it." But Tennyson did not approve of a man of Thackeray's genius undertaking editorial work. "I am sorry," the great poet wrote, "that you have engaged, for any quantity of money, to let your brains be sucked periodically by Smith, Elder & Co.; not that I don't like Smith, who seems, from the very little I have seen of him, liberal and kindly, but that so great an artist as you should go to work after this fashion."

This profound admiration of Thackeray has always been a tradition in the late Poet Laureate's family. Not long ago, the present Lord Tennyson remarked to a friend, "he always regarded Thackeray as the head of English literature of the Victorian Era."

This was one of Thackeray's most delightful friendships, and many charming interchanges of regard and affection passed between the poet and the novelist. "You don't know how pleased the girls were at Kensington t'other day," Thackeray wrote to him in 1859, "to hear you quote their father's little verses; and he, too, I daresay, was not disgusted.'' It is pleasant and right that a great poet and a great humourist should be able to appreciate each other's gifts, and speak of them generously.

Thackeray, indeed, was never sparing of praise for his contemporaries. Though he might belabour Byron* and Madame Sand, and tilt with considerable vigour against the ''Newgate'' novels, honestly believing *Don Juan*, *Spiridion*, *Eugene Aram*, *Oliver Twist*, *Jack Sheppard*, and similar creations, did considerable harm, he always spoke with great admiration of the two artists Cruikshank and Leech, who might, in some measure, be considered as his rivals in comic portraitures; and, both in his writings and his letters, wrote with appreciation, not necessarily unbounded, but certainly not too strictly critical, of Macaulay, and Washington Irving, of Hood (whose *Song of the Shirt* he declared the finest lyric ever written), of Lever, of Charlotte Brontë, and, above all, of Dickens. He praised Bulwer Lytton for the good example he set by being ''thoroughly literate,'' and admired Disraeli for his splendid talents. He reverenced ''the great old Goethe,'' and made frequent mention of Scott, whose *Ravenswood* he wrote down as the best thing he ever did. Dumas, whom he had met in

*Byron, who, though he died in 1824, can scarcely be called a contemporary, he heartily disliked. "Give me a fresh, dewy, healthy rose out of Somersetshire; not one of those superb, tawdry, unwholesome exotics, which are only good to make poems about," Thackeray wrote. "Lord Byron wrote more cant of this sort than any poet I know of. Think of 'the peasant girls with dark blue eyes' of the Rhine—the brown-faced, flat-nosed, thick-lipped, dirty wenches! Think of 'filling high a cup of Samian wine'; small beer is nectar compared to it, and Byron himself always drank gin. The man *never* wrote from his heart. He got up rapture and enthusiasm with an eye to the public. . . . Our native bard! *Mon Dieu! He* Shakspeare's, Milton's, Keats', Scott's native bard! Well, woe be to the man who denies the public gods."

Paris at the house of Gudin the painter, thoroughly aroused his enthusiasm. "All the forenoon," he wrote from Paris in 1849, "I read, with intense delight, a novel called *Le Viscomte de Bragelonne*, a continuation of the famous *Mousquetaires*, and just as interesting, keeping one panting from volume to volume, and longing for more." And afterwards, in America, he said to Mr. Cooke, "Dumas is charming. He is better than Walter Scott. . . . I came near writing a book on the same subject, *Les Trois Mousquetaires*, and taking Monsieur d'Artagnan for my hero. D'Artagnan was a real character of the age of Louis XIV., and wrote his own *Mémoires*. I remember picking up a dingy copy of them on an old bookstall in London, price sixpence, and intended to make something of it. But Dumas got ahead of me—he snaps up everything. He is wonderful!"

Thackeray was always happy when he could pay a compliment in his books to his friends. "The young Aga came for a pair of shoes; his contortions were so delightful as he tried them on that I remained with great pleasure, wishing for Leech to be at hand to sketch his lordship and his fat mamma, who sat on the counter," he wrote in *From Cornhill to Cairo*. And in the same volume, a little further on, he mentioned: "You can't put down in prose that delicious episode of natural poetry" [the bay of Glaucus]; "it ought to be done in a symphony, full of sweet strains of clear, crystal iambics, such as Milnes knows how to write." In one of his latest novels, *The Adventures of Philip*, he concluded a chapter: "There was a pretty group for the children to see, and for Mr. Walker to draw"; but the publishers, in their wisdom, have seen fit, in subsequent editions, to alter this to "for an artist to draw." He seemed to have a gift for discovering clever young men. "The time will come when you will lecture at Oxford," he said to Mr. Max Müller, though at the time (1856) nothing seemed more unlikely. And while he was in Rome, he wrote to Millais that he had met a versatile young man who would run him hard for the Presidentship one day. The versatile young man was Frederick Leighton, who not only ran Millais hard for the Presidentship, but actually won the race.

An amusing story had been told of Thackeray, who, with Millais and Dickens, was in the Park at Knoll, and came across some artists sketching. Millais went up to one of them, and said, "I beg your pardon, but your perspective is wrong." "Perhaps you can do it better yourself," the artist said. "I'll try," Millais answered; and he did so, and passed on to the next amateur. "Who's your friend?" said the instructed artist to Thackeray, who still stood beside him. "Millais," said Thackeray, leaving Dickens behind. "Who's that?" No. 1 artist said to Dickens, referring to Thackeray. He received the information. "And who are you?" the artist further inquired. "I'm Charles Dickens." "Really," said the amateur; "I wonder who you think I am?" And I grieve to have to say that he put his fingers up to his nose, performing the action commonly known as "cocking a snook."

Another good tale is told that, at an Academy dinner, several painters were talking together. "His glorious colouring is a fact about Titian," said one. "And his glorious drawing is another fact about Titian," said a second—when Carlyle, who had been listening, interrupted them. "And here I sit, a man made in the image of God, who knows nothing about Titian, and cares nothing about Titian—and that's another fact about Titian!" Thackeray, who was sipping claret at the moment, paused, and bowed courteously to Carlyle, and then remarked, "Pardon me, that is not a fact about Titian. But it is a fact—and a lamentable one—about Thomas Carlyle!" There was friendship between Carlyle and Thackeray, and much admiration and appreciation. I think their philosophy was in closer accord than either dreamt. "Thackeray," Carlyle said to Sir Charles Gavan Duffy, "had more reality in him, and would cut up into a dozen Dickens." And in 1853 he wrote to Emerson, "Thackeray has rarely come athwart me since his return. He is a big fellow, soul and body, of many gifts and qualities, particularly in the Hogarth line, with a dash of Sterne superadded, of enormous appetite withal, and very uncertain and chaotic in all points, except his outer breeding, which is fixed enough, and *perfect* according to the modern English style."

Monckton Milnes (Lord Houghton) was another old college friend, and in later days Thackeray was a visitor at Fryston, a house, he said to his host, which combines the freedom of the tavern with the elegancies of the château—the compliment was paid for permission to smoke everywhere but in young Milnes's own rooms. On his return from Paris after the failure of the *Constitutional* newspaper, Milnes was one of the first to be informed of his advent. "The young chevalier," he wrote, "is arrived, and to be heard of at the Bedford Hotel in Covent Garden, or at the Garrick Club, King Street. He accepts breakfasts—and dinners still more willingly." And we may be sure that many breakfasts and dinners were offered and taken. It was to Milnes,

I think, more than to any one else that he went for advice during the many years of weary waiting for success. "I was thinking of our acquaintance the other day, and how it had been marked, on your part, by constant kindness, along which I can trace it," he wrote, just before he left for the first journey to America. "Thank you for them, and let me shake your hand, and say *Vale* and *Salve*."

Thackeray went for the last time to Fryston during the Easter Recess of 1863; and on the fatal Christmas Eve Milnes received a simple sheet of note-paper, dated from Palace Green, Kensington, upon which no words were written, but which bore a little coloured sketch of a robin redbreast perched upon the coronet of a baron—it was Thackeray's farewell.

Milnes was much grieved at the death of his old friend, though not surprised, knowing how full of disease he was. He was, however, very angry that the authorities of the Abbey did not ask permission to bury him within the precincts; and he drew an *Historical Contrast* between this behaviour and the conduct of Dr. Sprat, the Bishop of Rochester and Dean of Westminster, on the death of Dryden, who

"Waited for no suggestive prayer,
But, ere one day had closed o'er the scene,
Craved as a boon to lay him there."

Then he paid tribute to the great humourist of his day in the following stanzas, which concluded the poem:—

"O gentler Censor of our age!
Prime master of our ampler tongue!
Whose word of wit and generous page
Were never wrath, except with wrong.

"Fielding—without the manner's dross,
Scott—with a spirit's larger room;—
What Prelate deems thy grave his loss?
What Halifax erects thy tomb?

"But, maybe, He—who so could draw
The hidden great, the humble wise,
Yielding with them to God's good law,
Makes the Pantheon where he lies."

Among other friends who have already been mentioned were Sir Frederick Pollock (Queen's Remembrancer), Anthony Stirling, Spedding, George Stovin Venables (a leader of the Parliamentary bar), and *Jacob Omnium* (of the *Times*).*

Of the friendly relations existing between Thackeray and the Cockran family I have spoken elsewhere. "When Cockran dies, he will go straight to heaven, and all the angels will turn out and present arms to him," the novelist declared.

Between the Bullers and himself there was great affection, and the death of Charles, his favourite, in 1848, was a great blow to him. "Isn't it an awful sudden summons? There go wit, fame, friendship, ambition, high repute!" he wrote to Mrs. Brookfield. And it was to this friend he alluded in the following exquisite lines:—

"Who knows the inscrutable design?
Blessed be he who took and gave!
Why should your mother, Charles, not mine,
Be weeping at her darling's grave?"

Mrs. Crowe and her children must also be mentioned among his intimates. In Paris, where he attended her evening receptions, and in London, when the family, in 1844, settled at Hampstead, where he rode on his short cob, he was a frequent visitor. "Once in our drawing-room he was apt to forget the hours," Sir Joseph has

*Thackeray told Dean Hole of a visit he paid with Mr. Higgins (*Jacob Omnium*), who was four or five inches the taller of the two, to see a Brobdingnagian on show, and how the man at the door had inquired "whether they were in the business, because, if so, no charge would be made!"

said in his Reminiscences; "would stop to partake of an early dinner, though bound to join a later festivity of the same kind elsewhere; and I recollect him now, as if it were yesterday, wiping his brow after trying vainly to help the leg of a tough fowl, and saying he was 'heaving a thigh.'" He was able, and delighted to be able, to render the younger members of the family many good services. When Charles Mackay, in 1854, asked him to go to the seat of war to furnish sketches and letters for the *Illustrated News*, he refused, but induced the editor to send Joseph Crowe in his place; and on the young man's return, he started a scheme for him to make money by lecturing on the war. I have already said how Eyre Crowe went out with him to America. "Six months tumbling about the world will do you no harm," he said to the young artist. And the sister Amy he took into his house, where she stayed, treated as a third daughter, until she married a distant cousin of his own, Colonel Edward Thackeray, V.C., and went to India, where the gallant soldier succumbed to the tropical climate.

Barry Cornwall and his wife were his friends; Mrs. Kemble, too; and Leech, and Landseer, and Macready (Megreedy, Thackeray called him), Dean Hole, Sir Theodore Martin and his wife (Helen Faucit, to whom he intended to dedicate *Denis Duval*), Father Prout, Sir Henry Cole (of the Science and Art Department, South Kensington), who inspired *Punch's* Parody:

> "I built my *Cole* a lordly treasure house;"

Morgan John O'Connell, of whose father, the great Daniel, he said, "He may be a humbug, but he is a great man—we owe to him Catholic Emancipation"; besides, in his earlier years, Dr. Maginn, Horace Smith, the part-author of *Rejected Addresses*, "that good, severe old man," and his daughters, were also among Thackeray's intimates. Mr. Merivale has related that it was to them he confided how he was bound to produce the first number of *Pendennis* within a few days, and had no plot, and no idea wherewith to start one; and how they then and there told him a true anecdote of Brighton life, which he took as the basis of his novel; and how, in gratitude, he christened his heroine Laura, after one of the sisters; and how, finally, when he visited them after the story was finished, the original Laura was very angry. "I'll never speak to you again, Mr. Thackeray," she declared; "you know I always meant to marry Warrington."

"My father held, I know, a large place in Thackeray's heart," Mr. Herman Merivale has written. "It was not a friendship to be talked of much, for the two men had too much of the quiet side in common. The same philosophy, the same deep sense of religion, the same reserve which unfits for general popularities and makes enemies where it is misunderstood, the same breadth of mental vision and incapacity for meaner things—above all, the same pole-star, the Vanitas—and the same blessing of the quality of Love, made the still bond between them very strong. Like many others, Thackeray was much in the habit of referring knotty questions to my father, and often have I listened, with boyish keenness, to the table-talk between them, by turns grave and gay, fanciful and deep."

Of the friends he made in later years were many Americans, of whom the chief were Mr. W. B. Reed, Mr. Bayard Taylor, and Mr. Fields and his wife.

Thackeray, indeed, seems to have left behind him the kindliest memories in America. What a genuine ring there is in the *In Memoriam* lines which appeared, when the news of his death reached New York, in *Harper's Magazine:*

> " Now that his noble form is clay,
> One word for good old Thackeray—
> One word for gentle Thackeray—
> Spite of his disbelieving eye
> True Thackeray, a man who would not lie.
> Among his fellows he was peer
> For any gentleman that ever was."

Mr. Follett Synge, Mr. Jeaffreson, Locker-Lampson, and Anthony Trollope, too, and James Hannay were also among his friends.

"Hannay is a boy after my heart!" the white-headed novelist said to me more than once. "He is a thoroughbred little fighting cock for pluck and endurance. He is a perfect bird of his particular sort. Examine him as closely as you please, you won't find a white feather in him." And before going to America he placed the manuscript to the *English Humourists* in the young man's hands to annotate during his absence, and on his return introduced him to the *Quarterly Review*. In Mr. Hannay's obituary notice he spoke of himself as "one whom Thackeray had loaded with benefits."

Thackeray's friendships were not many, which is only another way of saying that he preferred friends to acquaintances. "There was," says Mr. Hodder, "a constitutional reserve in his manner"; and it was not in the nature of such a man to become hail fellow well met with every one. But his loyalty as a friend and his love for his intimates deserved all the beautiful tributes that these few men and women have paid to his memory. "Ah!" he exclaimed, on hearing the news of Charles Buller's death, "*Aimons nous bien!* It seems to me that is the only thing we can carry away. When we go, let us have some who love us wherever we are."

CHAPTER XXIII

THACKERAY, THE MAN

CHAPTER XXIII

THACKERAY, THE MAN*

OF all characters, Thackeray's is one of the most difficult to understand. It is apparently so complex that the unravelling appears, at a first glance, almost impossible. Yet, when it is seriously and sympathetically approached, the task is found not to be so very difficult after all: the various wraps in which the sensitive man had covered his real self become unfolded, and he stands before us the simple-minded, honourable gentleman that he was.

In these days of *nil admirari*, it is accounted conclusive proof of a degenerate spirit to feel affection for anything or anybody, except oneself; but I devoutly trust that those who read even this imperfect Life of Thackeray will exclaim, as they lay it down, *He was a man!* There have been great men who, for goodness (in the right sense of the word), for kindness and tender-

*In that curiously interesting work, *The Man of Genius*, in which Professor Lombroso, with marvellous ability, attempts to demonstrate that not only are "great wits to madness near allied," but that Genius and Insanity are only different manifestations of the same abnormal psychical conditions, appears the following statement about the great size of Thackeray's head. It is difficult, I may say, to escape Professor Lombroso. If a man of genius have an abnormally small head, he is allied with idiots; and if a huge cranium, then he is classed with certain maniacs.

"It is certain that in Italy, Volta, Petrarch, Bordoni, Brunacci, St. Ambrose, and Fúsinari, all presented great cranial capacity. The same character is found to a still greater degree in Kant (1,740 c.c.). Thackeray (1,660 c.c.), Cuvier (1,830 c.c.), and Turgueneff (2,012 c.c.)"

ness and thoughtfulness, can be compared with him. There have been some men of genius as good, as kind, as tender, and as thoughtful; but, as far as I know, there have been none who have possessed these qualities in a greater degree. Had Thackeray been simply a good man in the ordinary sense of the word, I had written about him with no particular emotion; had I discovered that he was a regular church-goer, and a large subscriber to the "Missions to the Jews," or to the "Society for instructing the Tierra del Fuegians in the use of the knife, spoon, and fork," I should have remained perfectly untouched. There are many such men: men good, fairly virtuous, narrow-minded, not ungenerous, moderately amiable. But Thackeray was not like unto these. He was not always a regular church-goer (I state this, of course, not as a merit, but as a fact); neither was he interested in the conversion of the Jews, nor in the question of the clothing of the Hottentots in shoddy blankets—his philosophy was cast in a broader mould. He was a man of letters, who was, before all else, "pray God, a gentleman." As in his books this is to be observed in his fear of emphatic writing, and in the entire absence of the slightest taint of vulgarity, so in his life it may be detected in his natural delicacy, in his dread of appearing sentimental, even in converse with any but his most intimate friends, and in a hundred other ways that the reader cannot but have noticed.

Only a few of his letters have been published; but if every letter he had ever written were placed before the public, it would only be enabled to admire him the more. No one is perfect. Here is a witticism just a trifle too sharply launched; there, in private correspondence to a confidential friend, a heedless word thoughtlessly written. But these trivialities are ignored when we note the innumerable kindnesses, unostentatiously performed, for the most part then unknown except to the recipient, and, occasionally, and whenever practicable, unknown even to him. As a friend said of him: "His charity, like his religion, he was chary of mentioning, except to deprecate the idea that he was particularly beneficent." His letters show the man as he is known from his writings to all appreciative readers—the homeless man hungering after love and affection, the sensitive man that Anthony Trollope never comprehended. "A *big*, fierce, weeping man; not a strong one," as Carlyle so vividly described him.

When Thackeray, speaking of his works, said, "They have only bought so many of my new book"; or, "Have you seen the abuse of my new number?" or, "What am I to turn my hand to? They are getting tired of my novels," Mr. Trollope admitted that he could not understand. He knew authors who boasted of their thousands of copies sold, but he had never heard any other writer declare that no one would read his masterpiece, and that the world was becoming tired of him, and he was puzzled accordingly. Yet the cause of such depreciating remarks lay but little below the surface. Thackeray spoke so, I think, not because he was indifferent to success or the opinion of his contemporaries, but because the pain inflicted by these wounds would have been greater if he had thought any one else would sympathise with him. He preferred to say, "This book is a failure," rather than let any one else tell him he had not succeeded. He was anxious to disarm criticism by himself turning critic. He was a very proud, as well as a very sensitive man. Sometimes he was almost absurdly sensitive, as he showed in the attitude he took with reference to the *Town-Talk* article; and in Mr. Locker-Lampson's *Autobiography* there is a strange instance of this exaggerated susceptibility to criticism. "I happened to meet him as I was leaving the Travellers' Club," Mr. Locker-Lampson wrote. "Even now I think I could point out the particular flagstone on which the dear fellow was standing, as he gazed down on me through his spectacles with that dreary expression of his which his friends knew so well. He said, 'What do you think of the last number?' (No. 2 or 3 of *The Newcomes*.) He himself was evidently not satisfied with it. 'I like it immensely,' was my cordial rejoinder. A word or two more passed respecting the illustrations, which had been sharply criticised, and just as we parted I was tactless enough to add, 'But, my dear fellow, perhaps there may be some kind people who will say that you did the cuts and Doyle the letter-press.' On this Thackeray's jaw dropped, and he exclaimed bitterly, 'I—Oh! really, that's your opinion, is it?' I saw at once what a mistake I had made, but I could only reply, 'I spoke in fun, pure fun; you know perfectly well how much I admire your writings, and also Doyle's cuts.' But Thackeray would have none of it, and turned wrathfully away in the direction of Pimlico. However, his wrath, I presume, died away in the large and charitable air of the Green Park, for when I met him the day after he was as amiable as ever. The fact is I had so exalted an opinion of Thackeray and of his writing that it seemed impossible such a demi-god should care for aught anybody said; whereas, like Tennyson, he felt anything that everybody said."

Perhaps the most pleasing trait in his character was a

THE MARQUIS OF STEYNE.

Suppressed in the second and all subsequent editions.

marvellous affection for children—I speak not only of his own, but of all other little boys and girls.

> "There's something, even in his bitterest mood,
> That melts him at the sight of infanthood;
> Thank God that he can love the pure and good,"

he wrote of himself in *The Golden Pen;* and the instances of this tenderness for children are innumerable. When Fields, the American publisher, was in London, he was mentioning the various sights he had seen, when Thackeray, who happened to overhear him, broke in with, "But you haven't seen the greatest one yet. Go with me to-day to St. Paul's, and hear the charity children sing." "So we went," Mr. Fields relates, "and I saw the 'head cynic of literature,' the 'hater of humanity' as a critical dunce in the *Times* once called him, hiding his bowed head, wet with tears, while his whole frame shook with emotion, as the children of poverty rose to pour out their anthems of praise. Afterwards he wrote about it."

"There is one day in the year," Thackeray said, in one of the lectures on the Georges, "when I think St. Paul's presents the noblest sight in the whole world: when five thousand charity children like nosegays, and with sweet fresh voices, sing the hymn which makes every heart thrill with praise and happiness. I have seen a hundred grand sights in the world—coronations, Parisian splendours, Crystal Palace openings, Pope's chapels with their processions of long-tailed cardinals and quavering choirs of fat *soprani*—but think in all Christendom there is no such sight as Charity Children's Day. *Non Angli, sed angeli.* As one looks at that beautiful multitude of innocents; as the first note strikes;—indeed one may almost fancy that cherubs are singing." And elsewhere he has written, "To see a hundred boys marshalled in a chapel or old hall; to hear their sweet fresh voices when they chant, and look in their brave, calm faces; I say, does not the sight and sound of them smite you, somehow, with a pang of exquisite kindness?"

Every reference he made to children was in the same kindly spirit. He could never see a boy, he told Dickens, without wanting to give him a sovereign, and he always advocated, and even pleaded, for the tipping of schoolboys. "Ah! my dear sir," he wrote in a *Roundabout Paper*, "if you have any little friends at school, go and see them, and do the natural thing by them. You won't miss the sovereign. You don't know what a blessing it will be to them. Don't fancy they are too old—try 'em. And they will remember you and bless you in future days; and their gratitude shall accompany your dreary after-life, and they shall meet you kindly when thanks for kindness are scant. Oh mercy! shall I ever forget the sovereign you gave me, Captain Bob? . . . No. If you have any little friends at school, out with your half-crowns, my friend, and impart to those little ones the fleeting joys of their age." "It is all very well, my dear sir, to say that boys contract habits of expecting tips," he remarked on another occasion; "that they become avaricious and so forth. Fudge! Boys contract habits of tart and toffee-eating which they do not carry into after-life. On the contrary, I wish I *did* like tarts and toffee."

There was scarcely a boy of his acquaintance he had not tipped. On Founder's Day at Charterhouse, he would single out a name from the gown-boys' list: "Here's the son of dear old So-and-so; let's go and tip him." And one day, at the Exhibition of 1862, when

Good Dicky Snooks
Is fond of his books
And is loved by his Usher & Master
But naughty Tom Spry
Has got a black eye
And carries his nose in a plaster.

Miss Mary Knight
Has a small appetite
But Thomas her brothers a glutton
For breakfast he takes
Two pounds of beefsteaks
And for dinner a leg of roast Mutton

he was accompanied by Herman Merivale, he stopped a procession of school-girls and exclaimed, "Four-and-twenty little girls! They must have four-and-twenty bright little sixpences." And he spoke to the governess who was with them, and the little girls had their bright little sixpences.

He loved to draw caricatures for children—we know he commenced *The Rose and the Ring* to amuse a sick girl—and he loved to play with them, and to take them to the pantomime. There is a characteristic tale told of him, that he was once asked by a young man whom, as a boy, he had invited to dinner at his club, if he remembered the occasion. "Oh, yes!" said the great man, "and I remember what I gave you. Beefsteak and apricot omelette." The other was delighted that his host should remember even the details, and expressed his pleasure. "Yes," said Thackeray, twinkling in his own inimitable way, "I always gave boys beefsteaks and apricot omelette."

One of the most charming pictures of Thackeray has been presented in an article printed in *Temple Bar* for 1888, by Miss Henrietta Cockran, who knew him when she was a child of seven:—

"Amongst the many interesting people who gathered round my father and mother," she says, "none made such a vivid impression on my childish imagination as Thackeray. He is the central figure which stands out in bold relief from the dim surroundings. I can distinctly recall the big, white head, the spectacles, the rosy face, and the sweet, sunny smile which positively illumined his countenance and made it almost beautiful. I grew to love the broad, broken nose, and used to wonder how a boy at any period could have been so wildly audacious as to punch that feature. I wondered at the softness and the gentleness of his voice and manner, and why so great an author should care to come amongst us children in such a simple, friendly way. He had a formidable appearance, being over six feet, and broad in proportion. But evidently he was not too tall or too great to take an interest in our childish games. How often has he sat amongst us, enquiring tenderly after my dolls! He remembered all their names, and had made out a genealogical tree, so that every *poupée* had a distinct history of its own.

"One late afternoon, after having told us delightful stories, Mr. Thackeray remarked that he must leave at once, he was so terribly hungry. We coaxed him to remain, and told him we really could give him a good dinner.

"'There is nothing, my dears, you can give me,' he answered, with a funny little sigh; 'for I could only eat a chop of a rhinoceros or a slice from an elephant.'

"'Yes, I tan,' exclaimed my three-year-old sister; and we saw her disappear into a big cupboard. She emerged a few seconds after, with a look of triumph on her fat little face, holding in her hands a wooden rhinoceros and elephant from her Noah's Ark; and putting the two animals on a plate, she handed them with great gravity to Mr. Thackeray. Never can I forget the look of delight on the great man's face; how he laughed and rubbed his hands with glee; and then, taking the child up in his arms, kissed her, remarking, 'Ah, little rogue, you already know the value of a kiss.' Then he asked for a knife and fork, smacked his lips, and pretended to devour the elephant and rhinoceros.

"Another time when Mr. Thackeray called, we chil-

I tremble to write
The fate of Tom Knight
For here the poor fellow's in bed seen
And see how he takes
Instead of beef steaks
All sorts of the nastiest med'cine

Little Miss Perkins
Much loved pickled Gerkins
And went to the Cup board & stole some
But they gave her such pain
She ne'er ate them again
She found them so shocking unwholesome.

dren were in bed. I was the only one not asleep. I had been listening to his pleasant voice talking to my father and mother in the *salon*, when our bedroom door was cautiously opened, and in marched Mr. Thackeray, my mother following him with a candle. There were three little iron beds all in a row; I saw him smiling at us, and then, putting his hand in his pocket, he murmured, 'Now for the distribution of medals!' and chuckling, he deposited on each of our pillows a bright five-franc piece, remarking 'Precious little ones! they will think the fairies have been here.'

"Mr. Thackeray often made us little ones laugh heartily with his droll stories and ways. He one day spied my crinoline, which was on a chair in the nursery; he examined it carefully, and to my horror put his head through the aperture, and walked into the drawing-room with it round his neck, looking like Michael Angelo's statue of Moses.

"'I am an ogre now!' he exclaimed. 'Imagine, my dears, that I have a cropped red head, blue eyes, and very big *lunettes!*' and forthwith he related to us wonderful adventures, making us laugh and cry, just as he wished."

Next to his love of children came his charitable nature and his thoughtfulness for any one in trouble of any sort. His charity was only bounded by his means. He was not a man who waited to be asked to do a favour; his kindly heart would anticipate, not only the request, but frequently even the wish itself. How delicately, too, he dispensed his charities!

We are told by Miss Penny how he discovered some old acquaintance who—possibly through extravagance in money-making days—was in very reduced circumstances.

Thackeray mounted the many steps leading to the desolate chamber, administered some little rebuke on the thoughtlessness of not laying by some of the easily gained gold of youth or manhood and, slipping into a blotting book a hundred-pound note, hurried away. "I never saw him do it," said poor old P——. "I was very angry because he said I had been a reckless old goose—and then a hundred pounds falls out of my writing-book. God bless him!"

Nearly every one has heard how he was one day found in his room at a Paris hotel, writing on the lid of a pill-box, "One to be taken occasionally." He was asked what he was doing. "Well," he explained, "there is an old person here who says she is very ill and in distress, and I strongly suspect that this is the sort of medicine she wants. Dr. Thackeray intends to leave it with her himself." In the box, the pills had been replaced by napoleons.

Writing to a friend who was in low financial waters at the moment, and enclosing a cheque, he said: "I am sincerely sorry to hear of your position, and send this contribution which came so opportunely from another friend, whom I was enabled once to help. When you are well-to-do again I know you will pay it back, and I daresay somebody else will want the money, which is heartily at your service." Again, one morning Thackeray knocked at the door of Horace Mayhew's chambers in Regent Street, crying from without, "It's no use, Harry Mayhew; open the door." On entering he said cheerfully, "Well, young gentleman, you'll admit an old fogey," and when leaving he remarked: "By the way, how stupid! I was going away without doing part of the business of my visit. You spoke the other day of

Dear Suky ~~Otte~~ Jones
Though all skin & bones
Has a slim & an elegant figure
But Miss Mary Grig
Is as fat as a pig
And each day she grows bigger & bigger

poor George. Somebody — most unaccountably — has returned me a five-pound note I lent him a long time ago. I didn't expect it. So just hand it to George, and tell him when his pocket will bear it to pass it on to some poor fellow of his acquaintance. By-bye!" and he was gone.

And when an old *Punch* friend died in straitened circumstances, "Can't we, his old comrades, do something to show his poor widow and family our sense of his worth?" he wrote. "He has a son at Christ Church where, with the family's altered means, it may not be convenient to support the young man. Is the career likely to be serviceable to him? and would he desire to continue it? I shall be heartily glad to give £100 towards a fund for his maintenance at Oxford, should he think fit to remain there. Others of our friends, no doubt, would join in it."

There is the story told, I think by Mr. Herman Merivale, about Croker, whom Thackeray disliked on political and general grounds. "When Croker was dead a mutual friend told Thackeray how Croker had begged his wife to seek out some homeless boys, and let them stay with them from Saturday till Monday. 'They will destroy your flower-beds and upset my inkstands, but we can help them more than they can hurt us.' Thackeray choked, and went to see Mrs. Croker, and never spoke or thought ill of her husband again."

Instances could be multiplied without end, but added to one another they lack interest. As an example of thoughtfulness, who can forget his charming suggestion to his friend Brookfield, "to go off to poor Mrs. Crowe at Hampstead, and help him to cheer her up. I am going out myself to laugh and talk, and to the best of my ability soothe and cheer her, *but a word or two of kindness from a black coat* might make all the difference.''

Though proud, as I have said, he was the kindest of men to his inferiors. ''How dismal it must be for poor Eliza'' [the housekeeper] ''who has no friends to go to, who must stop in the kitchen all day. As I think of her I feel inclined to go back'' [from the Club] ''and sit in the kitchen with her, but I daresay I shouldn't amuse her much, and after she had told me about the cat, and how her father was, we should have nothing more to say to one another,'' he wrote to Mr. Brookfield whom, years after, when he was in America, he begged, ''If you are taking a drive some day, do go and pay a visit to my good cook and housekeeper Grey, and say you have heard from me, and that I am very well and making plenty of money, and that Charles'' [the valet] ''is well and is the greatest comfort to me. It will comfort the poor woman all alone in poor 36 yonder.'' ''I always write to him, Dear John,'' he said, speaking of an old attached servant in his mother's house. It was John who, on his own confession, taught Mrs. Ritchie as a child to sip porter out of a pint pot, and always took her part when she was naughty.

A proud, sensitive, charitable man, this; religious, too, and with the keenest sense of humour and a great sadness. Religion, though little mentioned in his books, was much in his thoughts. ''O awful, awful name of God! Light unbearable! Mystery unfathomable! Vastness immeasurable!'' he once exclaimed. But he rarely spoke of it.

''One Sunday evening in December,'' Dr. John Brown has recorded, ''Thackeray was walking with two friends along the Dean Road, to the west of Edinburgh—one of

Little Ned Torre
Thinks of nothing but war
Of helmet of sword & of trumpet
And when he can come
In the way of a drum
Our Neddy does no thing but thump it—

the noblest outlets to any city. It was a lovely evening; such a sunset as one never forgets; a rich dark bar of cloud hovered over the sky, going down behind the Highland Hills, lying bathed in amethystine bloom; between this cloud and the hills there was a narrow slip of the pure ether, of a tender cowslip colour, lucid, and as if it were the very body of heaven in its clearness; every object standing out as if etched upon the sky. The northwest end of Corstorphine Hill, with its trees and rocks, lay in the heart of this pure radiance, and there a wooden crane, used in the granary below, was so placed as to assume the figure of a cross; there it was, unmistakably lifted up against the crystalline sky. All three gazed at it silently. As they gazed, Thackeray gave utterance in a tremulous, gentle, and rapid voice, to what all were feeling, in the word 'Calvary!' The friends walked on in silence, and then turned to other things. All that evening he was very gentle and serious, speaking, as he seldom did, of divine things—of death, of sin, of eternity, of salvation, expressing his simple faith in God and in his Saviour."

Like all truly religious men, he had no fear of death. "Where can a good and pious man be better than in the presence of God," he said in a letter of condolence, written in 1849, "away from ill and temptation and care, and secure of reward? What comfort it is to think that he who was so good and so faithful here, must be called away to live among the good and just for ever! There never seems to me any cause for grief at the thought of a good man dying, beyond the sorrow for those who survive him, and, trusting in God's mercy and wisdom, infinite here and everywhere, await the day when they too shall be called away." Writing on the same subject four years later from Washington to Miss Perry, he said, "I don't pity anybody who leaves the world, not even a fair young girl in her prime; I pity those remaining. Out of our stormy life and brought nearer the divine light and warmth, there must be a serene climate. Can't you fancy sailing into the calm? Add a little more intelligence to that which we possess even as we are, and why shouldn't we? . . . Why presently, the body removed, shouldn't we personally be anywhere at will—properties of Creation, like the electric something (spark, is it?) that thrills all around the globe simultaneously? and if round the globe, why not *überall?* and the body being removed or elsewhere disposed of, and developed sorrow and its opposite, crime and the reverse, ease and disease, desire and dislike, etc., go along with the body—a lucid Intelligence remains, a Perception ubiquitous."

Yes! Thackeray had a fine faith; nothing narrow-minded about it, or bigoted; but a faith that nothing could disturb. The wrangle about Ritualistic practices did not worry him; it mattered little to him whether some deal boards were styled "altar," or "communion table." *His* mind did not, could not, descend to these petty immaterial details—he cared nothing for them. "It was about the origin of nations he" [Mr. Sortain] "spoke, one of those big themes on which a man can talk eternally, with a never-ending outpouring of words; and he talked magnificently, about Arabs for the most part, and tried to prove that because the Arabs acknowledged their descent from Ishmael or Esau, therefore the Old Testament History was true. But the Arabs may have had Esau for a father, and yet the bears may not have eaten up little children for quizzing Elisha's bald head."

These words explain his attitude to religion. The Bible might be inspired, or the Bible might not be inspired—but "God's in His Heaven." Against asceticism he tilted with zeal. "Blasphemous asceticism," he called it, "which is disposed to curse, hate, and undervalue the world altogether. Why should we? What we see here of this world is but an expression of God's will, so to speak—a beautiful earth and sky and sea—beautiful affections and sorrows, wonderful changes, and developments of creation, suns rising, stars shining, clouds and shadows changing and fading, people loving each other, smiling and crying, the multiplied phenomena of Nature, multiplied in fact and fancy, in Art and Science, in every way that a man's intellect or imagination can be brought to bear. . . . About my future state," he said, with true reverence, "I don't know. I leave it in the disposal of the awful Father—but for to-day I thank God that I can love you, and that you yonder and others besides are thinking of me with a tender regard."

There was another characteristic and emphatic outburst in a letter written on Christmas Day, 1849. "I stop in the middle of Costigan," he wrote, "with a remark applied to readers of Thomas à Kempis and others, which is, I think, that cushion-thumpers and High and Low Church ecstatics have often carried what they call their love for — to what seems impertinence to me. . . . Wretched little blindlings that we are, what do we know about Him? Who says we are to sacrifice the human affections as disrespectful to God? The liars, the wretched, canting fakirs of Christianity, the convent and the conventicle dervishes,—they are only less unreasonable now than the Emerites and holy women who whipped and starved themselves for the glory of God." Thackeray knew that his doctrines were opposed to the pious ascetics and religious mystics. "Why, you dear creature, what a history that is in the Thomas à Kempis book! The scheme of that book carried out would make the world the most wretched, useless, dreary, doting place of sojourn—there would be no manhood, no love, no tender ties of mother and child, no use in intellect, no trade or science, a set of selfish beings crawling about avoiding one another and howling a perpetual *miserere*."

Yet he was a man of a profoundly reverential spirit. The Very Reverend Reynolds Hole, the witty and eloquent Dean of Rochester, thus describes him:—

"He said so many good things, being the best talker I have ever listened to, when it pleased him to talk, that they trod down and suffocated each other; but I have a distinct recollection of one most interesting discussion that he had with a learned professor from Cambridge. The subject of debate, suggested by the publication of Buckle's *History of Civilisation*, was upon the powers of the human mind and the progress of scientific discovery to eliminate the sorrow and enlarge the happiness of mankind. The professor seemed to think that there would be hardly any limit to these attainments. Thackeray spoke as Newton spoke about gathering pebbles on the shore, and affirmed that one of the best results of knowledge was to convince man of his ignorance. He seemed to preach from the text, though he did not quote it, that the wisdom of this world is foolishness with God. It was a combat between pride and humility, and pride had its usual fall."

"Let us turn God's *to-day* to its best use," he said—and while monks were singing their litanies; while nuns were telling their beads; while clergymen were lecturing on the infallibility of the Bible, and the crowds flocked to hear them;—he was in some quiet spot, doing some kind action, or talking at the sick bed of an aunt, or sitting in sympathising silence with some broken-hearted man who had lost his son.

This, then, was Thackeray's creed, superb in its simplicity. Biblical criticism might proceed on its devastating career, it might prove that Jesus never uttered the Lord's Prayer and that the Sermon on the Mount was never delivered; Atheism might be rampant in the land, and the struggle between the churches of the earth become more and more embittered: but nothing of all this could touch his simple faith—"I believe in God the Father!"

I must now speak of Thackeray's extraordinary sense of fun. In all but his earliest writings, his broader humour is so covered with satire that it often passes unobserved; but the source from which *Major Gahagan* sprang never dried up, and all his life long he had a love for buffoonery. Mr. Locker-Lampson remembered to have seen him pirouette, wave his arms majestically, and declaim in burlesque—an intentionally awkward imitation of the ridiculous manner that is sometimes met with in French Opera; and he also recalled an occasion when, while he was talking to Thackeray's daughters, their father had put on his visitor's hat, and was strutting about flourishing it in the old Lord Cardigan style.

His power of impromptu rhyming was great and brilliant, and his fondness for this sort of exercise most constant. He was always rhyming and fooling, from his school-days till the last day of his life. A lady begged him to write a verse in her album—a practice to which he was always averse. Turning over the pages, however, he found the following:—

"Mont Blanc is the Monarch of Mountains,
They crowned him long ago,
But who they got to put it on,
Nobody seems to know.
"ALBERT SMITH."

Then, yielding to temptation, he took up a pen and wrote immediately underneath:—

"A HUMBLE SUGGESTION.

"I know that Albert wrote in hurry—
To criticise I scarce presume:
But yet, methinks that Lindley Murray
Instead of 'who' had written 'whom.'
"W. M. THACKERAY."

Mr. Merivale tells that, when a neighbour, knowing Thackeray to be a celebrated gourmand, asked him at the dinner-table what part of the fowl he preferred, he answered at once, and with great gravity:—

"'Oh! what's the best part of a fowl?'
My own Anastasia cried:
Then, giving a terrible howl,
She turned on her stomach and died."

He was always knocking off nonsense verses, such as the impromptu on Bishop Colenso:—

"This is the bold Bishop Colenso
Whose heresies seem to offend so,
Quoth Sam of the Soap,
'Bring fagot and rope,
For we know he ain't got no friends, oh!'"*

The famous *Little Billie* was chanted off one night quite impromptu, to the air of the then well-known song *Il y avait un petit navire*. And the following lines

*Sir M. E. Grant Duff's Diaries.

quoted in Mr. Trollope's volume were also an improvisation:—

"In the romantic little town of Highbury
My father kept a circulatin' library;
He followed in his youth that man immortal, who
Conquered the Frenchman on the plains of Waterloo.
Mamma was an inhabitant of Drogheda,
Very good she was to darn and to embroider.
In the famous island of Jamaica,
For thirty years I've been a sugar-baker;
And here I sit, the Muses' 'appy vot'ry,
A-cultivatin' every kind of po'try."

He was even addicted to puns. Every one remembers that Wagg asked Mrs. B. "Does your artist say he's a Frenchman?" and when that lady expressed ignorance, he replied, "Because if he does he's a *quizzin' yer*"; and who can forget Old Goody, with a "laugh like a parrot—you know they live to be as old as Methuselah, parrots do, and a parrot of a hundred is comparatively youthful (Ho! Ho! Ho!)"; and that dreadful "W. Empty House."

He made jokes at his own expense, or in an aside would chuckle at his critics. In *Mr. Brown's Letters* we learn that "Horner is asleep in the library at the Polyanthus: What is he reading? Hah! *Pendennis*, No. VIII.—hum, let us pass on," and on the page before is the drawing illustrative of the episode. "The heroine is not faultless (ah! that will be a great relief to some folks, for many writers' good women are, you know, so very insipid)," he said in *Lovel the Widower*, probably thinking of the strictures passed upon *Amelia* in *Vanity Fair;* and later in the same novel he wrote: "Some authors, who shall be nameless, are, I know, accused of depicting the most feeble, brainless, namby-pamby heroines, for ever whimpering tears, and prattling commonplaces."

Anecdotes, many spurious no doubt, are related. Sir Mountstuart Grant Duff told a story of Thackeray's remark one Sunday to his companion by a riverside, "If that d—d irreligious fish had been to afternoon church, we should not have caught him;" and it was of William Palmer Hale, who was a great beer-drinker, that he said to Mr. Yates, "Good Billy Hale, take him for half-and-half, we ne'er shall look upon his like again." Sometimes he would pay absurd compliments. "Among the notabilities," he wrote from Paris in 1850, "was Vicomte D'Arlincourt, a mad old romance writer, on whom I amused myself by pouring the most tremendous compliments I could invent. He said, 'J'ai vu l'Ecosse; mais Valler Scott n'y était plus, hélas!' I said 'Vous y étiez, Vicomte, c'etait bien assez d'un'—on which the old boy said I possessed French admirably, and knew how to speak the prettiest things in the prettiest manner." He told Janin that "In November you see every lamp-post on London Bridge with a man hanging to it"; and on one occasion when he and Macaulay were together in Paris, he wanted to be introduced as Macaulay and *vice versâ*—but the historian said solemnly that he did not approve of practical jokes, and so this sport did not come to pass.

Thackeray I think must have been in conversation something like Pendennis, as he appears in *Philip*, and probably "he seemed to be laughing at people, but he is a true friend, and when you know him his heart is good." He must have resembled Warrington somewhat, and I always think of him when I read the following: "Barnes said, with one of his accustomed curses, he did not know whether Mr. Warrington was 'chaffy' or not, and indeed he could never make out. Warrington replied that he could never make himself out, and if ever Mr. Barnes could, he would thank him for information on that subject." Probably often Thackeray could not make himself out.

But mere fun, mere farcical nonsense, he did not value highly. When he was asked if *Vanity Fair* would be funny, he retorted that it would be humorous; and he declared that while it is a real intellectual feat to write really good occasional verse, it was "easy enough to knock off that nonsense of *Pleaceman X.*" He had the same sense of the ridiculous that he bestowed upon *Becky Sharp*, and it was this, probably, that caused him to underestimate even his greatest books. He could not always take himself seriously as a great writer, and he was inclined to look down, not only on Dobbin, but even on Colonel Newcome and on Esmond himself.

But, as with every true humourist, the keynote to his character is *sadness*. "In much wisdom is much grief." And above all else, he was wise and very sad. He told Dr. John Brown how, on one occasion at Paris, he found himself in a great crowded *salon*, and looking from one end, across a sea of heads, being in Swift's place of calm in a crowd ("an inch or two above it"), he saw at the other end a strange visage, staring at him with an expression of comical woebegoneness; and how, after a little while, he found this rueful being was himself in the mirror. And he liked to relate the pathetic story of the sad-looking man in a decline, who, consulting a great physician, was recommended to go to the pantomime, where the sight of Harlequin would be sure to do him good, and cheer him up. "I am Harlequin," said the patient simply.

He loved his home, and his friends, and books, drawings, and music; he enjoyed a good dinner, and sometimes a jovial party. Yet he went through the world a spectator—a dignified Dobbin in the larger Vanity Fair—a melancholy, lonely man, a sad and splendid, a weary King Ecclesiast. He found sadness in humour, and a tear on the eyelid of every jest. "The best of your poems, instead of making me laugh, had quite the other effect," he wrote to Horace Smith. "All the best comic stuff so affects me. Sancho, Falstaff, even Fielding in *Amelia.*"

The world called to him, as it had done to Cruikshank, and so many others, "Make us laugh, or you and your children starve." He did his best, but he could not assume the *rôle* of *farceur* for very long at a time. He might be cutting the most amusing jokes in a private company, or writing the most comic verses for the public; but generally there can be found under the surface, a touch of pathos, or of melancholy. "What funny things I've written when fit to hang myself," he said in one letter to Mrs. Brookfield; and in another, "I did the doggerel verses, which were running in my head, when I last wrote you, and they are very lively. You'd say the author must have been in the height of good spirits! . . . No, you wouldn't, knowing his glum habit, and dismal views of life generally." His pen tells this to the album:—

> "I've helped him to pen many a line for bread;
> To joke, with sorrow aching in his heart;
> And make your laughter when his own heart bled."

Fate, dealing harshly with him, had made memory painful. It distressed him even to re-read his own writings. "Our books are diaries, in which our feelings must of necessity be set down," he said. "As we look to the page written last month, or ten years ago, we remember the day and its events; the child ill, mayhap, in the adjoining room, and the doubts and fears which racked the brain as it still pursued its work; the dear old friend who read the commencement of the tale, and whose gentle hand shall be laid in ours no more. I own, for my part, that in reading pages which this hand penned formerly, I often lose sight of the text under my eyes. It is not the words I see, but that past day; that bygone page of life's history; that tragedy, comedy it may be, which our little home company was enacting; that merry-making which we shared; that funeral which we followed; that bitter, bitter grief which we buried.''

In another place—*A Leaf out of a Sketch-Book*—he wrote very much the same thing: ''The sketch brings back, not only the scene, but the circumstances under which the scene was viewed. In taking up an old book, for instance, written in former days by your humble servant, he comes upon passages which are outwardly lively and facetious, but inspire the author with the most dismal melancholy. I lose all cognisance of the text sometimes, which is hustled and elbowed out of sight by the crowd of thoughts which throng forward, and which were alive and active at the time that text was born. Ah, my good sir, a man's books mayn't be interesting, . . . but if you knew all a writer's thoughts, how interesting his book would be!''*

*Compare these passages with a verse in Goethe's *Zuneigung zu Faust.*

> "Ihr bringt mit euch die Bilder froher Tage,
> Und manche liebe Schatten steigen auf:
> Gleich einer alten, halbgeklungnen Sage,
> Kommt erste Liebe und Freundschaft mit herauf;
> Der Schmerz wird neu, es wiederholt die Klage
> Des Lebens labyrinthisch erren Lauf
> Und nennt die Güten die, um schöne Stunden
> Vom Glück gelauscht, vor mir hinweggeschwunden."

Anthony Trollope said Thackeray was idle. Before it is possible to agree or dissent, let us consider Mr. Trollope's idea of idleness. His conception of industry was to rise at half-past five, and to write a certain number of words per hour for three or four hours; conversely it may be assumed that all writers who did not follow the main features of this plan were idle—that is, idle according to Anthony Trollope.

But that Thackeray was really idle—no! How *can* a man be called idle who does as Mr. Trollope himself admitted Thackeray did—a fair life's work? Even apart from quality, and taking only quantity into account, the great writer can make a good show. Twenty-six volumes of his selected works, with innumerable illustrations of his own; three or four supplementary volumes; and innumerable uncollected contributions to periodical literature;—were what the "idle" man produced during a little over thirty years. Yes! most people will support Mr. Trollope's statement that Thackeray "accomplished what must be considered as quite a sufficient life's work."

Mr. Trollope also says, in tones of reproof, that Thackeray wrote from hand to mouth, as it were, and that the printer's boy was often waiting in the passage for the last pages of "copy." Mr. Trollope knew that he himself, under such circumstances, would have been unable to do any work at all; but this clearly was not Thackeray's position, and the difference of the two cases is, to use a commercial metaphor, as that of two bills being presented for payment, under threat of legal proceedings, to two different persons, the first of whom has no available funds, the second having a mighty balance at his banker's. When we think of the wealth of Thackeray's brain, it is not difficult to understand how it was that the work produced by him, under pressure, is so excellent.

He was not a laborious writer, as a rule, though he laboured hard before producing both *Esmond* and *The Virginians*. He would read a book to obtain a paragraph, or visit a place for the sake of a description, or even inspect the complaint-books of the Reform and Athenæum Clubs in order to impart local colour to his Club snobs; but, with the exception of *Esmond*, he never drew up a plot, and he wrote from number to number, careless of what might follow. Indeed, he admitted that when he began a novel, he rarely knew how many people were to figure in it; and he told Mr. Jeaffreson that his plan was to create mentally two or three of his chief characters, and then to write right away from time to time, with intervals of repose between the times of industry, and go onward from chapter to chapter, with only a general notion of the course he would be taking a few chapters later. "I don't control my characters," he said. "I am in their hands, and they take me where they please." "I have been surprised at the observations made by some of my characters," he wrote in a *Roundabout Paper*. "It seems as if an occult power was moving the pen. The personage does or says something, and I ask, 'How the dickens did he come to think of that?' " Thus, when a friend remonstrated with him for having made Esmond marry "his mother-in-law," he only replied, "*I* didn't make him do it; they did it themselves." And most critics will admit that not to have married them would have been a mistake in Art.

That he was unmethodical I do not dispute. He had his stated hours for writing. He would take a quiet table at the Athenæum Club, and cover a few of those little slips of papers upon which he wrote his stories; and later in the day he would go to the Garrick Club, and devote some more time to his work. But he was easily tempted to go for a walk, or to join in an interesting conversation, and to put his sheets away until another time. Probably in this case, however, procrastination was a gift of the gods.

Again, those who charge him with idleness do not always remember that he suffered from a painful internal disease that frequently disinclined him to work, and actually often incapacitated him for writing altogether. He was a weary, disappointed man. Fame had come to him comparatively late in life, and his earlier years had been almost a continuous course of disappointments. He was *so* tired, and, he thought, worn out. "I am played out," he said to Mr. Jeaffreson. "All I can do now is to bring out my old puppets and put new bits of riband upon them. . . ." "What a wholesome thing fierce mental occupation is! Better than dissipation to take thoughts out of one; only one can't always fix the mind down, and other thoughts will bother it. Yesterday I sat for six hours, and could do no work; I wasn't sentimentalizing, but I couldn't get the pen to go, and, at four, rode out into the country," he wrote in 1850 to Mr. Brookfield. And Miss Henrietta Cockran, when he was editing the *Cornhill*, heard him complain, "My number is nearly due, but I cannot make it come. . . . Yes, I would like to rest my head in some quiet corner; I had a nice scene this morning, but 'tis all gone, and I cannot call to mind a bit of it now."

Such weariness was not the fruits of idleness.

It is strange how real his characters were to him while

he was working at them: he lived with them, shared their joys and sorrows, and spoke of them as of live personages. "Being entirely occupied with my two new friends, Mrs. Pendennis and her son Arthur Pendennis," he wrote to Mrs. Brookfield from Brighton in 1849, "I got up very early again this morning, and was with them for more than two hours before breakfast. He is a very good-natured, generous young fellow, and I begin to like him considerably. I wonder if he is interesting to me from selfish reasons, and because I fancy we resemble each other in many parts." "I wonder what will happen to Pendennis and Fanny Bolton," he asked in another letter to the same correspondent; "writing it and sending it to you, somehow it seems as if it were true."

Mrs. Ritchie remembers the morning Helen died. She entered her father's study in Young Street, but he motioned her away. An hour afterwards he went to the school-room, half-laughing and half-ashamed, and said, "I do not know what James can have thought of me when he came in with the tax-gatherer just after you left, and found me blubbering over Helen Pendennis's death."

He wrote from Brussels to Mrs. Brookfield: "to the Hotel de la Terrasse, where Becky used to live, and shall pass by Captain Osborne's lodgings;" adding of his own creations, "I believe perfectly in all those people, and feel quite an interest in the inn in which they lived." Years after, he pointed out to Mr. Hannay the house in Russell Square where the Sedleys lived.

The characters he created seemed to come to life, for he met several in later years. "In the novel of *Pendennis*, written ten years ago," he mentioned in *De Finibus*, "there is an account of a certain Costigan whom I had invented (as I suppose authors invent their personages out of scraps, heel-taps, odds and ends of characters). I was smoking in a tavern-parlour one night, and this Costigan came into the room alone—the very man—the most remarkable resemblance of the printed sketches of the man, of the rude drawings in which I had depicted him. He had the same little coat, the same battered hat, cocked on one eye, the same twinkle in that eye. 'Sir,' said I, knowing him to be an old friend whom I had met in unknown regions; 'Sir,' I said, 'may I offer you a glass of brandy and water?' '*Bedad, ye may*,' says he; '*and I'll sing ye a song tu.*' Of course, he spoke with an Irish accent. Of course, he had been in the army. In ten minutes he pulled out an Army Agent's account, whereon his name was written. A few months after, we read of him in a police-court."

Great interest has always been taken in Thackeray's originals. Much has been written about them that is well worth reading; much, I think, that is misleading. The novelist was personal sometimes—not a doubt of it—but it was seldom that he deliberately modelled a character on a man or woman of his acquaintance. He told his daughters that he never wilfully copied anybody. "Mr. Thackeray was only gently and skilfully assimilative and combinative in his characters. They passed through the alembic of his study and observation. The Marquis of Steyne is a sublimation of half-a-dozen characters, so is Captain Shandon, so are Costigan and the Mulligan. And the finest of Mr. Thackeray's characters—Becky, Dobbin, Jos Sedley, and Colonel Newcome—are wholly original, from the celebrity point of view at least."

The Manager from London

So wrote Mr. Sala some twenty years ago, and I am quite in agreement with his opinion.

Barry Lyndon's later career is founded on that of Andrew Robinson Storey Bowes, who married the widow of John, ninth Earl of Strathmore; and there is no doubt also a touch of Casanova. Many of the characters in *Esmond*, we know, are portraits of historical personages—the Duke of Hamilton, Lord Mohun, and Beatrix, for instance; but in the tales of modern life there are few characters that can be traced to any particular source.

"You know you are only a piece of Amelia. My mother is another half; my poor little wife—*y est pour beaucoup*," Thackeray told Mrs. Brookfield. Mr. Yates insisted that Wagg in *Pendennis* stood for Theodore Hook; that Lord Lonsdale, a very naughty old man, was the original of Major Pendennis's noble friend Lord Colchicum; and that Bunn was Thackeray's model for Dolphin the manager. Bunn was also held up to ridicule in the *National Standard*, and also in *Flore et Zéphyr*. It is said that Thackeray portrayed Mr. J. M. Evans in *The Kickleberrys on the Rhine;* that Leigh Hunt was the original of the Gandish whom he described in *The Newcomes;* and that Lord Steyne was the prototype of the Marquis of Hertford of that day. Mrs. Ritchie once saw the lady who was supposed to have suggested Becky Sharp to the novelist; and Carlyle and his wife knew the original Blanche Amory.

Charles Kingsley, in *Yeast*, told a good story that he had heard of his fellow-novelist. "I like your novel exceedingly," said a lady to Thackeray; "the characters are so natural, all but the baronet, and he is surely overdrawn: it is impossible to find such coarseness in his rank of life!" "That character," the author laughed, "is almost the only exact portrait in the whole book."

Concerning Colonel Newcome, Mrs. Ritchie distinctly avers the origin was composite. "Apparently there was no single original, but it was always understood that my step-grandfather, Major Carmichael Smyth, had many of his characteristics; and there was also a brother of the Major's, General Charles Carmichael, who was very like Colonel Newcome in looks; a third family Colonel Newcome, was Sir Richard Shakespear; and how many more are there not—present, and yet to come?"

Yet the following inscription on the memorial brass in the new Episcopal Church at Ayr would rather point to the fact that, in the Thackeray family, the novelist's step-father was the accepted original of Colonel Newcome. This memorial, I may add, was placed in the church by Lady Carmichael, and the inscription written by Mrs. Ritchie:

> SACRED TO THE MEMORY OF MAJOR WILLIAM HENRY CARMICHAEL SMYTH, OF THE BENGAL ENGINEERS, WHO DEPARTED THIS LIFE AT AYR, 9TH SEPTEMBER, 1861; AGED 81 YEARS.
>
> "*Adsum.*
>
> "And lo, he whose heart was as that of a little child had answered to his name, and stood in the presence of the Master."—*Newcomes*, vol. iii., chap. 26.
>
> On the rebuilding of the church, his grave was brought within the walls. He was laid to rest immediately beneath this place by his step-son, William Makepeace Thackeray. This memorial was put in 1887 by some members of the family.

Thackeray never thought lightly of his profession. Again and again he spoke of the sense of responsibility that an author should feel. "What a place it is to hold in the affections of man!" he wrote. "What an awful responsibility hanging over a writer! What man, holding such a place, and knowing that his words go forth to vast congregations of mankind—to grown folks, to their children, and, perhaps, to their children's children—but must think of his calling with a solemn and a humble heart! May love and truth guide such a man always! It is an awful prayer, and may Heaven further its fulfilment."

But he had no patience with the heaven-sent writers. "Away with this canting about great *motifs!* Let us not be too proud, and fancy ourselves martyrs of the truth, martyrs or apostles. We are but tradesmen, working for bread, and not for righteousness' sake. Let's try and work honestly, but don't let us be prating pompously about our sacred calling." What would he have said of Mr. R. M. Ballantyne, who, in his *Personal Reminiscences in Book-Making*, declared: "From what I have said, it will be seen that I have never aimed at achieving of this position" [of living by making story-books for young folks], "and I hope that it is not presumptuous of me to think—and to derive much comfort from the thought—that God led me into the particular path along which I have walked for so many years."

He regarded his profession with reverence, and he thought better of it than to accept it as an excuse for all sorts of licence.*

"Men of letters," he wrote in a *Roundabout Paper*, "cannot lay their hands on their hearts, and say, 'No,

*Thackeray did not regard letters as a profitable pursuit. On December 21, 1843, he wrote to a cousin of his: "It" [Literature] "is, however, a bad trade at the best. The prizes in it are fewer and worse than in any other professional lottery, but I know it's useless hampering a man who will be an author, whether or no—men are doomed, as it were, to the calling."

the fault' [that caused their intellectual inferiors to sneer at them] 'was Fortune's and the indifferent world's, not Goldsmith's or Fielding's.' There was no reason why Oliver should always be thriftless; why Fielding and Steele should sponge upon their friends; why Sterne should make love to his neighbours' wives. Swift, for a long while, was as poor as any wag that ever laughed, but he owed no penny to his neighbour; Addison, when he wore his most threadbare coat, could hold his head up and maintain his dignity; and, I dare vouch, neither of these gentlemen, when they were ever so poor, asked any man alive to pity their condition, and have a regard to the weaknesses incidental to the literary profession."

"What ought to be the literary man's point of honour nowadays?" he asked in the same paper. "Suppose, friendly reader, you are one of the craft, what legacy would you like to leave to your children? First of all (and by Heaven's gracious help), you would pray and strive to give them such an endowment of love as should last certainly for all their lives, and perhaps be transmitted to their children. You would (by the same aid and blessing) keep your honour pure, and transmit a name unstained to those who have a right to bear it. You would—though this faculty of giving is one of the easiest of the literary man's qualities—you would, out of your earnings, small or great, be able to help a poor brother in need, to dress his wounds, and, if it were but twopence, to give him succour. Is the money which the noble Macaulay gave to the poor lost to his family? God forbid! To the loving hearts of his kindred is it not rather the most precious part of their inheritance? It was invested in love and righteous doing, and it bears interest in Heaven. You will, if letters be your vocation, find saving harder than giving and spending. To save be your endeavour, too, against the night's coming, when no man may work; when the arm is weary with the long day's labour; when the brain perhaps grows dark; when the old, who can labour no more, want warmth and rest, and the young ones call for supper."

If a young man of letters came to him for advice as to the course he should pursue, he said, "Bear Scott's words in your mind: '*Be good, my dear.*'" "It may not be our chance, brother scribe, to be endowed with such merit or rewarded with such fame," he concluded his appreciation of Macaulay and Washington Irving. "But the rewards of these men are rewards paid to *our service*. We may not win the *bâton* or *epaulettes*, but God give us strength to guard the honour of the flag!"

It is pleasing to think that he, who was so much greater than either of these contemporaries upon whom he bestowed such lavish praise, was in the foremost rank of those who pressed forward to fight for the honour of the flag!

"I have been earning my own bread with my pen for near twenty years now," he wrote to M. Forgues; "and sometimes very hardly too, but in the worst time, please God, never lost my own respect."*

*Mrs. Ritchie's Introduction to *Esmond*.

CHAPTER XXIV

THACKERAY AND THE THEATRE

CHAPTER XXIV

THACKERAY AND THE THEATRE

WHILE *The Newcomes* was coming out in monthly numbers Thackeray turned his attention towards the drama. He had always been a lover of the play, and a frequenter of the theatre. Even as a small boy [1828] he had played Fusbos in *Bombastes Furioso* in a performance promoted by some Charterhouse school-fellows. In the album of Thackeray's letters and drawings are many references to plays, and quite a little gallery of theatrical portraits and scenes. His famous novels teem with allusions to plays and players.

"Do you remember, dear M——, oh, friend of my youth," he wrote in *Vanity Fair*, "how one blissful night five-and-twenty years since, the *Hypocrite* being acted, Elliston being manager, Dowton and Liston performers, two boys had leave from their loyal masters to go out from Slaughter House School, where they were educated, and to appear on Drury Lane stage, amongst a crowd which assembled there to greet the king? THE KING! There he was. Beef-eaters were before the august box. The Marquis of Steyne (Lord of the Powder Closet) and other great officers of state were behind the chair on which he sat—*He* sat—florid of face, portly of person, covered with orders, and in a rich curling head of hair. How we sang God save him! How the house rocked and shouted with that magnificent music! How they cheered, and cried, and waved handkerchiefs! Ladies wept; mothers clasped their children; some fainted with emotion. People were suffocated in the pit, shrieks and groans rising up amidst the writhing and shouting mass there of his people who were, and, indeed, showed themselves almost to be, ready to die for him. Yes, we saw him. Fate cannot deprive us of *that*. Others have seen Napoleon. Some few still exist who have beheld Frederick the Great, Doctor Johnson, Marie Antoinette, etc.—be it our reasonable boast to our children that we saw George the Good, the Magnificent, the Great."

As he grew up, his liking did not decrease. When he was reading with Mr. Taprell, he wrote to his mother: "As for the theatre, I scarcely go there more than once a week, which is moderate for me. In a few days come the Pantomimes. Huzza!" And when, years after, he asked a friend if *he* loved "the play," and was answered "Ye-es; I like a good play," he retorted, "Oh, get out! I said *the* play. You don't even understand what I mean."

In Weimar his letters tell how frequently he went to the theatre. Opera was given there, though the orchestra, under the direction of Hummel, was, in his opinion, far superior to the singers. During the winter he heard *Medea*, *The Barber of Seville*, *Il Flauto Magico*, Beethoven's *Battle of Victoria*, and *Fidelio*, in the last of which Madame Schröder-Devrient sang. He saw *Hernani* played, and recommended his family to read it; went with an actor to Enfürt to see Schiller's *Die Räuber* (which play was thought too patriotic and free for the Weimar Court Theatre); and admired Devrient's mag-

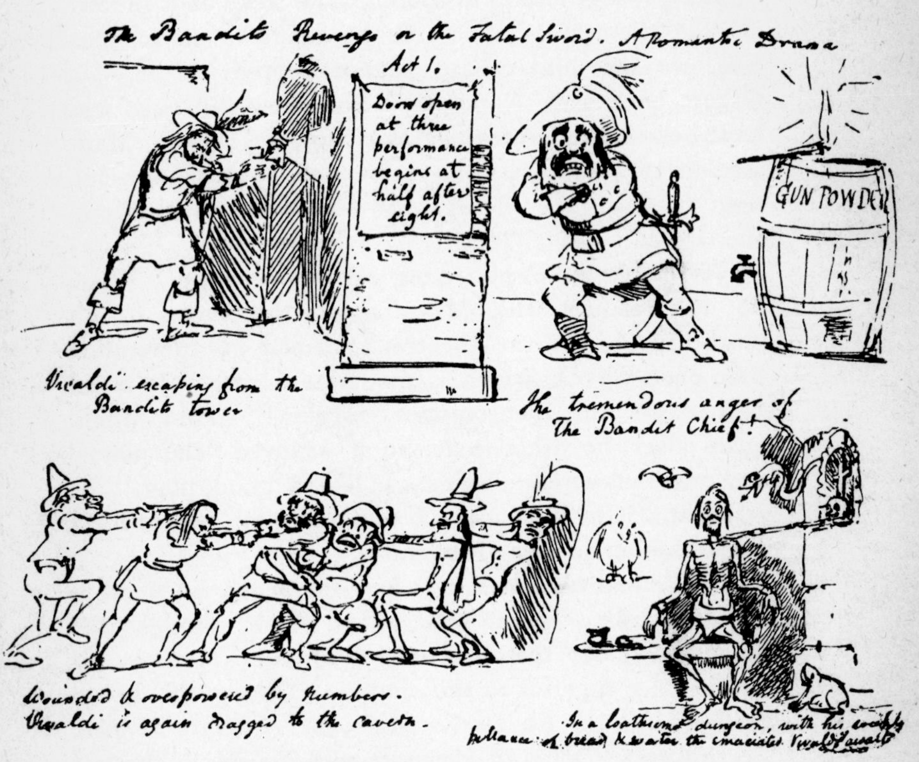

THE BANDITS' REVENGE; OR, THE FATAL SWORD.

Act 1. A Romantic Drama.

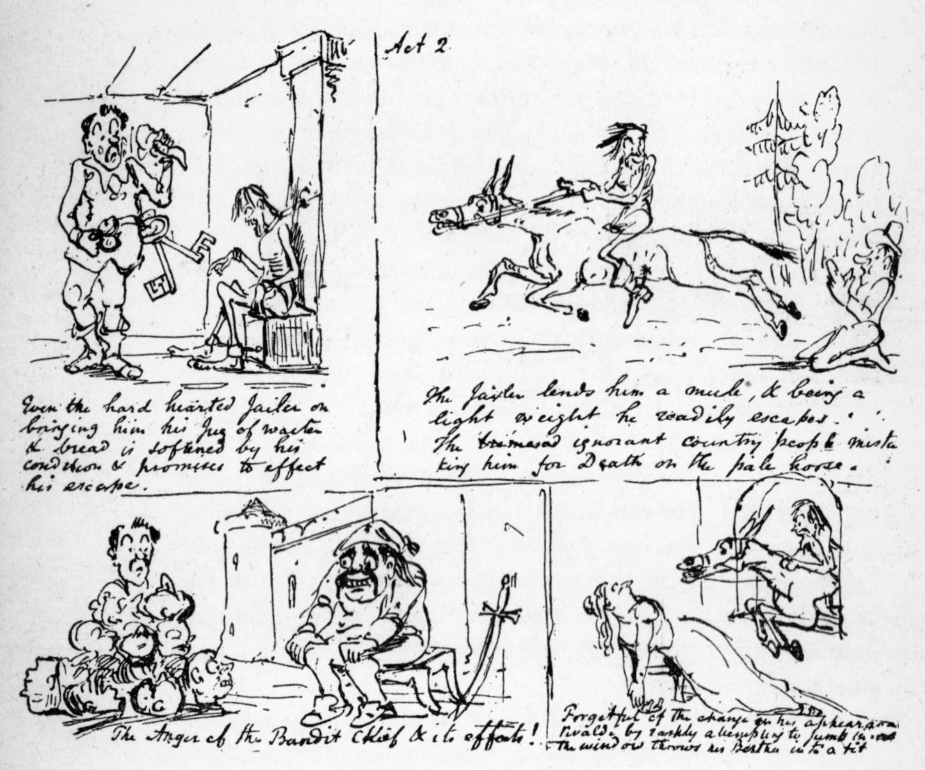

THE BANDITS' REVENGE.

Act 2.

nificent performance of *Franz Moor*. "I never saw anything so horrible in my life," he wrote home. Afterwards he was introduced to the great actor, who, it may still be remembered by many, came to London in 1852 for a season at the St. James's Theatre.

His letters are full of allusions to "the play." He writes that he has seen Mademoiselle Mars in *Valerie*, Madame Dejazet in *Napoleon à Brienne*, and that he went with his father and mother to Covent Garden to hear the *Barber of Seville* (when he observed that Miss Inverarity sang charmingly, but had a mouth big enough to sing two songs at once; and noted that Wilson had one of the freshest voices he ever heard). He saw *King Lear* in 1847, and found the play a bore. "We are the most superstitious people in England," he remarked. "It is almost blasphemy to say a play of Shakespeare is bad, but I can't help it if I think so; and there are other pieces of book-slating that make me mad."

During his stay at Paris he was a student of the drama, and he wrote sensibly and interestingly of plays and players. He saw Rachel, who was trying to revive the taste for Racine, and was sure that she could only galvanise the corpse, not revivify it. He is glad of it, for he would rather go to Madame Saqui, or see Deburan dancing on a rope; his lines are quite as natural and poetical.

He would like Scribe, I think, if all the characters in the plays did not break the seventh commandment.

"Of the drama, Victor Hugo and Dumas are the well-known and respectable guardians," he wrote in the article on *French Dramas and Melodramas*. "Every piece Victor Hugo has written since *Hernani* has contained a monster—a delightful monster, saved by one virtue. There is Triboulet, a foolish monster, Lucrèce Borgia, a maternal monster; Mary Tudor, a religious monster; Monsieur Quasimodo, a hump-backed monster; and others that might be named whose monstrosities we are induced to pardon—nay, admiringly to witness—because they are agreeably mingled with some exquisite display of affection. And, as the great Hugo has one monster to each play, the great Dumas has, ordinarily, half-a-dozen, to whom murder is nothing; common intrigue, and simple breakage of that before-mentioned commandment, nothing; but who live and move in a vast, delightful complication of crime that cannot be easily conceived in England, much less described. When I think over the number of crimes that I have seen Mademoiselle Georges, for instance, commit, I am filled with wonder at her greatness, and the greatness of the poets who have conceived these charming horrors for her. I have seen her make love to and murder her sons in the *Tour de Nesle*. I have seen her poison a company of no less than nine gentlemen, at Ferrara, with an affectionate son in the number. I have seen her, as Madame de Brinvilliers, kill off numbers of respectable relations in the first four acts; and, at the last, be actually burned at the stake, to which she comes shuddering, ghastly, barefooted, and in a white sheet. Sweet excitement of tender sympathy! Such tragedies are not so good as a real, downright execution, but, in point of interest, the next thing to it. With what a number of moral emotions do they fill the breast; with what a hatred for vice, and yet a true pity and respect for that grain of virtue that is to be found in us all; our bloody, daughter-loving Brinvilliers; our warm-hearted, poisonous Lucretia Borgia; above all, what a smart appetite

THE BANDITS' REVENGE.

Act 3.

THE BANDITS' REVENGE.

for a cool supper afterwards at the Café Anglais, when the horrors of the play act as a piquant sauce to the supper!"

The "Catholic reaction" affected the drama as well as the literature and the art of the day; and Thackeray denounced the plays with as much vigour as he employed against the books and pictures. He devoted much space to analysing those plays in which Dumas brought a vast quantity of religion before the footlights—*Caligula*, and *Don Juan de Marana*, and similar productions. The *Festin de Belthazar* and the *Juif Errant*, for instance, meet with harsh treatment at his hands. On the other hand, *La Duchesse de la Vauballière*, which obtained a great success at the Porte St. Martin, and *Hermann d' Ivrogne*, rather pleased him, because, though not very refined, they are at least moral in their teachings.

He only laughed at *Kean*, in which Dumas introduces Lord Melbourn, Sir Brougham, Sir Hardinge, the Secretary-at-War, and the "Coal Hole," with a company of Englishwomen wearing pinafores (as if the British female were in the invariable habit of wearing the outer garment, or slobbering her gown without it); and he rings down the curtain upon the first act of the *Naufrage de la Méduse*, where the scene is laid on board an English ship-of-war, with all the officers in light blue or green coats (the lamp-light prevented his distinguishing the colour accurately) and TOP-BOOTS!

Then he summed up the state of the French stage of the late 'thirties: "While the drama of Victor Hugo, Dumas, and the enlightened classes, is profoundly immoral and absurd, the drama of the common people is absurd, if you will, but good and right-hearted."

The theatre is often mentioned in his stories and in

his novels—nearly everybody goes to the play-house, and nearly everybody loves "the play."

In *Vanity Fair*, Cuff (whom Dobbin thrashed), the great chief and dandy of the Swishtail Seminary, goes to the opera, and knows the merits of the principal actors, preferring Mr. Kean to Mr. Kemble. In later years, little George Osborne, with Rawson the footman, visited all the principal theatres of the metropolis, knew the names of all the actors from Drury Lane to Sadler's Wells, and performed, indeed, many of the plays to the Todd family and their youthful friends, with West's famous characters, in their pasteboard theatre. His father, on the eve of his departure for Belgium in 1815, had gone off to half-price to see Kean as *Shylock;* and Dobbin, on the evening of his return from India, treated himself to a seat at the Haymarket, where, let us hope, he enjoyed himself.

During the Waterloo campaign, everybody in Brussels went to the opera, where it was almost like being in old England, for the house was filled with familiar British faces; but the *coup d'œil* of the Brussels opera-house did not strike Mrs. O'Dowd as being so fine as the theatre in Fishamble Street, Dublin, nor was French music at all equal, in her opinion, to the melodies of her native country. Here it was on a certain memorable evening, when Mr. and Mrs. George Osborne, Dobbin, and Mrs. O'Dowd were in a box facing another occupied by Mr. and Mrs. Rawdon Crawley and General Tufto, that Becky played Osborne against the General—and won them both.

Becky had her little box on the third tier of the opera-house in London, too, and in the crush-room was cut by Lady Bareacres and Lady de la Mole, both of

THE BANDITS' REVENGE.

Emblematic Vision.

The Triumph of Clytemnestra.

whom she had known in Brussels, though, after her presentation at Court, she made things equal by refusing to recognise Lady Crackenbury and Mrs. Washington White, whose invitations she had once eagerly sought. She (the daughter of a French opera dancer) acted in the charades at Gaunt House, where she made such a success as *Clytemnestra* ("Mrs. Rawdon Crawley was quite killing in the part," said Lord Steyne), and, as a French Marquise in the second charade she sang *The Rose upon my Balcony* from Sir George Thrum's opera, *The Brigand's Wife*—this was also a favourite song of the Ravenswing (Mrs. Hooker Walker). It is hinted that Becky may have been the Madame Rebecque whose appearance in the opera of *La Dame Blanche* at Strasburg in 1830 gave rise to a furious uproar in the theatre there.

Finally, during their continental tour, Amelia and her boy, George, and Dobbin, and Jos were frequent visitors to the Pumpernickel Staats-Theatre. "They went to the Opera often of evenings," we are told, "to those many unassuming dear old operas in the German towns, where the noblesse sits and cries, and knits stockings on the one side, over against the *bourgeoisie* on the other; and His Transparency the Duke and his Transparent family, all very fat and good-natured, come and occupy the great box in the middle, and the pit is full of the most elegant slim-waisted officers with straw-coloured moustachios, and twopence a day in full pay. Here it was that Emmy found her delight, and was introduced for the first time to the wonders of Mozart and Cimarosa. The Major's musical taste has been before alluded to, and his performances on the flute commended. But perhaps the chief pleasure he had in these operas was in watching Emmy's rapture while listening to them. A new world of love and beauty broke upon her when she was introduced to those divine compositions: this lady had the keenest and finest sensibility, and how could she be indifferent when she heard Mozart? The tender parts of *Don Juan* awakened in her raptures so exquisite that she would ask herself when she went to say her prayers of a night, whether it was not wicked to feel so much delight as that with which *Vedrai Carino* and *Batti Batti* filled her gentle little bosom? But the Major, whom she consulted upon this head, as her theological adviser (and who himself had a pious and reverent soul) said that, for his part, every beauty of art and nature made him thankful as well as happy, and that the greatest pleasure to be had is listening to fine music, as in looking at the stars in the sky, or at a beautiful landscape or picture, was a benefit for which we might thank Heaven as sincerely as for any other worldly blessing."

During a part of *Pendennis* the interest is almost entirely placed in stage-land. We are introduced to the full strength of Mr. Bingley's stock company at the Theatre Royal Chatteris, from Mr. Bows the first violinist in the orchestra, and Mrs. Dropsicum (Bingley's mother-in-law, great in *Macbeth*) who takes the money at the door to the leading lady herself, Miss "Milly" Fotheringay. Foker and Pendennis attend a performance of the *Stranger* in which Miss Fotheringay's *Mary Haller* is supported by the *Countess Wintersen* of Mrs. Bingley, the *Baron Steinforth* of Garbetts, the *Tobias* of Goll; by Hicks and Miss Thackthwaite; and by the *Stranger* of Bingley, who was attired in light pantaloons and Hessian boots, and had the stage jewellery on too, and allowed his little finger to quiver out of his cloak with a sham diamond ring covering the first joint of the

Extract from the Crumpton Weekly Journal.

Yesterday a Melodrama from the pen of the worthy Manager was produced at the Theatre We went at five to secure a good place but were sorry to find (although the house was a respectable one) that we had no need of coming so early. The plot of the piece is as follows. Rivaldi (charmingly played by the Manager Mr. Blatherington) is taken prisoner by Ferocio Mr Fogle Biggs, & in a ferocious manner did he perform his part Rivaldi escapes is again taken & confined in the Wizards tower (this is a charming scene painted by Mr F. Biggs & assistants) he mollifies the Gaoler escapes a second time & after destroying in a novel manner, the whole of the banditti is united to his bride Bertha, charmingly personified by Mrs Dilke Flinders we are glad to see her husband an old favorite of ours by the way again on our boards. We trust that the peccadilloes reported of Mr D. F are not so serious as to cause any final separation between 2 of the most delightful performers on our Stage – Mr Blatherington introduced "On to the battle field" in the prison scene aptly enough; but we must confess our old friend Swags song in D flat – was d – flat!

By the by we have heard it reported that Blatherington has lost twelve shillings by the season – we hope not

From the Crumpton Independant Miscellany –

Our very absurd contemporary has been exhausting the epithets of charming, delightful – upon an unfortunate melodrama brought out at our Theatre, & never repeated.

There was we confess some good scenery & acting in it – Biggs was clever – very – as he always is. but

OPINIONS OF THE PRESS ON THE BANDITS' REVENGE.

really Mr. Blatherington shd. give up lovers parts – he is too old & too fat, & when he acts with Mrs Dilke Flinders is "like a pearl on an Ethiops ear" to use the words of the eternal bard – but how can we sufficiently praise her. the lovely the gentle & the impassioned Flinders why in poetry to be sure so here goes.

I saw thee – & my feelings gushed
  In one tumultuous tide
My eyes was dim, my ear was hushed
  To every thing beside –
I thought my heart was withered
But from out its mouldering cinders
~~There sprang~~ a mighty flame there gathered
For thee my love. my Flinders –

I gaze on thee. I gaze on thee
  At morn & eventide.
I mark thee as with twinkling feet
  Along the stage you stride –
At night I pace before thy gate
  And linger at thy windows
For I am very desolate
  For want of thee my Flinders.

A 2nd Extract from the Weekly Journal –

"Off with her head. So much for Buckingham
A very few of our readers Hamlet! may be aware that there exists in the town a very small weekly publication whose only attributes are vulgar profligacy & insignificant impertinence – The witty Journal alluded to contained last week a critique on the new melodrama – & some impudent observations on ourselves. these we pass by in contempt but of the former we wd. make mention – Mr. Blatherington's acting they say is so bad when it is put in comparison with the brighter talents of Mrs Flinders that it is like – what? – why gentle reader – a pearl in an Althiops ear! – Now wh. is the pearl & which is the ear? – Mr B. seems to be the pearl & Mrs F the ear poor ear thou art cruelly boxed indeed! – There are some verses in wh. the author's ear, ears again, is hushed! Mrs F strides across the stage & her name is made to rhyme with winders!!! A winder used at school to be a violent blow on the ribs wh. suspended the breath ~~as we bearterly~~ with it inflicted on the individual

finger and twiddling in the faces of the pit—this had belonged to George Frederick Cook, who had it from Mr. Quin, who may have bought it for a shilling. After this Pendennis, falling in love with Miss Fotheringay, went to the theatre nearly every night, and on the occasion of that lady's Benefit took his mother and little Laura and Mr. Smirke to see *Hamlet*. Miss Fotheringay, of course, was the *Ophelia*, and Mr. Hornbull from London was the *Hamlet* of the night, Mr. Bingley modestly contenting himself with *Horatio*, reserving his full strength for *William* in *Black Ey'd Susan*, which was the second piece, and in this the *bénéficiare* played *Susan*, Mr. Goll the *Admiral*, and Mr. Garbetts *Captain Boldweather*. Later, through the instrumentality of Major Pendennis, who wished to separate the nephew from the woman he thought he loved, Lord Steyne sent down to Chatteris Dolphin, the London manager, who also figures in *Lovel the Widower* as the employer of the ballet girl, Bessy Bellenden. Dolphin, then running the Museum Theatre under the patronage of the most noble Marquis, came, attended by his secretary Mr. William Minns, saw a performance of *Pizarro*, and was so delighted with Miss Fotheringay's impersonation of *Cora* that he forthwith gave her an engagement to play in London at once. And with her departure Pendennis's interest in the Chatteris theatre ceased—and so does ours. When he saw her again she was the wife of the old beau Sir Charles Mirabel, and he wondered how he could ever have loved her.

In *Esmond* the hero accompanied Lord Castlewood and Lord Mohun to Duke Play-House in Lincoln's Inn Fields, where the play was one of Mr. Wycherley's, *Love in a Wood*. Mrs. Bracegirdle performed the girl's part in the comedy, and, disguised as a page, stood before the gentlemen as they sat on the stage and looked over her shoulder with a pair of arch black eyes, and laughed at my lord, and asked what ailed the gentleman from the country, and had he had bad news from Bullock Fair? Between the acts of the play the gentlemen crossed over and conversed freely. There were two of Lord Mohun's party, Captain Macartney, in a military habit, and a gentleman in a suit of blue velvet and silver in a fair periwig, with a rich fall of point of Venice lace—my Lord the Earl of Warwick and Holland. My lord had a paper of oranges, which he ate, and offered to the actresses, joking with them. And Mrs. Bracegirdle, when my Lord Mohun said something rude, turned on him, and asked him what he did there, and whether he and his friends had come to stab anybody else, as they did poor Will Montford? My lord's dark face grew darker at this taunt, and wore a mischievous, fatal look. They that saw it remembered it, and said so afterwards.

"The picture is impressive, although one or two of its details may be questioned," Mr. Dutton Cook commented in his interesting paper on Thackeray. "Perhaps the play was not *Love in a Wood*, but some other comedy. The disguise of a page is not worn by any of the ladies in Mr. Wycherley's comedy, and Mrs. Bracegirdle is not known ever to have sustained any part in that work, which was revived at *Drury Lane* in 1718, the play-bills stating that it had not been represented for thirty years. And perhaps in Queen Anne's time the theatre in Lincoln's Inn Fields had ceased to be called after the Duke of York, who had become James II., and had abdicated his throne. Moreover, Lord Mohun, whose Christian name, by-the-bye, was Charles, and not

Henry, appears, from his portrait by Kneller, to have been a man of fair complexion.''

Mr. Esmond, after he quitted the army, betook himself to literature for a relaxation, and composed a play, whereof the prompter's copy, once in the possession of Mrs. Rachel Esmond Warrington, is docketed *The Faithful Fool, a comedy, as it was performed by her Majesty's Servants.* It was a very sentimental piece, and Mr. Steele, who had more of that kind of sentiment than Mr. Addison, admired it, whilst the other rather sneered at the performance; though he owned that, here and there, it contained some pretty strokes. He was bringing out his own play of *Cato* at the time, the blaze of which quite extinguished Esmond's farthing candle; and his name was never put to the piece, which was printed as by a Person of Quality. Only nine copies were sold, though Mr. Dennis, the great critic, praised it, and said it was a work of great merit; and Colonel Esmond had the whole impression burned one day, in a rage, by Jack Lockwood, his man. The piece perished on the third night, with only half-a-dozen persons to behold its agonies.

In *The Virginians* the Warrington brothers, and the Lambert family go to Covent Garden Theatre to see a performance of Mr. John Howe's immortal tragedy of *Douglas*, in which Mr. Spranger-Barry is magnificently attired as *Norval*, and the beautiful Mrs. Washington makes all the ladies, and even the grenadiers on guard on each side of the stage, weep visibly.

Like grandfather, like grandchild—George Warrington wrote a play which he read at Mr. Spencer's chambers in Fig Tree Court to a party that included Mr. Johnson himself, who recollected that he had read in

Meteranus, in the *Theatrum Universum*, the story of Mr. Warrington's tragedy. *Carpezan* eventually was produced with great success by Mr. Rich at Covent Garden. "The part of Carpezan was filled by Barry,"—I quote from the chronicles of the House of Warrington—"Shuter was the old nobleman, Reddish, I need scarcely say, made an excellent Ulric, and the King of Bohemia was by a young actor from Dublin, Mr. Geoghegan, or Hagan, as he was on the stage, and who looked and performed the part to perfection. Mrs. Woffington looked too old in the first acts as the heroine; but her murder in the fourth act, about which great doubts were expressed, went off to the terror and delight of the audience. Miss Wayn sang the ballad, which is supposed to be sung by the King's page, just at the moment of the unhappy wife's execution, and all agreed that Barry was very terrible and pathetic as Carpezan, especially in the execution scene. The piece was put very elegantly on the stage by Mr. Rich, though there was some doubt whether, in the march of Janissaries in the last" [act] "the manager was correct in introducing a favourite elephant, which had figured in various pantomimes, and by which one of Mr. Warrington's black servants marched in a Turkish habit. . . . Mr. Barry, amidst general applause, announced the play for repetition, and that it was the work of a young gentleman of Virginia, his first attempt in the dramatic style."

George's second attempt was less fortunate. It was a poetical tragedy, entitled *Pocahontas*, and was produced at Drury Lane by Garrick, with Hagan as Sir Walter Raleigh, and Miss Pritchard in the title *rôle*. In the front boxes sat Samuel Johnson, who could not see, and Reynolds, who could not hear, and who had come good-naturedly, *à deux*, to form an opinion of the play. But, while at first everything went smoothly enough, just at the moment when the heroine rushes to the prisoner's arms, and a number of people were actually in tears, a fellow in the pit bawled out, "Bedad! There's the Belle Savage kissing the Saracen's Head"—the ignorant people not knowing that Pocahontas herself was the very Belle Savage from which the tavern took its name. The gentleman in the pit repeated it *ad nauseum* during the performance, and, as each new character appeared, saluted him by the name of some tavern—for instance, the English gentleman (with a long beard), he called the "Goat and Boots"; his lieutenant (Barker), whose face certainly was broad, the "Bull and Mouth," and so on! And the curtain descended amidst a shrill storm of whistling and hisses.

Yellowplush, with the celebrated Mr. Smith, his friend, goes to see *The Sea-Captain*, and is not impressed with Mr. Lytton's dramatic powers. Mr. Brown the elder liked to see children enjoying a pantomime; Mr. Spec mentions how he fulfilled a solemn engagement made during the midsummer holidays to go with his friend, Augustus Jones, to a Christmas pantomime at Covent Garden Theatre; and Solomon Pacifico himself went to the Conservatoire at Paris to hear Madame Sontag. Miss Budge, so well known to the admirers of the festive dance on the other side of the water as Miss Delancy, even after her marriage with Crump, could never forget her earlier love, and went at least four times a week to the "Wells" and the "Cobourg," and even to the "Lane" and the "Market." Her daughter Morgiana (so named after that celebrated part in *The Forty Thieves* which Miss Budge performed with unbounded applause both at the "Surrey" and the "Wells") also had a grand enthusiasm for the stage, and had appeared many and many a time at the Theatre in Catherine Street, in minor parts first, and then in *Little Pickle*, in Desdemona, in Rosina, and in Miss Footes' part, where she used to dance. For the particulars of Miss Morgiana's later operatic successes, the reader is respectfully referred to the works of the eminent society historian, Mr. George Savage Fitzboodle.

But while Thackeray has written so much *of* the stage, he has written very little *for* the stage. There is a little one-act piece, *King Glumpus*, probably written for an amateur performance—a burlesque, somewhat after the style of *Bombastes Furioso*. Mr. Theodore Taylor thought he composed the libretto of John Barrett's opera *The Mountain Sylph*, and in the British Museum catalogue there is ascribed to him a French melodrama *The Abbaye de Pemarch*, founded on Southey's *Mary the Maid of the Inn;* but I do not believe it was written by the great novelist. Again, when Sir Frederick Pollock was editing Macready's *Journal* he was puzzled by an entry in 1831 or 1832: Received Thackeray's tragedy, with some such name as *Retribution*. But Fitzgerald told Pollock he was sure it was not W. M. T., who, especially at that time, had more turn to burlesque than real tragedy: and sure that he would have told him of it then, whether accepted or rejected—as rejected it was. However, Sir Frederick became assured it was by some other Thackeray, probably the one mentioned by Planché as a dramatic *dilletante*.

To Mr. C. P. Johnson credit is due for having discovered a piece that is undoubtedly from Thackeray's pen. This most indefatigable literary explorer found (and

KING GLUMPUS.

republished in 1891 as Number 27 of *The Sette of Odd Volumes*) in the *Brittania* for May, 1841, under the heading of *Loose Sketches*, which may be taken to indicate the intention of writing a series of similar tales, *Reading a Poem. A Sketch by M. A. Titmarsh.* The sketch is in two parts or scenes, and deals with the days when "Bungay" and "Bacon" issued *Keepsakes* and *Spring Annuals*, and would pay large sums to obtain the poems—or the *names*—of titled ladies and gentlemen.

As the playette is at present practically unattainable, I reprint here, as a curiosity, and to show how Thackerayesque it is, the *dramatis personæ:*—

LORD DAUDLEY. . The Earl of Bagwig's eldest son, a "Worshipper of the Muses"; in a dressing-gown, with his shirt collar turned down.

MR. BOGLE. . . . The celebrated publisher, in a publisher's costume of deep black.

MR. BLUCHYER. . An English gentleman of the Press. Editor of the *Weekly Bravo;* green coat, red velvet waistcoat, dirty blue satin cravat, dirty trousers, dirty boots. (This actor should smell very much of stale smoke, and need not shave for two or three days before performing the part.)

MR. DISHWASH. . An English gentleman of the Press: editor of the *Castalian Magazine;* very neat in black and a diamond pin.

MR. YELLOWPLUSH. My lord's body servant; in an elegant livery.

The scene is Lord Daudley's drawing-room in the Albany.

That Thackeray ever attempted to have this performed I think unlikely, but it is certainly amusing; and in the quaint satire on the remarkably ephemeral *Annuals* there are discernible many touches of the hand that afterward wrote *Pendennis*.

It was not, however, until twelve or thirteen years later that he made his first and only really serious attempt to write a play. In 1854 he submitted to Buckstone of the Haymarket, and to Wigan of the Olympic Theatre, a comedy entitled *The Wolves and the Lamb*. Neither of these managers, despite the fact that it was by the author of *Esmond*, would produce it, and I think they were quite right. "I thought I could write a play," Thackeray is reported to have said, "and I find I can't"; and I think he was quite right too. The play is well written, the dialogue delightful, and the characters grandly drawn; only there is too much dialogue, too little action, and no dramatic incident. It would be delightful everywhere but on the stage: it is a novel, with faint dramatic possibilities, written in the form of a comedy.

This is the view Thackeray eventually must have taken, for, retaining much of the original dialogue, though making many minor alterations, altering the names of the characters—(Captain Touchit in the play is Mr. Batchelor in the novel; Millikin is Mr. Lovel; Lady Kicklebury, Lady Baker; Howell, Bedford; and Julia, Bessy)—introducing Dr. Drencher, and changing the scene from Richmond to Putney, he converted *The Wolves and the Lamb* into *Lovel the Widower*.

It is interesting to note that while the play was refused, as soon as it was turned into a story some one saw the possibility of a play in it. The following letter was printed in the *Theatre* for 1891:—

"56, ONSLOW SQUARE, *January* 20, 1862.

"Is *Lovel the Widower* the story which you propose to dramatise for Miss Sedgwick and Mr. Robson? I wrote it originally as a drama myself, having Mr. Robson in my eye for the principal character. Mr. Wigan, however, did not think the piece suitable for his theatre, and declined it; as also did Mr. Buckstone, unless I would make alterations, which I did not choose to do.

"We are going to have a private representation of this piece by some of my friends and family, and I had it printed to save the trouble of copying. The conversations at the commencement seem needlessly long, and probably are unsuitable for the stage, but these could surely be curtailed; the last act is so very lively and amusing that I cannot but think Mr. Wigan and Mr. Buckstone were wrong concerning it.

"Will Mr. Robson have the kindness to read it over? It seems to me that he and Miss Sedgwick will be excellent representatives of the two principal characters.

"Believe me,

"Your very faithful servant,

"W. M. THACKERAY.

"CECIL HOWARD, ESQ."

The private representations took place when Thackeray gave a house-warming after his removal from Onslow Square to Palace Green. Thackeray, Mr. Merivale, the acting manager, tells us, declined a speaking part on the ground that he couldn't possibly learn such poor words, and only appeared with a cigar as the clerical papa (Mr. Bonnington) just before the fall of the curtain, to hold out his hands and say in pantomime to actors and audience, "Bless you, my children."*

*The cast included Hermann Merivale, Sir Charles Young (author of *Jim the Penman*), Morgan O'Connell (the Liberator's son), Follett Synge, Quintin Twiss (the then well-known amateur low comedian), Mrs. Caulfield, two daughters of Sir Henry Cole; and Thackeray's younger girl.

Dramatists, wandering from the more glorious paths of original inspiration into the more profitable business of adaptation, from time to time have devoted their unwelcome attentions to Thackeray. *The Diary of C. Jeames de la Pluche, Esq.* was dramatised even before it had completed its course in *Punch*, where the close of the narrative left *Jeames* happy and contented, save in one respect. "A witless version of his adventures has been produced at the Princess's Theatre, etc." Later, on August 27, 1878, Mr. Hollingshead produced at the "Gaiety" *Jeames, a New and Original Comedy*, with Mr. Edward Terry as "Jeames," and Miss Ellen Farren as "Mary Ann Higgins." The author was Mr. Burnand, of *Punch* fame, who issued the following curious and rather unnecessary note:—

"*Jeames's Diary* is included under the head of Thackeray's burlesques. In adapting this story to the stage, I have availed myself of all the exaggerations of character and incident which are of the essence of original caricature, and I have merely made such alterations as seemed to me necessary in order to suit the circumstances of the present time. Mining speculation is not absolutely parallel with the railway mania in the days of King Hudson; but, with recent events still fresh in our memory, it is near enough for dramatic purposes—that is, where, as in this exceptional instance, exaggeration is permissible. The episode of the presentation at Court in the uniform of the Cingbar Yeomanry is purely Thackerayan. The names of the characters I have generally retained, but I have given Jeames a house in Mayfair instead of bachelor's quarters in the 'Halbany.' With this preface I submit the 'Domestic's drama' to the judgment of the public. The description 'New and Original' I use advisedly as applied to the subject and its treatment, while I only profess to use the term of 'Comedy' in the broadest sense in which it can be applied to the present piece." The play was not enthusiastically received, and it was withdrawn after a run of about eight weeks.

The Rose and the Ring was adapted for representation on the stage by Mr. H. Savile Clarke, and set to music by Mr. Walter Slaughter. It was produced on the afternoon of December 20, 1890, at the Prince of Wales's Theatre, with Miss Violet Cameron, Mr. John le Hay, and Mr. Harry Monkhouse in the cast; and it was played until the end of the following January.

Vanity Fair was next mutilated by no less a person than Mr. J. M. Barrie, who had taken from the novel the scene which shows Becky fallen upon evil days, with the Pumpernickel students for companions, making her last attempt upon the susceptible but slippery Jos Sedley, and, by showing a love-letter that the faithless George has written, bringing Amelia and Dobbin together. This piece was produced in June or July, 1893, at Terry's Theatre, with an exceptionally strong cast.

Becky Sharp . .	MISS JANET ACHURCH.
Major Dobbin . .	MR. CHARLES CHARRINGTON.
Amelia . . .	MISS ANNIE HUGHES.
Jos Sedley . . .	MR. EDMUND MAURICE.

Esmond has had by far the worst fate in this respect, for it has been dramatised at least three times. Mr. E. H. Sothern had a version written for him; Mr. W. H. Wills wrote another for Mr. and Mrs. Kendal, who disposed of the play to Sir Henry (then Mr.) Irving, by whom it was handed over to the amateur dramatic club that bears his name, and by them was once performed, in June, 1893; and Mr. Edward Compton, on March 5, 1897, produced at Edinburgh yet a third version, prepared for him by Mr. T. Edgar Pemberton.

"Mr. Edward Compton's production on November 26, for the first time near London, of Mr. T. Edgar Pemberton's version of Thackeray's *Esmond* calls, I think, for some remark," I wrote at the time, protesting. "To the lovers of pure literature, *Esmond* is a great and beautiful work, from which nothing can be taken away, and to which nothing may be added. To such of us, therefore, the news that some of the most dramatic scenes have been taken bodily from the book in order to allow Mr. Pemberton to compile a play is almost too horrid to contemplate, however admirable the play as a play may be. One proof of the greatness of a play is that as a whole it is better than its finest passages; thus the soliloquy 'To be or not to be' is more appreciated when spoken in its place in *Hamlet* than when delivered by some irresponsible mummer upon a platform. So, too, is a great novel one in which the most dramatic passages come as the result of a natural sequence of events, from which it follows that the beauty of the scenes is in great part destroyed when they stand away from the context.

"Then again, a play depends for its success upon strong situations and effective curtains, whereas a novel, on the contrary, relies on the daintiness of its expression and on the delicacy and subtlety of its treatment. To understand this statement is to admit that a great gulf, which cannot be bridged over without much severe damage to the original, separates the novel from the play.

"I would abandon to the adaptor—if fed he must be—works of no importance to the lover of literature.

But *Esmond!* It had been thought that the masterpieces of fiction would remain untouched by the desecrating hand.

"What should we say of the Goth who turned *The School for Scandal* into a novel? We might, perhaps, admire his courage, but we should most certainly deplore his audacity. As for the result, as lief let us read the expurgated edition of *Tom Jones!* Should the Vandal who dramatises the greatest historical romance in the language go scot free? I have read that 'Mr. Pemberton loves his Thackeray, and in that spirit set about his dramatisation of *Esmond.*' I would point out to him that there is a love so passionate that by very force of its passion it brings about the ruin of the object of its affection. *Esmond* stands on a pedestal from which it cannot be dragged, even by its most injudicious admirers; and it may therefore be urged that there is no cause for complaint. For those who say so I have no answer, if they cannot find it for themselves in the announcement: '*Esmond,* a novel, written by Thackeray, dramatised by Mr. T. E. Pemberton.' "

Thackeray's novels, of all writings extant, cannot be dramatised successfully. *Esmond,* for instance, is the love-story of half a lifetime. His dialogue, written for the study, is impossible on the stage. If the play-maker uses the dialogue, he ruins his play; if he does not use it, he loses the atmosphere of the story—for who but Thackeray can write as Thackeray? If he follows the lines of the book, he can scarcely have a play at all, for there is very little action, certainly little dramatic plot, in any of the novels; if he abandons the book— . . . The adaptor may impale himself on any of the horns of either of these dilemmas.

CHAPTER XXV

THACKERAY AS A PUBLIC SPEAKER

CHAPTER XXV

THACKERAY AS A PUBLIC SPEAKER

A MOST finished *lecturer*, Thackeray often made a very poor appearance when he attempted to deliver a speech to a large audience. Probably he spoke best at the Garrick Club dinners and on similar occasions, when he felt more or less at home. Certainly at all other times he was terribly self-conscious, and went through hours of agony before the dinner-hour arrived. It was long before he could speak without anxiety as to the result, though after the courses of lectures had been delivered he became more self-possessed, and in 1857 made a really fine speech at Edinburgh in defence of his loyalty.

No complete list of his speeches has ever been compiled, nor is there any particular need for such a list. He was no orator, and, though he carefully prepared his speeches, he rarely delivered them as they were written. Usually he broke down after the first two or three sentences. The demand for a speech from Thackeray at such dinners and meetings as he attended did not arise until after *Vanity Fair* had marked him as a great man. Then he was called upon to speak at the Royal Academy banquets, at the Royal Literary Fund meetings, and at such institutions. His political speeches were strictly limited to the Oxford utterances.*

* "He" [Mr. Green] "gave me, too, the most remarkable account of canvassing Oxford with Thackeray, whose want of power of public speaking seems to have been perfectly extraordinary. On the

Mr. Hodder, in his *Memoirs*, has related how one morning, when acting as the novelist's secretary and amanuensis, he went into Thackeray's bedroom, and found him in bed, where he had passed a very restless night. "I'm sorry you do not seem very well this morning," Mr. Hodder said to him. "*Well*," he murmured; "no, I am not well. I have got to make that confounded speech to-night." [He was to preside at the annual dinner of the General Theatrical Fund.] "Don't let that trouble you; you will be all right when the time comes," the secretary said, soothingly. "Nonsense," Thackeray replied; "it won't come all right; I can't make a speech, confound it! That fellow Jackson let me in for this. Why don't they get Dickens to take the chair? *He can* make a speech, and a good one. . . . *I'm* of no use. . . . They little think how nervous I am; and Dickens doesn't know the meaning of the word."

At the Literary Fund meeting in 1850 he had been cajoled into a promise to speak. He wrote from "the little G." to Mrs. Brookfield later in the evening. "I have made an awful smash at the Literary Fund, and have tumbled into Evins knows where. It was a tremendous exhibition of imbecility. I hope you two are sound asleep. Why isn't there somebody that I could go and smoke a pipe to? *Bon soir.* But O! what a smash I have made! I am talking quite loud to myself at the Garrick sentences I intended to have uttered; but they wouldn't come in time."

In a letter dated a few days later he made reference

hustings he utterly broke down, and Green heard him say to himself, 'If I could only go into the Mayor's parlour for five minutes, I could write this out quite well.'"—SIR M. E. GRANT DUFF.

to another speech: "To-night I am going to the bar dinner, and shall probably make another speech; I don't mind about failing there, so I shall go pretty well." And at the farewell banquet on March 1, 1851, to Macready, on his retirement from the stage, when Lytton was in the chair, he was one of the stewards—the others were Tennyson, Macaulay, Milnes, Landseer, Jerrold, Dickens, Mark Lemon, Maclise, Samuel Rogers, and Mr. Brookfield—and in the course of the evening proposed the health of Mrs. Macready and her family. "The gentlemen of the G.," he wrote to Mrs. Brookfield, "tell me and another auditor from the Macready dinner that my style of oratory was conspicuous for consummate ease and impudence, I all the while feeling in so terrible a panic that I scarcely knew at the time what I was uttering, and didn't know at all when I sat down."

Probably he never spoke quite as badly as he imagined, and even when he spoke well Mr. Bayard Taylor says he always insisted it was by accident.

Mr. Fields has declared that it never disturbed Thackeray that he made a woeful picture as a speaker, but that he sat down with such cool serenity, if he found he could not recall what he wished to say, that his audience could not help joining in smiling when he came to a standstill. "Once he asked me to travel with him from London to Manchester to hear a great speech he was going to make at the Founding of the Free Library Institution in that city," Mr. Fields has related. "All the way down he was discoursing of certain effects he intended to produce on the Manchester dons by his eloquent appeals to their pockets. This passage was to have great influence with the rich merchants, this one with the clergy, and so on. He said that although

Dickens, and Bulwer, and Sir James Stephen—all eloquent speakers—were to precede him, he intended to beat each of them on this special occasion. He insisted that I should be seated directly in front of him so that I should have the full force of his magic eloquence. . . . Sir John Potter, who presided, then rose, and after some complimentary allusions to the author of *Vanity Fair*, introduced him to the crowd, who received him with ringing plaudits. As he rose, he gave me a half-wink from under his spectacles, as if to say, 'Now for it; the others have done very well, but I will show 'em a grace beyond the reach of their art.' He began in a clear and charming manner, and was absolutely perfect for three minutes. In the midst of a most earnest and elaborate sentence he suddenly stopped, gave a look of comic despair at the ceiling, crammed both hands into his trousers pockets, and deliberately sat down. . . . He continued to sit on the platform in a perfectly composed manner; and when the meeting was over, he said to me, without a sign of discomfiture, 'My boy, you have accidentally missed hearing one of the finest speeches ever composed for delivery by a great British orator.' "

Thackeray himself, in a letter to his youngest daughter, mentioned the occasion. "Last week I was away at Manchester," he wrote, "when I broke down in a speech before three thousand ladies and gentlemen. I felt very foolish, but I tried again at night and did better; and as there is nothing more wicked in breaking down in a speech than in slipping on a bit of orange-peel and breaking one's nose, why, I got up again, and made another speech at night without breaking down. It is all custom, and most people can no more do it than they can play the piano without learning."

Mr. Bright, who was present, also wrote about it many years later, and told the Misses Thackeray that he took their father to another meeting, where there were no fal-lal folks, but a set of good, honest working men. And he spoke there, and Mr. Bright declared that he never heard a better speech in all his life. "It was a capital speech," he said, "and they were all delighted with him."*

Again, on the morning of the banquet given to him before he went to America in 1855, he was in a state of great nervous anxiety. "It is very kind of my friends to give me a dinner," he said, "but I wish it was over, for such things set me trembling. Besides," he exclaimed to Mr. Hodder, "I have to make a speech, and what am I to say? Here, take a pen in your hand and sit down, and I'll see if I can hammer out something. It's hammering now; I'm afraid it will be stammering by-and-bye." It is astonishing how opinions differ as to how he spoke on that night. Mr. Edmund Yates thought "Thackeray was plainly moved, so much so that his reply was very short; he tried to pass off his emotion with some joke about the coming voyage and the steward, but it was too much for him." Sir Frederick Pollock declared that the speech was "not very felicitous"; while another critic reported that "Thackeray, who is far from a good speaker, outdid himself. There was his usual hesitation, but this hesitation becomes his manner of speaking and his matter, and is never unpleasant, though it is . . . most irksome to himself." Finally Mr. Hodder said, "I believe I am right in saying that the speech as delivered fell far short of the speech as written."

**Chapters from Some Unwritten Memoirs.*

Later, in 1857, besides the Edinburgh and Oxford speeches, he spoke in London at the Commercial Travellers' dinner; and on December 1, 1863, three weeks before his death, he made an appeal at a meeting called by Canon Sinclair in aid of the Lancashire Cotton Famine Fund.

I conclude this chapter with the report of some of his speeches.*

I

1849

"If the approbation which my profession receives is such as Mr. Adolphus" [the previous speaker] "is pleased to say it has been, I can only say that we are nearly as happy in this country as our brother literary men are in foreign countries, and that we have all but arrived at the state of dethroning you all. I don't wish that this catastrophe should be brought about for the sake of personal quiet; for one, I am desirous to read my books, write my articles, and get my money. I don't wish that that should take place; but if I survey mankind, not from China to Peru, but over the map of Europe, with that cursory glance which novel-writers can afford to take, I see nothing but literary men who seem to be superintending the affairs of the Continent, and only our happy island which is exempt from the literary despotism. Look to Italy, towards the boot of which I turn my eyes, and first I find that a great number of novelists and literary men are *bouleversing* the country from toe to heel, turning about Naples, and kicking Rome here and there, and causing a sudden

*The first five speeches are reported in Mr. Theodore Taylor's volume, and the last in Mr. Hodder's *Memoirs*.

onward impetus of the monarchy of the great Carlo Alberto himself. If I go to France, I find that men, and more particularly men of my own profession and Mr. James's profession, are governing the country; I find that writers of fiction and authors in general are ruling over the destinies of the empire; that Pegasus is, as it were, the charger of the first citizen of the Republic. But arriving at my own country, I beseech you to remember that there was a time, a little while ago, on the 10th of April last, when a great novelist—a man of my own profession—was standing upon Kennington Common in the van of liberty, prepared to assume any responsibility, to take upon himself any direction of government, to decorate himself with the tricolor sash or the Robespierre waistcoat; and but for the timely, and I may say 'special,' interposition of many who are here present, you might have been at present commanded by a president of a literary republic instead of by our present sovereign. I doubt whether any presidents of any literary republics would contribute as much to the funds of this society. I don't believe that the country as yet requires so much of our literary men; but in the meantime I suppose it must be the task and endeavour of all of us light practitioners of literature to do our best, to say our little say in the honestest way we may, to tell the truth as heartily and as simply as we are able to tell it, to expose the humbug, and to support the honest man."

II

1840

"I suppose, Mr. Chairman, years ago, when you had a duty to perform, you did not think much about, or look to, what men of genius and men of eloquence might say of you, but you went and you did your best with all your power; and what was the result? You determined to do your best on the next occasion. I believe that is the philosophy of what I have been doing in the course of my life; I don't know whether it has tended to fame, or to laughter, or to seriousness; but I have tried to say the truth, and, as far as I know, I have tried to describe what I saw before me, as well as I best might, and to like my neighbour as well as my neighbour would let me like him. All the rest of the speech which I had prepared has fled into thin air; the only part of it which I remember was an apology for, or rather an encomium of, the profession of us novelists, which I am bound to say, for the honour of our calling, ought to rank with the very greatest literary occupations. Why should historians take precedence of us? Our personages are as real as theirs. For instance, I maintain that our friends Parson Adams and Dr. Primrose are characters as authentic as Dr. Sacheverell, or Dr. Warburton, or any reverend personage of their times. Gil Blas is quite as real and as good a man as the Duke of Serma, and, I believe, a great deal more so. I was thinking, too, that Don Quixote was, to my mind, as real a man as Don John or the Duke of Alva; and then I was turning to the history of a gentleman of whom I am particularly fond—a school-fellow of mine before Dr. Russell's time. I was turning to the life and history of one with whom we are all acquainted, and that is one Mr. Joseph Addison, who, I remember, was made Under-Secretary of State at one period of his life, under another celebrated man, Sir Charles Hedges, I think it was, but it is now so long ago, I am not sure; but I have no doubt Mr. Addison was much more proud of his connection with Sir Charles Hedges and his place in Downing Street, and his red box and his quarter's salary, punctually and regularly paid; I daresay he was much more proud of these than of any of the literary honours which he received, such as being the author of the *Tour to Italy* and *The Campaign*. But after all, though he was undoubtedly connected with Sir Charles Hedges, there was another knight with whom he was much more connected, and that was a certain Sir Roger de Coverley, whom we have always loved and believed in a thousand times better than a thousand Sir Charles Hedges. And as I look round at this table, gentlemen, I cannot but perceive that the materials for my favourite romances are never likely to be wanting to future authors. I don't know that anything I have written has been generally romantic; but if I were disposed to write a romance, I think I should like to try an Indian tale, and I should take for the heroes of it—or for some of the heroes of it—I would take the noble lord whom I see opposite to me" [Lord Hardinge] "with the Sutlej flowing behind him, and the enemy in his front, and himself riding before the British army, with his son Arthur and his son Charles by his side. I am sure, in all the regions of romance, I could find nothing more noble and affecting than that story, and I hope some of these days some more able novelist will undertake it."

III

AUTHORS AND THEIR PATRONS

DELIVERED 1851

"Literary men are not by any means, at this present time, that most unfortunate and most degraded set of people whom they are sometimes represented to be. If foreign gentlemen should, by any chance, go to see *The Rivals* represented at one of our theatres, they will see Captain Absolute and Miss Lydia Languish making love to one another and conversing, if not in the costume of the present day, or such as gentlemen and ladies are accustomed to use, at any rate in something near it; whereas when the old father Sir Anthony Absolute comes in, nothing will content the stage but that he should appear with red heels, large buckles, and an immense Ramillies wig. This is the stage tradition: they won't believe in an old man unless he appears in this dress and with this wig; nor in an old lady unless she comes forward in a quilted petticoat and high-heeled shoes; nor in Hamlet's grave digger unless he wears some four-and-twenty waistcoats; and so on. In my trade, in my especial branch of literature, the same tradition exists; and certain persons are constantly apt to bring forward or to believe in the existence, at this moment, of the miserable old literary hack of the time of George II., and bring him before us as the literary man of this day. I say that that disreputable old phantom ought to be hissed out of society. I don't believe in the literary man being obliged to resort to ignoble artifices and mean flatteries to get places at the tables of the great, and to enter into society upon sufferance. I don't believe in the patrons of this present day, except such patrons as I am happy to have in you, and as any honest man might be proud to have and shake by the hand—be shaken by the hand by. Therefore I propose from this day forth that the oppressed literary man should disappear from among us. The times are altered, the people don't exist; 'the patron and the jail,' praise God, are vanished from out our institutions. It may be possible that the eminent Mr. Edmund Curll stood in the pillory in the time of Queen Anne, who, thank God, is dead; it may be that in the reign of another celebrated monarch of these realms, Queen Elizabeth, authors who abused the persons of honour would have their arms cut off on the first offence, and be hanged on the second. Gentlemen, what would be the position of my august friend and patron, Mr. Punch, if that were now the case? Where would be his hands, and his neck, and his ears, and his bowels? He would be disembowelled, and his members cast about the land. We don't want patrons, we want friends; and I thank God we have them. And as for any idea that our calling is despised by the world, I do, for my part, protest against and deny the whole statement. I have been in all sorts of society in this world, and I have never been despised that I know of. I don't believe there has been a literary man of the slightest merit or of the slightest mark who did not greatly advance himself by his literary labours. I see along this august table gentlemen whom I have had the honour of shaking by the hand, and gentlemen whom I should never have called my friends but for the humble literary labours I have been engaged in. And therefore, I say, don't let us be pitied any more. As for pity being employed upon authors, especially if you will but look at the novelist of the present day, I think you will see it is altogether out of the question to pity them. We will take, in the first place, if you please, a great novelist who is the great head of a great party in a great assembly in this country. When this celebrated man went into his county to be proposed to represent it, and he was asked on what interest he stood, he nobly said he stood on his *head*. And who can question the gallantry and brilliancy of that eminent crest of his? and what man will deny the great merit of Mr. Disraeli? Take next another novelist, who writes from his ancestral hall, and addresses John Bull in letters on matters of politics; and John Bull buys eight editions of those letters. Is not this a prospect for a novelist? There is a third, who is employed upon this very evening, head and hand, heart and voice, I may say, in a work of charity. And what is the consequence? The Queen of the realm, the greatest nobles of the empire, all the great of the world,—will assemble to see him and to do him honour. I say, therefore, don't let us have pity. I don't want it till I really *do* want it. Of course it is impossible for us to settle the mere prices by which the works of those who amuse the public are to be paid. I am perfectly aware that Signor Twankeydillo, of the Italian Opera, and Mademoiselle Petitpas, of the Haymarket, will get a great deal more money in a week for the skilful exercise of their chest and toes than I, or you, or any gentleman, should be able to get by our brains and by weeks of hard labour. We cannot help these differences in payment—we know there must be high and low payments in our trade, as in all trades; that there must be gluts of the market, and over-production; that there must be successful machinery, and rivals, and brilliant importations from foreign countries; that there must be hands out of employ, and tribulation of workmen. But these ill-winds which afflict us blow fortunes to our successors. They are natural evils. It is the progress of the world rather than any evil which we can remedy, and that is why I say this society acts most wisely and justly in endeavouring to remedy, not the chronic distress, but the temporary evil; that it finds a man at the moment of the pinch ot necessity, helps him a little, and gives him a 'God-speed,' and sends him on his way. For my own part, I have felt that necessity, and bent under that calamity; and it is because I have found friends who have nobly, with God's blessing, helped me at that moment of distress that I feel deeply interested in the ends of a Society which has for its object to help my brother in similar need."

IV

ROYAL LITERARY FUND DINNER

"We, from this end of the table, speak humbly and from afar off. We are the usefuls of the company, who over and over again perform our little part, deliver our little messages, and then sit down; whereas you yonder are the great stars of the evening;—you are collected with much care, and skill, and ingenuity, by the manager of this benefit performance; you perform Macbeth and Hamlet, we are the Rosencrantzes and Guildensterns; we are the Banquos—as I know a Banquo who has shaken his gory old mug at Drury Lane at a dozen Macbeths. We resemble the individual in plush, whom gentlemen may have seen at the opera, who comes forward and demurely waters the stage, to the applause of the audience—never mind who is the great Taglioni, or the Lind, or the Wagner, who is to receive all the glory. For my part, I am happy to fulfil that humble office, and to make my little speech, and to return, and leave the place for a greater and more able performer. How like British charity is to British valour! It must always be well fed before it comes into action! We see before us a ceremony of this sort, which Britons always undergo with pleasure. There is no tax which the Briton pays so cheerfully as the dinner-tax. Every man here, I have no doubt, who is a little acquainted with the world must have received, in the course of the last month, a basketful of tickets inviting him to meet in this place for some purpose or other. We have all rapped upon this table, either admiring the speaker for his eloquence, or at any rate applauding him when he sits down. We all of us know—we have had it a hundred times—the celebrated flavour of the old Freemasons' mock-turtle, and the celebrated Freemasons' sherry; and if I seem to laugh at the usage, the honest, good old English usage, of eating and drinking, which brings us all together for all sorts of good purposes—do not suppose that I laugh at it any more than I would at good old honest John Bull, who has, under his good, huge, boisterous exterior, a great deal of kindness and goodness at the heart of him. Our festival may be compared with such a person; men meet here and shake hands, kind hearts grow kinder over the table, and a silent almoner issues forth from it, the festival over, and gratifies poor people, and relieves the suffering of the poor, which would never be relieved but for your kindness. So that there is a grace that follows after your meat and sanctifies it. We have heard the historians and their calling worthily exalted just now; but it seems to me that my calling will be the very longest and the last of those of all the literary gentlemen I see before me. Long after the present generation is dead—of readers and authors of books—there must be kindness and generosity, and folly and fidelity, and love, and heroism, and humbug, in all the world; and as long as they last, my successors, or the successors of the novelists who come long after us, will have plenty to do, and plenty of subjects to write upon. There may chance to be a time when wars will be over, and the 'decisive battles' of the world will not need a historian. There may arrive a time when the Court of Chancery itself will be extinguished; and, as perhaps you are all aware, there is a certain author of a certain work called *Bleak House* who, for the past three months, has been assaulting the Court of Chancery in a manner that I cannot conceive that ancient institution will survive. There may be a time when the Court of Chancery will cease to exist, and when the historian of *The Lives of the Lord Chancellors* will have no calling. I have often speculated upon what the successors of the novelists in future ages may have to do; and I have fancied them occupied with the times and people of our own age. If I could fancy a man so occupied hereafter and busied, we will say, with a heroic story, I would take the story which I heard hinted at the other night by the honoured, the oldest, the bravest, and the greatest man in this country—I would take the great and glorious action of Cape Danger, when, striking to the powers above alone, the *Birkenhead* went down—when, with heroic courage and endurance, the men remained on the decks, and the women and children were allowed to go away safe, as the people cheered them, and died doing their duty! I know of no victory so sublime in the annals of the feats of English valour—I know of no story that could inspire a great author or novelist better than that. Or suppose we should take the story of an individual of the present day, whose name has been already mentioned; we might have a literary hero not less literary then Mr. David Copperfield, or Mr. Arthur Pendennis, who is defunct; we might have a literary hero who, at twenty years of age, astonished the world with his brilliant story of *Vivian Grey;* who, in a little time afterwards, and still in the youthful period of his life, amazed and delighted the public with *The Wondrous Tale of Alroy;* who, presently following up the course of his career and the development of his philosophical culture, explained to a breathless and listening world the great Caucasian mystery; who, quitting literature, then went into politics; met, faced, and fought, and conquered, the great political giant and great orator of those days; who subsequently led thanes and earls to battle, and caused reluctant squires to carry his lance; and who, but the other day, went in a gold coat to kiss the hand of his Sovereign as Leader of the House of Commons and Chancellor of Her Majesty's Exchequer. What a hero that will be for some future novelist, and what a magnificent climax for the third volume of his story!"

V

THE COMMERCIAL TRAVELLERS' DINNER, 1857

"I feel it needful for me to be particularly cautious whenever I come to any meeting in the City which has to do with money and monetary affairs. It is seldom that I appear at all in these regions, unless, indeed, it be occasionally to pay a pleasing visit to Messrs. Bradbury & Evans in Bouverie Street, or to Messrs. Smith & Co. of Cornhill. But I read my paper like every good Briton, and from that I gather a lesson of profound caution in speaking to mercantile men on subjects of this kind. Supposing, for instance, that I have shares in the Bundelcund Banking Company, or in the Royal British Diddlesex Bank! I come down to a meeting of the shareholders, and hear an honoured treasurer and an admirable president making the most flourishing reports on the state of our concern, showing to us enormous dividends, accompanied with the most elegant bonuses, and proving to us that our funds are invested in the most secure way at Bogleywallak Bundelcund and Branksea Castle—go away delighted at the happy prospect before my wife and family, feeling perfect confidence that those innocent beings will be comfortable for the rest of their lives. What, then, is my horror when in one brief fortnight after, instead of those enormous dividends and elegant bonuses, I am served with a notice to pay up a most prodigious sum; when I find that our estates at Bogleywallak Bundelcund have been ravaged by the Bengal tiger; that the island of Branksea is under water; that our respected president is obliged to go to Spain for the benefit of his health, and our elegant treasurer cannot abide the London fog. You see I must be a little careful. But, granted that the accounts we have here have not, like our dinner, been subjected to an ingenious culinary process; granted that you have spent, as I read in your report, £25,000 in raising a noble school and grounds; that you have collected around you the happy juvenile faces which I see smiling on yonder benches to be the objects of your Christian kindness;—granting all this to be true, then, gentlemen, I am your most humble servant, and no words that I can find can express my enthusiastic admiration for what you have done. I sincerely wish, on behalf of my own class, the literary profession, that we could boast of anything as good. I wish that we had an institution to which we could confide our children, instead of having to send them about to schools as we do, at an awful risk. When the respected Mr. Squeers, of Do-the-boys Hall, announces that he proposes to take a limited number of pupils—I should rather say a number of very limited pupils—it is not because he is in love with the little darlings that he does it, but because he deigns to extract a profit out of them. It always pains me to think of the profits to be screwed out of the bellies of the poor little innocents. Why have we not, as men of letters, some such association as that which you have got up? I appeal to my literary brethren, if any of them are present, whether we, the men of the pen, cannot emulate the men of the road? A while ago, a friend engaged in my own profession, making his £1,000 a year, showed me his half-yearly account of his two little boys at school. These little heroes of six and seven, who are at an excellent school, where they are well provided for, came home with a little bill in their pocket which amounted to the sum of £75 for the half-year. Now think of this poor paterfamilias, earning his moderate £1,000 a year, out of which he has his life-assurance, his income-tax, and his house rent to pay, with three or four poor relations to support—for doubtless we are all blessed with those appendages—with the heavy bills of his wife and daughters for millinery and mantua-making to meet, especially at their present enormous makes and sizes;—think of this overburdened man having to pay £75 for one half-year's schooling for his little boys! Let the gentlemen of the press, then, try to devise some scheme which shall benefit them, as you have undoubtedly benefited by what you have accomplished for yourselves. We are all travellers and voyagers who must embark on life's ocean; and before you send your boys to sea, you teach them to swim, to navigate the ship, and guide her into port. The last time

I visited America, two years ago, I sailed on board the *Africa*, with Captain Harrison. As she was steaming out of Liverpool one fine blowy October day, and was hardly over the bar, when, animated by those peculiar sensations not uncommon to landsmen at the commencement of a sea-voyage, I was holding on amidship, up comes a quick-eyed, shrewd-looking little man, who holds on to the next rope to me, and says, 'Mr. Thackeray, I am the representative of the house of Appleton & Co., of Broadway, New York—a most liberal and enterprising firm, who will be most happy to do business with you.' I don't know that we then did any business in the line thus delicately hinted at, because at that particular juncture we were both of us called, by a heavy lurch of the ship, to a casting up of accounts of a far less agreeable character."

And now, lastly, I quote the *outline* of the speech Thackeray dictated to Mr. Hodder, which was to have been delivered at the farewell banquet in 1855, and which conclusively proves that he *should* have acquitted himself to the general satisfaction.

"I know great quantities of us here present have been invited to a neighbouring palace, where turtle, champagne, and all good things are all plentiful almost as here, and where there reigns a civic monarch with a splendid court of officers, etc.; the sort of greeting that I had myself to-day—this splendour, etc.—the bevy in the ante-room—have filled my bosom with an elation with which no doubt Sir Francis Graham Moon's" [Lord Mayor] "throbs. I am surrounded by respectful friends, etc.—and I feel myself like a Lord Mayor. To his lordship's delight and magnificence there is a drawback. In the fountain of his pleasure there surges a bitter. He is thinking about the 9th of November, and I about the 13th of October." [When Thackeray was to leave for America.] "Some years since, when I was younger, and used to frequent jolly assemblies, I wrote a Bacchanalian song, to be chanted after dinner, etc. I wish some one would sing that song now to the tune of the Dead March in *Saul*, etc.—not for me—I am miserable enough; but for you, who seem in a great deal too good spirits. I tell you I am not—all the drink in Mr. Bathe's cellars" [Bathe was the proprietor of the London tavern where the dinner was held] "won't make me. There may be sherry five hundred years old—Columbus may have taken it out from Cadiz with him when he went to discover America, and it won't make me jolly, etc.; and yet entirely unsatisfactory as this feast is to me, I should like some more. Why can't you give me some more? I don't care about them costing two guineas a head. It is not the trouble I value. Let us go to Simpson's fish ordinary—or to Bertolini's or John o' Groats, etc.: I don't want to go away—I cling round the mahogany tree.

"In the course of my profound and extensive reading I have found it is the habit of the English nation to give dinners to the unfortunate. I have been dining lately with some worthy singular fellows a hundred and fifty or a hundred and sixty years old. I find that upon certain occasions the greatest attention was always paid them. They might call for anything they liked for dinner. My friend Simon Frazer, Lord Lovat" [beheaded for treason, 1747], "about a hundred years since, I think, partook very cheerfully of minced veal and sack before he was going on his journey—Lord Ferrars, rice" [executed for murder, 1760]—"and I could tell you a dozen jolly stories about feasts of this sort. I remember a particularly jolly one at which I was present, and which took place at least nine hundred years ago. My friend Mr. Macready gave it at Forres Castle, North Britain, Covent Garden. That was a magnificent affair indeed. The tables were piled with the most splendid fruits; gorgeous dish-covers glittered in endless perspective. Macbeth—Macready, I mean—taking up a huge gold beaker, shining with enormous gems that must have been worth many hundred millions of money, filled it out of a gold six-gallon jar, and drank courteously to the general health of the whole table. Why did he put it down? What made him, in the midst of that jolly party, appear so haggard and melancholy? It was because he saw before him the ghost of John Cooper, with chalked face and an immense streak of vermilion painted across his throat. No wonder he was disturbed. In like manner I have before me at this minute the horrid figure of a steward with a basin or a glass of brandy and water, which he will press me to drink, and which I shall try and swallow, and which won't make me any better—I know it won't. Then there's the dinner, which we all of us must remember in our school-boy days, and which took place twice or thrice a year at home, on the day before Dr. Birch expected his young friends to reassemble at his academy, Rodwell Regis. Don't you remember how that morning was spent?—how you went about taking leave of the garden, and the old mare and foal and the paddock, and the pointers in the kennel; and how your little sister kept wistfully at your side all day; and how you went and looked at that confounded trunk which old Martha was packing with the new shirts, and at that heavy cake packed up in the play-box; and how kind 'the governor' was all day; and how at dinner he said, 'Jack,'—or 'Tom'—'pass the bottle' in a very cheery voice; and how your mother had got the dishes she knew you liked best; and how you had the wing instead of the leg, which used to be your ordinary share; and how that dear, delightful, hot, raspberry rolly-polly pudding, good as it was, and fondly beloved by you, yet somehow had the effect of the notorious school stick-jaw, and choked you and stuck in your throat; and how the gig came; and then, how you heard the whirl of mail-coach wheels and the tooting of the guard's horn as, with an extraordinary punctuality, the mail and the four horses came galloping over the hill. Shake hands, good-bye! God bless everybody! Don't cry, sister; away we go! and to-morrow we begin with Dr. Birch and six months at Rodwell Regis. But after six months'' [Thackeray expected to be away for this length of time] ''come the holidays again! etc., etc., etc.''

CHAPTER XXVI

THACKERAY AS ARTIST

CHAPTER XXVI

THACKERAY AS ARTIST

THACKERAY'S literary work has so overshadowed his drawings that I have no doubt the great majority of his readers is unaware of the amount of time he devoted to the pencil—the number of caricatures, and vignettes, and initials, and tail-pieces, he sketched; and has not paused to remember that he stands almost alone as a great author who has illustrated his own books. Many have forgotten, if they ever knew, that he produced the designs on copper and steel and wood for the *Paris Sketch-Book, Comic Tales and Sketches* (excepting *The Fatal Boots*, which is illustrated by Cruikshank), *The Great Hoggarty Diamond, The Irish Sketch-Book, From Cornhill to Grand Cairo, Vanity Fair, Mrs. Perkyn's Ball, Our Street, Pendennis, Dr. Birch and his Young Friends, The Kickleburys on the Rhine, The Rose and the Ring, The Virginians, Lovel the Widower*, and the *Roundabout Papers;* and that he contributed nearly four hundred drawings to *Punch*.

The *Fitzboodle Papers, Barry Lyndon, Esmond*, and the *Lectures*, were published without illustrations. He had intended to illustrate *The Newcomes* himself, and actually commenced two sketches for the first number; but for some reason or other it was decided that Doyle should furnish the drawings, and the two sketches already designed were adopted and redrawn by him. "He does beautifully easily what I want to do and can't," Thackeray declared. But I think Doyle did not draw much better than Thackeray, and was in no degree his superior in originality of design.

Again Thackeray finding it troublesome to draw on the wood the illustrations for *The Adventures of Philip*, when the story was appearing in *Cornhill*, some of the drawings were made on paper and then redrawn on wood, but not to his satisfaction. Mr. Frederick Walker was then introduced to him by Mr. George Smith; but this talented young artist, after redrawing a few of Thackeray's sketches, declared himself capable of better work, and declined to continue the job. Eventually the work was left in his hands with only written suggestions, sometimes a rough pen-and-ink sketch by the author; probably the *Good Samaritans* was the first executed on his own responsibility. The following is the last letter that passed between the novelist and his illustrator in reference to this book:—

"DEAR MR. WALKER,—In August. Philip. The Little Sister and the two little children saying this prayer in an old-fashioned church pew, not Gothic. The church is the one in Queen Square, Bloomsbury, if you are curious to be exact. The motto PRO CONCESSIS BENEFICIIS, and that will bring the story to an end. I am sorry it's over. And you?

"Always yours,

"W. M. THACKERAY."*

All his life he preferred the pencil to the pen. As I have already said, he often found writing wearisome and

* *The Life and Letters of Frederick Walker.*

the strain of composition irksome; there were times even when he almost hated the chain that held him to the desk. But he always turned to the drawing-board with pleasure.

"The sketches as they are given here are scarcely to be counted work," Mrs. Ritchie wrote in the preface to the volume of drawings published as *The Orphans of Pimlico*. "The hours which he spent upon his drawing-blocks and sketch-books brought no fatigue or weariness; they were of endless interest and amusement to him, and rested him when he was tired. It was only when he came to etch upon steel or to draw for the engraver upon wood that he complained of effort and want of ease; and we used often to wish that his drawings could be given as they were first made, without the various transmigrations of wood and steel, and engraver's toil and printer's ink."

His feeling for art was precocious, and at a very early age he both drew and painted. At Charterhouse on the leaves of his class-books he would draw caricatures of the masters, and he ornamented with various illustrations and sketches his copies of *Don Quixote*, *The Castle of Otranto* (in which is an intensely amusing drawing of Manfred clapping the door against Matilda), *Rollin's Ancient History*, *Robinson Crusoe*, *Joseph Andrews*, *Ainsworth's Latin Dictionary* (which he bought second-hand for a shilling, and which sold at his death for nearly five pounds), the *Eton Latin Grammar*, and no doubt many other books.*

*"O Scottish chiefs, didn't we weep over you! O mysteries of Udolpho, didn't I and Briggs (minor) draw pictures out of you! Efforts feeble indeed, but still giving pleasure to ourselves and our friends. 'I say, old boy, draw us Vivaldi tortured in the Inquisition,' or 'Draw us Don Quixote and the windmills,' amateurs would say to boys who had a love of drawing."—*De Juventute*.

The *Death of Marmion*, *Hector and Andromeda*, *The Minstrel Boy*, *Old King Cole*, *Getting Fat*, *Strike*, *Strike the Light Guitar*, and many other drawings, showing signs of originality, have been preserved, and reproduced in an interesting volume entitled *Thackerayana*. Besides these, the Rev. Charles Oldfield remembered a series of his pen-and-ink sketches labelled *Fine Arts* by the schoolboy designer: Painting, which was illustrated by a young ragamuffin, shoeless himself, laying blacking on a boot, the blacking-bottle, very big, with label to match, "Warren's Best"; carving, represented by a pimple-faced man of strong Jewish features going in with a large knife and fork at a similarly exaggerated ham; and "Music," showing an Italian of the stage-bandit type, slouch-hatted, gaitered, and monkeyed, grinding a hurdy-gurdy.

At Cambridge, he drew, among other things, a droll series descriptive of university life—*The Mathematic Lecturer*, *The Classman*, *The Plodder*, *The Grinder*, etc., and, best of all, two sketches entitled *First Term*, a student hard at work, and *Second Term*, the same student in the well of a sofa, the back of which is turned to the spectator, who can only see the cigar and boots of the lounger. There are two sketches, under the same names, and similar in subject, but not nearly so amusing, in the *Etchings* done while at Cambridge, and published by Sotheran in 1878, of which collection those most worthy of mention are the *Departure for Cambridge*, and the *Arrival from Cambridge*. At Weimar Thackeray found his principal delight in drawing caricatures for children; and he has himself recorded how he was touched to find on his second visit, more than twenty years after, that many of the sketches had been preserved—*Legal Defini-*

tions (*by one who may be called to the Bar*) are the best of the few I have seen.

At first he drew only for the amusement of his friends. "If I had only kept the drawings from his pen which used to be chucked about as though they were worth nothing!" more than one person said to Anthony Trollope, who was shown an album of drawings and letters which, in the course of twenty years, from 1829 to 1849, were despatched from Thackeray to his old friend Edward Fitzgerald. But one day he determined to seek a market for his caricatures; and he did eventually find a Mr. Gibb, who offered to dispose of them for him, though whether he was able to do so I cannot say.

Of his life in the Paris studios I have written in an earlier chapter;* and so, after mentioning that he contributed to the *National Standard* alleged portraits of Louis Phillipe, Braham, Rothschild, Alfred Bunn, and Sir Peter Laurie, I may pass on to the year 1836, when, in Macready's diary, on April 27, there is an entry: "At Garrick Club, when I dined and saw the papers. Met Thackeray, who has spent all his fortune, and is now about to settle at Paris as an artist."

Henry Reeve wrote to his mother (Paris, January 14, 1835): "Thackeray is flourishing, and after the opera we took tea and had a long talk of the doings of French artists. He complains of the impurity of their ideas, and of the jargon of a corrupt life, which they so unwisely admit into their painting-rooms. Thackeray's drawings—if I may judge by his note-book—are as pure

*"Drawing appeared to be his favourite amusement," Planché—who knew him when he was a slim young man, rather taciturn, in Paris—has said, "and he often sat by my side while I was reading or writing, covering every scrap of paper lying about with the most splendid sketches and amusing caricatures."

and accurate as any I have seen. He is a man whom I would willingly set to copy a picture of Raphael's, as far, at least, as the drawing goes; but he does not seem likely to get into a system of massive colouring, if I may judge by what he said."

Thackeray, however, soon abandoned the hope of being a serious painter, though to the end of his days he never ceased to practise the lighter veins of his art. In 1834 he had illustrated Edward Fitzgerald's *Undine* with fourteen little coloured drawings; and in March two years later he published simultaneously in London (Mitchel, Bond Street) and Paris (Rittner & Goupil, Boulevard Montmartre), a small folio, consisting of his six drawings (slightly tinted and drawn on the stone by Edward Norton, brother of the author of *Box and Cox*) entitled *Flore et Zéphyr.*

How thoroughly Thackeray's sense of humour was developed, even at this time, may be gathered from the following criticism by Dr. John Brown, in the *North British Review.* "It is," says Dr. Brown, "a small folio, with six lithographs, slightly tinted, entitled *Flore et Zéphyr. Ballet Mythologique dédié à* ——, *par Théophile Wagstaffe!* Between '*à*' and '*par*' on the cover is the exquisite Flore herself, all alone in some rosy and bedizened bower. She has the old jaded smirk, and, with eyebrows up and eyelids dropped, she is looking down with modesty and glory. Her nose, which is long, and has a ripe droop, gives to the semi-circular smirk of the large mouth, down upon the centre of which it comes in the funniest way, an indescribably sentimental absurdity. Her thin, sinewy arms and large hands are crossed on her breast, and her petticoat stands out like an inverted white tulip of muslin, out of which come her professional

PEN'S STAIRCASE. I.

A little Dinner.

PEN'S STAIRCASE. 2

A few little Bills.

legs, in the only position which human nature never puts its legs into; it is her special *pose*. Of course, also, you are aware, by that smirk, that look of being looked at, that though alone in maiden meditation in this her bower, and sighing for her Zephyr, she is in front of some thousand pairs of eyes, and under the fire of many double-barrelled *lorgnettes*, of which she is the focus. In the first place, *La Danse fait ses Offrandes sur l' Autel de l'Harmonie*, in the shape of Flore and Zephyr coming tripping to the footlight, and having no manner of regard to the altar of harmony, represented by a fiddle with an old and dreary face, and a laurel-wreath on its head, and very great regard for the unseen but perfectly understood 'house.'

"Next is *Triste et Abattu, les Séductions des Nymphes, le (Zéphyr) tentent en Vain*, Zephyr looking theatrically sad.

"Then Flore (with one lower extremity at more than a right angle to the other) *Déplore l' Absence de Zéphyr*.

"Next Zephyr has his turn, and *Dans un Pas Seul exprime sa suprême Désespoir*—the extremity of despair being expressed by doubling one leg so as to touch the knee of the other, and then wholly whirling round so as to suggest the regulator of a steam-engine run off.

"Next is the rapturous reconciliation, when the faithful creature bounds into his arms, and is held up to the 'house' by the waist in the wonted fashion.

"Then there is *La Retraite de Flore*, where we find her with her mother and two admirers—Zephyr, of course, not one. This is in Thackeray's strong, unflinching line. One lover is a young dandy, without forehead or chin, sitting idiotically astride his chair. To him the old lady, who has her slight *rouge* too, and is in a homely shawl and muff, having walked, is making faded love.

In the centre is the fair darling herself, still on tiptoe, and wrapped up, but not too much, for her *fiacre*. With his back to the comfortable fire, and staring wickedly at her, is the other lover, a big, burly, elderly man, probably well-to-do on the Bourse, and with a wife and family at home in their beds.

"The last exhibits *Les Délassements de Zéphyr*. That hard-working and homely personage is resting his arm on the chimney-piece, taking a huge pinch of snuff from the box of a friend, with a refreshing expression of satisfaction—the only bit of nature as yet. A dear little innocent pot-boy, such as only Thackeray knew how to draw, is gazing and waiting upon the two, holding up a tray from the nearest tavern, on which is a great pewter-pot of foaming porter for Zephyr, and a rummer of steaming brandy-and-water for his friend, who has come in from the cold air."

The sketches are indeed admirable, and will well repay a visit to the Library of the British Museum, where there is one of the few known copies. The venture, however, met with no commercial success.

Undeterred by this failure, he soon made another attempt to make money by his pencil. It was at the time when Dickens was writing *Pickwick*. Robert Seymour, the inventor of the original crude design of *Pickwick*, was the illustrator; but when he had only completed the drawings for the first two or three numbers, on the morning of Thursday, April 20 [1836], in a fit of temporary insanity he committed suicide. His place was filled by Mr. R. W. Buss, with whose work, however, Dickens was not satisfied. A new artist was wanted, and Thackeray, applying for the post, met Dickens for the first time. Years after, at a Royal Academy dinner,

A morning visit at tea-time

Thackeray, in responding to the toast of "Literature," with which his name and Dickens's were associated, spoke of his now famous offer, the refusal of which he would persist in calling "Mr. Pickwick's lucky escape."

"Had it not been for the direct act of my friend who has just sat down," he said, "I should most likely never have been included in the toast which you have been pleased to drink; and I should have tried to be not a writer, but a painter, or designer of pictures. That was the object of my early ambition; and I can remember when Mr. Dickens was a very young man, and had commenced delighting the world with some charming humourous works, of which I cannot mention the name, but which were coloured light green, and came out once a month, that this young man wanted an artist to illustrate his writings; and I recollect walking up to his chambers in Furnival's Inn with two or three drawings in my hand, which, strange to say, he did not find suitable. But for the unfortunate blight which came over my artistical existence, it would have been my pride and pleasure to have endeavoured one day to find a place on these walls for one of my performances. This disappointment caused me to direct my attention to a different walk of art, and now I can only hope to be 'translated' on these walls, as I have been, thanks to my talented friend Mr. Egg."

"On Saturday," Thackeray had written in April to Mrs. Brookfield, "when you go to Oxbridge, I shall console myself by a grand dinner at the Royal Academy, if you please, to which they have invited me on a great card like a tea-tray. That's a great honour; none but bishops, purchasers, and other big-wigs are asked. I daresay I shall have to make an impromptu speech.

Shall I come to rehearse it to you on Friday?" The *Illustrated London News* wished to publish an engraving of this banquet, but as the officials would give no facilities, the artist (Mr. John Gilbert) had only the report of the *Times* to depend on. When the rough outline sketch was drawn, Mr. Vizetelly sent it to Thackeray, asking if it were accurate. "Your arrangement of the company at the Academy dinner is all wrong, Jupiter" [the *Times*] "notwithstanding," Thackeray replied. "The plan I have roughly sketched out will show you where most of the big and little stars twinkled. It was a cold and formal affair—almost as full as my Lord Carlisle's late patronising spread given to certain well-known gents from Grub Street." This referred to a dinner given to some of the *Punch* staff and other literary men, which was a fearfully, dreadfully dismal meal. "Of course," Thackeray said to Mr. Vizetelly afterwards, "we all knew each other's pet stories, and all the dear old jokes, and this acted as a wet blanket upon us. No one would have thought of trotting out a good new story simply for one of his *confrères* to crib for his next magazine article. If Lord Carlisle had asked half a dozen literary men and half a dozen lords, we should in this case have fit audience found, and been able to amuse the quality at the trifling expense of boring ourselves."

He then made the drawing known as *The History of Dionysius Diddler*, and the series, perhaps after Hogarth's *Marriage à la Mode*, entitled *The Count and Countess des Dragées*, which were first published in 1864 in the *Autographic Mirror*. Among his other drawings, not illustrations of his own books, are the twelve plates of illustrations to Douglas Jerrold's *Men of Character;* the illustrations to *Lord Bateman:* a ballad; and *Sketches by*

Sketches by Spec. No. 1. *Published by H. Cunningham, 3 St James' Square*

BRITANNIA PROTECTING THE DRAMA.

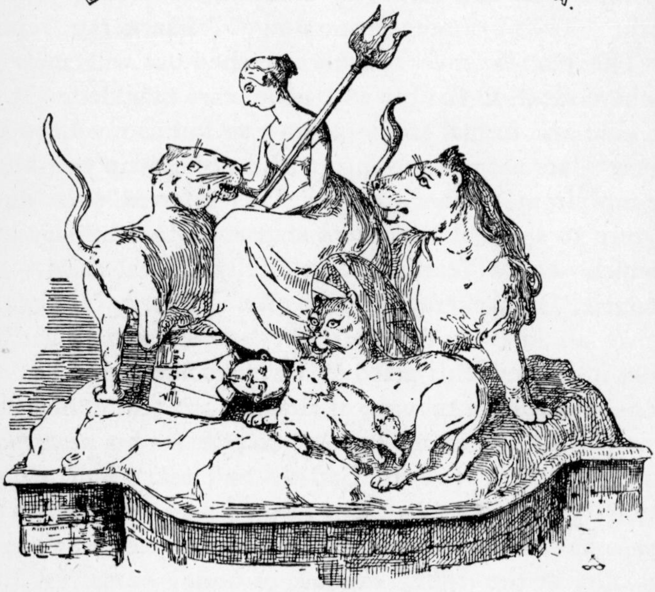

EXPLANATION OF THE HALLEGORY.

This Ladies and Gentlemen is a Hallegory, and represents Britanny patronising hof the Drama — Look at the Drama laying at her feet & over it remark the Lioness is lifting hof her leg

That's Britanny — she's holding hof a pitch fork (as well she may in sich company) and the hanimals round about her why, they are the principal hactors. For some parts (especially for **BLOODY TRAGEDY**) *they beat the Commongarden ones hollow. and that's why Brittanny mostly goes to Drury Lane*

Look at the Lamb (hemblem of hinnocence!) hes lying betwixt the legs of the Panther, and thinking of the kind souls who got him hof the situation. Britanny's caressing the Lioness, for shes cumspicuous for humanity, & theres no sich proof of kindness as being fond of the brute beastesses

The figure of Britanny is taken from the reverse of that famous coin the British Halfpenny: some people think it would apply to coins more valuable and is the wery thing for the **REWERSE of A SOVERING.**

Spec.—No. 1: Britannia Protecting the Drama, which was published by Cunningham not later than 1840, and has been reproduced by the Autotype Company from the only known copy, now in the possession of Mr. C. P. Johnson.

Eleven years after Thackeray's death, Messrs. Chatto & Windus published a volume, *Thackerayana,* which contained reproductions of a great number of his Charterhouse, Cambridge, and Weimar drawings.* Mrs. Ritchie, however, thought the book did not give a fair example of her father's feeling for art, and deemed it advisable to publish some of his later drawings, which should more adequately represent his gift. This later volume was published by Messrs. Smith & Elder in 1876, under the title of *The Orphan of Pimlico.*

"A dozen years ago I entreated Annie Thackeray, Smith, Elder, etc., to bring out a volume of Thackeray's better drawings," Edward Fitzgerald told Mr. Aldis Wright early in 1875. "Of course they wouldn't. Now Chatto & Windus have, you know, brought out a volume of his inferior: and now Annie T., S. & E. prepare a volume—when it is not so certain to pay, at any rate, as when W. M. T. was the hero of the day. However, I send them all I have; pretty confident they will select the worst: of course, for my own part, I would rather have any other than copies of what I have; but I should like the world to acknowledge he could do something besides the ugly and the ridiculous." And on December 29, Fitzgerald wrote to Frederick Tennyson: "In the midst of all this mourning" [for Minnie Thackeray (Mrs. Leslie Stephen)] "comes out a new volume of

*This was suppressed, as it contained a great amount of copyright matter; but it has since been republished.

Thackeray's drawings—or sketches—as I foresaw it would be, too much caricature, not so good as much of his old *Punch;* and with none of the better things I wanted them to put in—for his sake, as well as the community's. I do not wonder at the publisher's obstinacy, but I wonder that Annie T. did not direct otherwise. I am convinced I can hear Thackeray saying, when such a book as this was proposed to him, 'Oh, come, there has been enough of all this,' and crumbling up the proof in that little hand of his. For a curiously little hand he had, uncharacteristic of the grasp of his mind: I used to consider it half inherited from the Hindoo people among whom he was born."

There is no doubt but that Fitzgerald was right. *The Orphan of Pimlico* is interesting, as any collection of Thackeray's writings or drawings always must be, but it contains many rough, unfinished sketches—several, too, that he deliberately left out of his books, probably because he did not consider them good enough. Greater interest would have been excited by a volume containing a selection of his drawings from *Punch*.

He was at his best when illustrating his own writings. There has rarely been an artist who could make his drawings so helpful to the text. His characters are as truly depicted by the pencil as by the pen, and they tell the story together. His drawing may not always have been quite accurate, the perspective may have occasionally been wrong, and an arm may have slightly resembled a fin, or a leg have been slightly out of correct drawing; but for quaint fancy and humour they have rarely been surpassed. Take *Vanity Fair*—the most profusely and perhaps the best illustrated of all his books—and study the pictorial work, from the opening initial W to the

Venus preparing the armour of Mars

"Finis" tail-piece. Look at Becky showing off her doll (Miss Jemmy) to her father's rather dissolute Bohemian friends, or, all alone, building a house of cards that we know will tumble down after the fashion of such structures; or look at her fishing, and trying to entangle Mr. Jos; or at Dobbin and Cuff fighting (in a capital C); or at Sir Pitt with his new governess's box on his shoulders; or at that governess in the schoolroom (paying just as much attention to her charges as we expected); or at Moss arresting Rawdon Crawley in Gaunt Square (observe Moss's companion whistling to a cabman). Then glance at the end of chapter ix., and you will find a delightful sketch of a rather sad jester, Thackeray himself. Turn over the pages as far as chapter xxx., and you may compare Becky, sleeping comfortably, with Mrs. O'Dowd, as Venus, preparing the Armour of Moss, before Waterloo. Nine chapters later see Miss Horrocks playing the piano with the sycophant Hester by her side, and then glance at Sir Pitt nursed by the now bullying Hester. Note, elsewhere, the two appearances of Becky in the character of Clytemnestra.*

Then take *Pendennis* and go through it carefully, observing especially the three cuts, *A Morning Visit at Tea-Time*, *Rowena Visits Rebecca*, and *Blanche Playing to Foker;* and so look through all the volumes. After which, pause. Consider the originality of the drawings,

*"There is one mystery about her" [Becky Sharp] "which I should like to have cleared up. Nearly at the end of the book there is a picture of Jo Sedley in his night-dress seated—a sick old man—in his chamber; and behind the curtain is Becky, glaring and ghastly, grasping a dagger. Beneath the picture is the single word 'Clytemnestra.' Did Becky kill him, Mr. Thackeray?" This question seemed to afford the person to whom it was addressed matter for profound reflection. He smoked meditatively, appeared to be engaged in endeavouring to arrive at the solution of some problem, and then with a sarcastic expression—a "slow smile" dawning on his face—replied: "I don't know."—J. E. Cooke, *An Hour with Thackeray*.

the fancy, the suggestiveness, the power of bringing a whole scene before the spectator in a few carefully chosen outlines. If *that* is not art, *then* Thackeray was not an artist.

Flore et Zéphyr must be ranked high among his creations. After which I may mention the illustrations to *The Rose and the Ring;* the frontispiece to *Comic Tales and Sketches;* the portrait in *Punch* of Adolphus Simcoe, Esq. (the translator of the well-known ballad of King Canute from the Anglo-Saxon); the three companion pictures, also in *Punch*—"Sherry, perhaps," "Rum, I hope," "*Tracts, by Jove*"; the title-pages of *Vanity Fair* and *Pendennis;* the portrait, in *The Virginians*, of the founder of the family, Henry Esmond; and lastly, and in my opinion the best of all, the *Rex—Ludovicus-Ludovicus Rex* in *The Paris Sketch-Book.**

Thackeray, I think, was under no misapprehension as to the value of his sketches. True, when he was living in Paris he wrote desponding letters, expressing doubts whether he would ever be able to make a living by his pencil—but that was when he was thinking of "serious" painting. But then, just as he often belittled his literary genius, so, too, he depreciated his artistic gifts. For instance, when a man said to him in all good faith, "But you can draw," he unjustly wrote him down as a snob. He made fun of himself as a "serious" painter in his *Fraser* articles; and one day wrote, "You have a new artist on *The Train*, I see, dear Yates. I

*Until 1843 Thackeray's drawings were generally unsigned, though the frontispiece of *Comic Tales and Sketches* was signed W. M. T., and a few later sketches W. T. for William Thackeray. It was not until the letter to *Punch* from Alongo Spec, Historical Painter, enclosing two designs, that the "spectacles" (⚯) which were to become as famous as the leech in a bottle, made their first appearance.

ADOLPHUS SIMCOE, ESQ.

have been looking at his work, and I have solved a problem. I find there *is* a man alive who draws worse than myself." Mr. Cockran, calling on him one morning, found him fretting over a drawing of his own. "Look," the host said, "now G. (mentioning a clever draughtsman), by a few touches, throwing some light or shadow here and there, would make this a picture. How it is I know not, but I certainly cannot do it at all."

On another occasion Thackeray showed Mr. Marcus Stone some proofs of initial letters which he had done himself. In one the people all wore muffs instead of heads. "Well, young shaver, do you know what that means?" he asked, and to spare him the humiliation of saying, perhaps, the wrong thing, he added immediately: "I mean they are all muffs." Then he paid the young man a pretty compliment. He asked him where he got his pencils, for, he said, "My pencils don't draw like yours."

He was certainly aware of his lack of technical skill as an etcher. He asked Mr. Vizetelly to find him some one who would etch the frontispiece to the *Cairo* drawing from his water-colour sketch, and the job was given to a young man named Thwaites, who subsequently put a number of the drawings for *Mrs. Perkyn's Ball* on the wood. "I return the drawings after making a few alterations in them," he wrote to Mr. Vizetelly on one occasion. "Present Mr. Titmarsh's compliments to your talented young man and say M. A. T. would take it as a great favour if he would kindly confine his improvements to the Mulligans and Mrs. Perkyn's other guests' extremities. In your young gentleman's otherwise praiseworthy corrections of my vile drawings, a certain *je ne sais quoi*, which I flatter myself exists in the original sketches, seems to have given him the slip, and I have tried in vain to recapture it. Somehow I prefer my own Nuremberg dolls to Mr. Thwaites's." Vizetelly said Thackeray was almost as fastidious as Mr. Ruskin in regard to the manner in which his sketches were transferred to the wood, and Thackeray himself once complained to Mr. Hollingshead: "I'm not a first-rate artist, I know; but I'm not half as bad as those fellows, the woodcutters, make me." It is, indeed, more than probable that much of the delicacy of expression and drawing has been lost in the cuts.

"It may be doubted, however, whether any degree of assiduity would have enabled him to excel in the money-making branches," Mr. Hayward wrote in 1848, "for his talent was altogether of the Hogarth kind, and was principally remarkable for the pen-and-ink sketches of character and situation which he dashed off for the amusement of his friends." Certainly his talent was of the Hogarth kind; but the works of Hogarth, who certainly made money, have not been adjudged valueless. Though Thackeray lacked academic correctness and technical mastery, the undeniable originality and humour of his drawings will secure for them a very long lease of life, and I think have placed him in the ranks of caricaturists above Doyle, and not far below Leech and Cruikshank himself.

It may be thought that I have over-praised, and altogether ranked Thackeray too high as an artist. But I am happy, at any rate, to find myself "in good company," for Charlotte Brontë, writing to Mr. S. Williams (March 11, 1848), sums up her impressions of Thackeray as a draughtsman and book-illustrator in these eulogistic words, with which I most cordially and entirely agree:—

Becky's second appearance in the character of Clytemnestra.

"You will not easily find a second Thackeray. How he can render, with a few black lines and dots, shades of expression, so fine, so real; traits of character so minute, so subtle, so difficult to seize and fix, I cannot tell—I can only wonder and admire. Thackeray may not be a painter, but he is a wizard of a draughtsman; touched with his pencil, paper lives. And then his drawing is so refreshing: after the wooden limbs one is accustomed to see portrayed by commonplace illustrators, his shapes of bone and muscle clothed with flesh, correct in proportion and anatomy, are a real relief. All is true in Thackeray. If Truth were again a goddess, Thackeray should be her high priest."*

**Charlotte Brontë and Her Circle.*

CHAPTER XXVII

THACKERAY AS ART-CRITIC

CHAPTER XXVII

THACKERAY AS ART-CRITIC

"THACKERAY was one of the best of art-critics. He had the true instinct and relish, and the nicety and directness, necessary for just as well as high criticism: the white light of his intellect found its way into this as into every region of his work. . . . It would not be easy to imagine better criticisms of art than those from Mr. Thackeray's hand. His art 'has its seat in reason,' and he is more objective, cool, and critical than Mr. Ruskin,"—so wrote Dr. John Brown; and few who have studied Thackeray's papers on art in *Fraser*, in *Ainsworth*, in the *Pictorial Times*, in M. Marvy's volume of engravings,* and elsewhere, will be inclined to dispute this judgment.

His fame as an art-critic was not even confined to England.

"When Thackeray was in this city," Charles Sumner wrote from Washington, "we visited, among the earlier

*During 1848, Louis Marvy, a young French artist, in whose *atelier* in Paris, and with whose family Thackeray had spent many happy hours, fled to England to take refuge from the revolutionary storm. Here he had engraved some *Sketches after English Landscape Painters*, hoping, by this means, to obtain enough money to enable him to pursue his more ambitious designs. The publisher to whom the engraving had been submitted would not entertain the proposal of the skilful but unknown painter, unless the letterpress was written by Thackeray, who agreed readily enough, and furnished a number of short notices of Turner, Calcott, Redgrave, Cattermole, Constable, Gainsborough, and other famous painters.

places, the capitol rotunda. Thackeray was an artist by birthright, and his judgment was beyond chance or question. He took a quiet turn around the rotunda, and in a few words gave each picture its perfectly correct rank and art valuation. 'Trumbull is your painter,' he said; 'never neglect Trumbull.' Other places of interest were then seen, after which we started homeward. He had not yet been at my house, and my chief anxiety was to coach him safely past that Jackson statue. The conversation hung persistently upon art matters, which made it certain that I was to have trouble when we should come in view of that particular excrescence. We turned the dreadful corner at last, when, to my astonishment, Mr. Thackeray held straight past the hideous figure, moving his head neither to the right nor left, and chatting as airily as though we were strolling through an English park. Now I knew that the instant we came in sight of poor Jackson's caricature he saw it, realised its accumulated terrors at a glance, and, in the charity of his great heart, took all pains to avoid having a word said about it. Ah, but he was a man of rare consideration."*

On matters artistic he laid down the law again and again with no uncertain voice. His courage was prodigious. As it was said of Disraeli that, even at the beginning of his career, both in his political writings and when speaking in the House, he always attacked men of bigger standing than himself, so may it be said of Thackeray that he made it a rule to tilt against men of recog-

*At a private house Thackeray spoke of the statue. "The hero was sitting in an impossible attitude," he said, "on an impossible horse with an impossible tail"; and the artist's defence, that he had never seen an equestrian statue, did not cause him to alter his opinion.

nised position, and let the smaller fry escape with a word or two. His criticisms made him unpopular, as Fitzgerald's letter (quoted in an earlier chapter), shows, but to his credit it must be said that he never deviated from his opinions, which, except in isolated instances, have been accepted by the critics of later generations.

He wrote of French artists, and, while telling of his love for their Bohemianism, showed clearly that he was not blinded to the faults of their works. He objected strongly to the so-called "Classical school"—the slavish imitation of the old Masters. "It is the study of Nature surely that profits us, and not of these imitations of her," was the sound maxim he urged. "Because," he continued, "certain mighty men of old could make heroical statues and plays, must we be told there is no other beauty but classical beauty?—must not every whipster of a French poet chalk you out plays, *Henriades*, and such like, and vow that here was the real thing, the undeniable Kalon?" He went to see the prize pictures at the École Royale des Beaux-Arts. "The subjects," he said, "are almost all what are called classical: Orestes pursued by every variety of Furies; numbers of little wolf-suckling Romuluses; Hectors and Andromaches in a complication of parting embraces, and so forth; for it was the absurd maxim of our forefathers that because these subjects had been the fashion twenty centuries ago, they must remain so *in sæcula sæculorum;* because to these lofty heights giants had scaled, behold the race of pigmies must get upon stilts and jump at them likewise! and on the canvas and in the theatre, the French frogs (excuse the pleasantry) were instructed to swell out and roar as much as possible."

The pictures at the Luxembourg pleased him better, though he noticed that the chief specimens of the sublime are in the way of murder—and he gives a list to prove his contention.

Some of his individual criticisms are interesting. He admired Delacroix, especially his *Medea*, and found in him the stamp of genius and a great heart. "A score of shipwrecked men are in this boat, on a great, wide, swollen, interminable sea—no hope, no speck of sail—and they are drawing lots which shall be killed and eaten," he wrote of another picture of this artist. "A burly seaman, with a red beard, has just put his hand into the hat, and is touching his own to the officer. One fellow sits with his hands clasped, and gazing—gazing into the great void before him. By jingo, his eyes are unfathomable! he is looking at miles and miles of lead-coloured, bitter, pitiless brine! Indeed, one can't bear to look at him long; nor at that poor woman, so sickly and so beautiful, whom they may as well kill at once, or she will save them the trouble of drawing straws; and give up to their maws that poor, white, faded, delicate, shrivelled carcase. Ah, what a thing it is to be hungry! Oh, Eugenius Delacroix! how can you manage, with a few paint-bladders, and a dirty brush, and a careless hand, to dash down such savage histories as these, and fill people's minds with thoughts so dreadful? Ay, there it is; whenever I go through that part of the gallery where M. Delacroix's picture is, I always turn away now, and look at a fat woman with a parroquet opposite. For what's the use of being uncomfortable?"

"Another great picture," he continued, "is one of about four inches square — *The Chess-players*, by M. Meissonier—truly an astonishing piece of workmanship.

No silly tricks of effect and abrupt, startling shadow and light, but a picture painted with the minuteness and accuracy of a daguerreotype, and as near as possible perfect in its kind. Two men are playing at chess, and the chessmen are no bigger than pin-heads; every one of them an accurate portrait, with all the light, shadow, roundness, character, and colour, belonging to it."

Delaroche's *Death of Elizabeth* did not appeal to him, but his *Enfans d'Edouard*, though pathetic and gloomy, was more to his taste. Horace Vernet, the father-in-law of Delaroche, is written down as the King of French battle-painters. Court's *Death of Cæsar*, Jacquand's *Death of Adelaide de Cominges*, and Decaisne's *Guardian Angel*, were all praised; so, too, Gudin's sea-pieces, a landscape of Giroux, the *Prometheus* of Aligny, and Flandrine's *Jesus Christ and the Children*—which last, however, he set down as imitations of Poussin's *Polyphemus* and the Roman Schools respectively. Jacques Louis David was admired to a certain extent. Greuze was mentioned as marvellously graceful and delicate, and Claude and Watteau as delightful and refreshing; while in the statue-room Jouffley's *Jeune Fille confiant son Premier Secret à Venus* quite aroused his enthusiasm.

On the other hand, the so-called "Christian" or "Catholic" art, in his eyes, was humbug, and he hated it accordingly.

"Here, for instance, is Chevalier Ziegler's picture of *St. Luke painting the Virgin*," he wrote of it. "St. Luke has a monk's dress on, embroidered, however, smartly round the sleeves. The Virgin sits in an immense yellow-ochre halo, with her son in her arms. She looks preternaturally solemn; as does St. Luke, who is eyeing his paint-brush with an intense, ominous, mystical look. They call this Catholic art. There is nothing, my dear friend, more easy in life. First take your colours, and rub them down clear — bright carmine, bright yellow, bright sienna, bright ultramarine, bright green. Make your costumes as much as possible like the costumes of the early part of the fifteenth century. Paint them in with the above colours, and if on a gold ground, the more 'Catholic' your art is. Dress your Apostles like priests before the altar; and remember to have a good commodity of crosiers, censers, and other such gimcracks as you may see in the Catholic chapels, in Sutton Street, or elsewhere. Deal in Virgins, and dress them like a burgomaster's wife by Cranach or Van Eyck. Give them all long twisted tails to their gowns, and proper angular draperies. Place all their heads on one side, with the eyes shut and the proper solemn simper. At the back of the head, draw, and gild with gold-leaf, a halo, or glory, of the exact shape of a cart-wheel: and you have the thing done. It is Catholic art *tout craché;* as Louis Phillippe says."

He would have had fewer historical painters if dispensing with these would have increased the number of those who devoted themselves to landscape. "Herein lies the vast privilege of the landscape-painter," he suggested, "he does not address you with one particular subject or expression, but with a thousand never contemplated by himself, and which only arise out of occasion. You may always be looking at a natural landscape as at a fine pictorial imitation of one; it seems eternally producing new thoughts in your bosom as it does fresh beauties for its own. I cannot fancy more delightful, cheerful, silent companions for a man than half a dozen landscapes hung round his study. Portraits, on the contrary, and large pieces of figures, have a painful, fixed, staring look, which must jar upon the mind in many of its moods. Fancy living in a room with David's sans-cullotte 'Leonidas' staring perpetually in your face! For," he added, "an ordinary man would be whirled away in a fever, or would hobble off this mortal stage in a premature gout-fit, if he too early, or too often, indulged in such tremendous drink. I think in my heart I am fonder of pretty third-rate pictures than of your great thundering first-rates. Confess how many times you have read Béranger, and how many Milton! If you go to the 'Star and Garter,' don't you grow sick of that vast, luscious landscape, and long for the sight of a couple of cows, or a donkey, and a few yards of common? Donkeys, my dear MacGilp, since we come to this subject, say not so: Richmond Hill for them. Milton they never grow tired of, and are as familiar with Raphael as Bottom with exquisite Titania. Let us thank Heaven, my dear sir, for according to us the power to taste and appreciate the pleasures of mediocrity. I have never heard that we were great geniuses. Earthy we are, and of the earth; glimpses of the sublime are but rare to us; leave we them to great geniuses, and to the donkeys; and if nothing profit us, *aërias tentasse domus* along with them, let us thankfully remain below, being merry and humble."

He wrote of other foreign artists in the last article of his that deals with art—the *Notes of a Week's Holiday*, written in one of the later years of his life. The most noticeable references are to Paul Peter Rubens, and Hans Hemmelinck.

"Better see Rubens anywhere than in a church," he said. "At the Academy, for example, where you may study him at your leisure. But at Church? I would as soon ask Alexandre Dumas for a sermon. Either would paint you a martyrdom very fiercely and picturesquely—writhing muscles, flaming coals, scowling captains and executioners, swarming groups, and light, shade, colour, most dexterously brilliant or dark; but in Rubens I am admiring the performer rather than the piece. With what astonishing rapidity he travels over his canvas; how tellingly the cool lights and warm shadows are made to contrast and relieve each other; how that blazing, blowsy penitent in yellow satin and glittering hair carries down the stream of light across the picture! This is the way to work, my boys, and earn a hundred florins a day! See! I am as sure of my line as a skater of making his figure eight! and down with a sweep goes a brawny arm, or a flowing curl of drapery. The figures arrange themselves as if by magic. The paint-pots are exhausted in furnishing brown shadows. The pupils look wondering on as the master careers over the canvas. Isabel or Helena, wife No. 1 or No. 2, is sitting by, buxom, exuberant, ready to be painted; and the children are boxing in the corner, waiting till they are wanted to figure as cherubs in the picture. Grave burghers and gentlefolks come in on a visit. There are oysters and Rhenish always ready on yonder table. Was there ever such a painter?

"And Hans Hemmelinck at Bruges?" he continued in the same paper, but in a different tone. "Have you never seen that dear old hospital of St. John, on passing the gate of which you enter into the fifteenth century? I see the wounded soldier still lingering in the house, and tended by the kind grey sisters. His little panel on its easel is placed at the light. He covers his board with the most wondrous, beautiful little figures, in robes as bright as rubies and amethysts. I think he must have a magic glass, in which he catches the reflection of little cherubs with many-coloured wings, very little and bright. Angels, in long, crisp robes of white, surrounded with halos of gold, come and flutter across the mirror, and he draws them."

He wrote several articles on English art. His principal paper, published in the *Westminster Review*, was on Cruikshank, whom he probably first met at a Club called the "Rationals." Mr. Church says the members used to assemble on Saturday afternoons during the years 1837 and 1838 at the "Wrekin," in Broad Court, Drury Lane, a tavern which, in those days, was much frequented by authors, actors, journalists, and artists. The "Wrekin" seems to have been famous chiefly for Shrewsbury cakes and Tewkesbury ales, until the "Rationals" added to its fame by the distinguished company that assembled there to the four-o'clock Saturday afternoon dinner, where among the visitors were Thackeray, Cruikshank, Jerrold, Robert Keeley, Benjamin Webster, Paul Bedford, George Dance, Captain Addison, Clarkson Stanfield, Mark Lemon, and Henry Mayhew.

"Many artists, we hear, hold his work rather cheaply," Thackeray wrote of Cruikshank. "They prate about bad drawing, want of scientific knowledge:—they would have something vastly more neat, regular, anatomical.

"Not one of the whole band most likely but can paint an Academy figure better than himself; nay, or a portrait of an alderman's lady and family of children. But look down the list of painters, and tell us who are they? How many among these men are *poets* (makers), possessing the faculty to create, the greatest among the gifts with which Providence has endowed the mind of man? See how many there are; count up what they have done; and see what, in the course of some nine-and-twenty years, has been done by this indefatigable man.

"What amazing energetic fecundity do we find in him! As a boy he began to fight for bread, has been hungry (twice a day, we trust) ever since, and has been obliged to sell his wit for his bread week by week. And his wit, sterling gold as it is, will find no such purchasers as the fashionable painter's thin pinchbeck, who can live comfortably for six weeks when paid for painting a portrait, and fancies his mind prodigiously occupied all the while. There was an artist in Paris—an artist hair-dresser—who used to be fatigued and take restoratives after inventing a new *coiffure*. By no such gentle operation of hair-dressing has Cruikshank lived; time was (so we are told in print) when for a picture with thirty heads in it he was paid three guineas—a poor week's pittance truly, and a dire week's work. We made no doubt that the same labour would at present bring him twenty times the sum; but whether it be ill-paid or well, what labour has Mr. Cruikshank's been? Week by week, for thirty years, to produce something new—some smiling offspring of painful labour quite independent and distinct from its ten thousand jovial brethren; in what hours of sorrow and ill-health to be told by the world, 'Make us laugh, or you starve. Give us fresh fun; we have eaten up the old, and are hungry.' And all this has he been obliged to do—to wring laughter day by day, sometimes, perhaps, out of want, often certainly from ill-health or depression—to keep the fire of his brain perpetually alight: for the greedy public will give it no leisure to cool. This he has done, and done well. He has told a thousand truths in as many strange and fascinating ways; he has given a thousand new and pleasant thoughts to millions of people; he has never used his wit dishonestly; he has never, in all the exuberance of his frolicsome humour, caused a single painful or guilty blush. How little do we think of the extraordinary power of this man, and how ungrateful we are to him!

"Here, as we come round to the charge of ingratitude, the starting post from which we set out, perhaps we had better conclude. The reader will perhaps wonder at the high-flown tone in which we speak of the services and merits of an individual whom he considers a humble scraper on steel, that is wonderfully popular already. But none of us remember all the benefits we owe him; they have come one by one, one driving out the memory of the other; it is only when we come to examine them altogether, as the writer has done, who has a pile of books on the table before him—a heap of personal kindness from George Cruikshank (not presents, if you please, for we bought, borrowed, or stole, every one of them)—that we feel what we owe him. Look at one of Mr. Cruikshank's works, and we pronounce him an excellent humourist. Look at all: his reputation is increased by a kind of geometrical progression—as a whole diamond is a hundred times more valuable than the hundred splinters into which it might be broken would be. A fine rough English diamond is this about which we have been writing."*

*"When Cruikshank was engaged on the *Omnibus*, he asked Thackeray to contribute. Thackeray sent him a fairly long contribution, I forget on what subject, and Cruikshank returned him a sovereign in full satisfaction. Thackeray laughed good-naturedly as he told a friend of this. 'You may suppose after that I did not trouble George with any more of my poems,' he added."

The article in the *Quarterly* on Leech, which caused a temporary estrangement between Thackeray and the *Punch* staff, is referred to elsewhere. "This book is better than plum-cake at Christmas," he wrote of a volume of Leech's drawings. "It is an enduring plum-cake, which you may eat, and which you may slice and deliver to your friends; and to which, having cut it, you may come again and welcome, from year's end to year's end. . . . Leech is the sort of man who appears once in a century."

In his other papers on art he devoted his attention to the National Gallery, and to the annual exhibitions of the Royal Academy, the Water Colour Society, the New Water Colour Society, and the Gallery in Suffolk Street.

Writing in 1838, he suggested an artist's peerage:

1. Baron Briggs. (At the very least he is out and out the best portrait-painter of the set.)

2. Daniel Prince Maclise. (His Royal Highness's pictures place him very near to the throne indeed.)

3. Edwin, Earl of Landseer.

4. The Lord Charles Landseer.

5. The Duke of Etty.

6. Archbishop Eastlake.

7. His Majesty KING MULREADY, whose picture *All the World's a Stage* he held to be the crowning picture of the year; and he accompanied his opinion with a cut: *Titmarsh placing the Laurel Wreath on the Brows of Mulready*.

Of this same artist he wrote again in a later article. "Mr. Mulready has an art, too, which is not inferior, and, though he commonly takes, like the before-mentioned gentleman" [Eastlake], "some very simple, homely subject to illustrate, manages to affect and delight one as much as painter can. Mr. Mulready calls his picture *The Ford;* Mr. Eastlake styles his *Sisters*. The *Sisters* are two young ladies looking over a balcony; *The Ford* is a stream through which some boys are carrying a girl! and how is a critic to describe the beauty in such subjects as these? It would be easy to say these pictures are exquisitely drawn, beautifully coloured, and so forth; but that is not the reason of their beauty: on the contrary, any man who has a mind may find fault with the drawing and colouring of both. Well, there is a charm about them seemingly independent of drawing and colouring; and what is it? There's no footrule that I know of to measure it; and the very wisest lecturer on art might define and define, and be not a whit nearer the truth. I can't tell you why I like to hear a blackbird sing; it is certainly not so clear as a piping bullfinch." He especially admired Eastlake's *Christ and the Little Children*, and *The Salutation of the Aged Friar*. "There is," he thought, "in almost everything Mr. Eastlake does (in spite of a little feebleness of hand and primness of mannerism) a purity which is to us quite angelical, so that we can't look at one of his pictures without being touched and purified by it.

"Sir David Wilkie does everything for a picture nowadays but the *drawing*. Who knows?" he adds quaintly. "Perhaps it is as well left out." "What can one say more," he wrote of *Queen Victoria holding her First Council*, "but admire the artist who has made out of such unpoetical materials as a table of red cloth and fifty unoccupied, middle-aged gentlemen a beautiful and charming picture?" "The artists say there is very fine painting in Sir David Wilkie's great *Sir David Baird*," he mentioned later; "for my part, I think very little. You see a great quantity of brown paint; in this is a great flashing of torches, feathers, and bayonets. You see in the foreground, huddled up on a rich heap of corpses and drapery, Tippoo Sahib; and swaggering over him on a step, waving a sword for no earthly purpose, and wearing a red jacket and buckskins, the figure of Sir David Baird. The canvas is poor, feeble, theatrical. And I would as soon have Mr. Hart's great canvas of *Lady Jane Grey* (which is worth exactly twopence-halfpenny) as Sir David's poor picture of *Seringapatam.* Some of Sir David's portraits are worse even than his historical compositions; they seem to be painted with snuff and tallow-grease: the faces are merely indicated, and without individuality; the forms only half-drawn, and almost always wrong."

As early as 1832 he wrote that "Mr. Haydon, by dint of telling all the world he is a great painter, has made them believe it. *The Mock Election* is very forced and bad, *Xenophon* so-so, and the rest of the pictures about as good as *The Mock Election.*" He never saw any reason to alter his juvenile judgment. "Among the heroic pictures, of course Mr. Haydon's ranks the first; its size and pretensions call for that place," he said in *Fraser,* thirteen years after. "It roars out too, as it were, with a Titanic voice from among all the competition to public favour, 'Come and look at me.' A broad-shouldered, swaggering, hulking archangel, with those rolling eyes and distending nostrils which belong to the species of sublime caricature, stands scowling on a sphere from which the devil is just descending, bound earthwards. Planets, comets, and other astronomical phenomena roll and blaze round the pair, and flame in the new blue sky. There is something burly and bold in this resolute genius which will attack only enormous subjects, which will deal with nothing but the epic—something respectable even in the defeat of such characters. . . . Let us hope somebody will buy; who, I cannot tell. It will not do for a chapel; it is too big for a house; I have it—it might answer to hang up over a caravan at a fair, if a travelling orrery were exhibited inside."

Of Maclise he spoke frequently, and with much admiration and discernment. The picture of *Christmas*, with five hundred figures on the canvas, is the first to be considered. "I wish you could see the wonderful accuracy with which all these figures are drawn, and the extraordinary skill with which the artist has managed to throw into a hundred different faces a hundred different characters and individualities of joy. Every one of these little people is smiling, but each has his own particular smile. As for the colouring of the picture, it is, between ourselves, atrocious; but a man cannot have all the merits at once. Mr. Maclise has for his share humour such as few painters ever possessed, and a form of drawing such as never was possessed by *any other*—no, not by one, from Albert Dürer downwards. . . . What might not this man do, if he would read and meditate a little, and profit by the works of men whose taste and education are superior to his own?"

In another paper he gave a very carefully weighed opinion of the artist's *Macbeth*.

"A large part of this vast picture Mr. Maclise has painted very finely," he wrote. "The lords are all there in gloomy state—fierce, stalwart men in steel; the variety of attitude and light in which the different groups are placed, the wonderful knowledge and firmness with which each individual figure and feature is placed down upon the canvas, will be understood and admired by the public, but by the artist still more, who knows the difficulty of these things, which seem so easy, which are so easy, no doubt, to a man of Mr. Maclise's extraordinary gifts. How fine is yonder group at the farthest table, lighted up by the reflected light from the armour of one of them! The effect, as far as we know, is entirely new; the figures drawn with exquisite minuteness and clearness, not in the least interrupting the general harmony of the picture. Look at the two women standing near Lady Macbeth's throne, and those beautiful little hands of one of them placed over the state-chair; the science, workmanship, feeling, in those figures are alike wonderful. The face, bust, attitude, of Lady Macbeth are grandly designed; the figures to her right, with looks of stern doubt and wonder, are nobly designed and arranged. The main figure of Macbeth, I confess, does not please; nor the object which has occasioned the frightful convulsive attitude in which he stands. He sees not the ghost of Banquo, but a huge, indistinct, gory shadow, which seems to shake its bloody locks, and frown upon him. Through this shade, intercepted only by its lurid transparency, you see the figures of the guests; they are looking towards it and *through* it. The skill with which this point is made is unquestionable; there is something there and nothing. The spectators feel this as well as the painted actors of the scene: there are times when, in looking at the picture, one loses sight of the shade altogether, and begins to wonder, with Rosse, Lennox, and the rest.

"The idea, then, as far as it goes, is as excellently

worked out as it is daringly conceived. But is it a just one? I think not. I should say it was a grim piece of comedy rather than tragedy. One is puzzled by this piece of *diablerie*—not deeply awe-stricken, as in the midst of such heroical characters and circumstances one should be.

> "'Avaunt, and quit my sight! Let the earth hide thee!
> Thy bones are marrowless—thy blood is cold!
> Thou hast no speculation in those eyes
> Which thou dost glare with.'

"Before the poet's eyes, at least, the actual figure of the ghost stood complete—an actual visible body, with the life gone out of it; an image far more grand and dreadful than the painter's fantastical shadow, because more simple. The shadow is an awful object—granted; but the most sublime, beautiful, fearful sight in all nature is surely the face of a man, wonderful in all its expressions of grief or joy, daring or endurance, thought, hope, love, or pain. How Shakespeare painted all these! with what careful thought and brooding were all his imaginary creatures made!"

He never let pass an opportunity of expressing admiration of Dickens; and when Maclise exhibited in 1840 a portrait of his great rival, he made it the subject for praise, both for the sitter and the painter.

"Look at the portrait of Mr. Dickens—well arranged as a picture, good in colour, and light, and shadow, and, as a likeness perfectly amazing; a looking-glass could not render a better fac-simile," he wrote. "Here we have the real identical man Dickens; the artist must have understood the inward Boz as well as the outward before he made this admirable representation of him. What cheerful intelligence there is about the man's eyes and large forehead! The mouth is too large and full, too eager and active perhaps; the smile is very sweet and generous. If Monsieur de Balzac, that voluminous physiognomist, could examine his head, he would, no doubt, interpret every line and wrinkle in it: the nose firm and well placed; the nostrils wide and full, as are the nostrils of all men of genius (this is Monsieur Balzac's maxim). The past, the future, says Jean Paul, are written in every countenance. I think we may promise ourselves a brilliant future for this one. There seems to be no flagging as yet in it, no sense of fatigue, or consciousness of decaying power. Long mayest thou, O Boz! reign over thy comic kingdom; long may we pay tribute, whether of threepence weekly or of a shilling monthly it matters not. Mighty prince, at thy imperial feet Titmarsh, humblest of thy servants, offers his vows of loyalty and his humble tribute of praise."

Etty he could never bring himself wholly to admire. He admitted that his luscious pencil has covered a hundred glowing canvases which every artist must love, but he could not forgive him his indelicacy. He had no objection to figure-painting, but he hated Etty's licentious and lascivious Andromedas and Venuses. But it was one of Etty's paintings that called forth the following beautiful passage:—

"Here is a far nobler painting—the prodigal kneeling down lonely in the stormy evening, and praying to Heaven for pardon. It is a grand and touching picture, and looks as large as if the three-foot canvas had been twenty. His wan, wretched figure and clasped hands are lighted up by the sunset; the clouds are livid and heavy; and the wind is howling over the solitary common, and numbing the chill limbs of the poor wanderer.

A goat and a boar are looking at him with horrid obscene eyes. They are the demons of Lust and Gluttony which have brought him to this sad pass. And there seems no hope, no succour, no Ear for the prayer of this wretched, way-worn, miserable man, who kneels there alone, shuddering. Only above, in the grisly blue sky, you see a glistering, peaceful silver star, which points to home and hope as clearly as if the little star were a sign-post, and home at the very next turn of the road."

Marcus Stone, who was so angry with Thackeray's criticisms, had little cause to be angry on his own account.

Landseer is often mentioned, and nearly always in terms of admiration.

"We must not take leave of the compositions without mentioning Mr. Landseer's wonderful *Shoeing*, and *Stag*—the latter the most poetical, the former the most dexterous, perhaps, of the works of this accomplished painter," he wrote in 1844. "The latter picture, at a little distance, expands almost into the size of nature. The enormous stag, by the side of a great blue northern lake, stalks over the snow down to the shore, whither his mate is coming through the water to join him. Snowy mountains bend round the lonely landscape; the stars are shining out keenly in a deep icy blue overhead."

The highest praise, however, was reserved for two artists of very dissimilar schools—Turner and Hunt.

Of the former he spoke in terms so well chosen, and with such nice judgment, that Ruskin himself never bettered the criticisms.

In *A Second Lecture on the Fine Arts* he wrote: "I must request you to turn your attention to a noble river by J.M.W. Turner, Esq., R.A., *The Fighting Téméraire*—as grand a painting as ever figured on the walls of any

Academy, or came from the easel of any painter. The old Téméraire is dragged to her last home by a little spiteful, diabolical steamer. A mighty red sun, amidst a host of flaring clouds, sinks to rest on one side of the picture, and illumines a river that seems interminable, and a countless navy that fades away into such a wonderful distance as never was painted before. The little demon of a steamer is belching out a volume (why do I say a volume? not a hundred volumes could express it) of foul, lurid, red-hot, malignant smoke, paddling furiously, and lashing up the water about it; while behind it (a cold grey moon looking down on it), slow, sad, and majestic, follows the brave old ship, with death, as it were, written on her. . . .

"It is absurd, you will say (and with a great deal of reason), for Titmarsh, or any other Briton, to grow so politically enthusiastic about a four-foot canvas, representing a ship, a steamer, a river, and a sunset. But herein surely lies the power of the great artist. He makes you see and think of a great deal more than the objects before you. He knows how to soothe or to intoxicate, to fire or to depress, by a few notes, or forms, or colours, of which we cannot trace the effects to the source, but only acknowledge the power. I recollect some years ago, at the theatre at Weimar, hearing Beethoven's *Battle of Vittoria*, in which, amidst a storm of glorious music, the air of 'God save the King,' was introduced. The very instant it began, every Englishman in the house was bolt upright, and so stood reverently until the air was played out. Why so? From some such thrill of excitement as makes us glow and rejoice over Mr. Turner and his *Fighting Téméraire*, which, I am sure, when the art of translating colours into music or poetry shall be discovered, will be found to be a magnificent natural ode or piece of music.''

He did not appreciate other of this marvellous painter's works*—*Cicero at his Villa*, and *Agrippina with the Ashes of Germanicus*, for instance; and *Pluto and Proserpino* called forth the following protest:—

''O ye gods! why will he not stick to copying her majestic countenance, instead of daubing it with some absurd antics and freaks of his own? Fancy pea-green skies, crimson-lake trees, and orange and purple grass—fancy cataracts, rainbows, suns, moons, and thunderbolts—shake them up well, with a quantity of gamboge, and you will have an idea of a fancy picture by Turner. It is worth a shilling alone to go and see *Pluto and Proserpino*. Such a landscape! such figures! such a little red-hot coal-scuttle of a chariot!''

He did not know whether the *Slave-Trader* is sublime or ridiculous, but he had no doubt as to the merits of *Rain—Steam—Speed*.

''Mr. Turner has out-prodigied almost all former prodigies,'' he said of this picture in *May Gambols*. ''He has made a picture with real rain, behind which is real sunshine, and you expect a rainbow every minute. Meanwhile there comes a train down upon you, really moving at the rate of fifty miles an hour, and which the reader had best make haste to see, lest it should dash out of the picture, and be away up Charing Cross

*Mr. Thornbury, in his *Life of J. M. W. Turner*, wrote: "I am afraid the tradition is too true that that great and bitter satirist of poor humanity's weaknesses, Mr. Thackeray, had more than a finger in thus lashing the dotage of a great man's genius. Long after, I have heard that Mr. Thackeray was shown some of Turner's finest water-colour drawings, upon which he exclaimed: 'I will never run down Turner again.' But the blows had already gone to the great man's heart, and it did no good to lament them."

through the wall opposite. All these wonders are performed with means not less wonderful than the effects are. The rain, in the astounding picture called *Rain—Steam—Speed*, is composed of dabs of dirty putty *slapped* on to the canvas with a trowel; the sunshine scintillates out of the very thick, smeary lumps of chrome yellow. The shadows are produced by cool tones of crimson lake, and quiet glazings of vermilion; although the fire in the steam-engine *looks* as if it were red—I am not prepared to say that it is not painted with cobalt and pea-green. And as for the manner in which the *Speed* is done, of that the less said the better—only it is a positive fact that there is a steam-coach going fifty miles an hour. The world has never seen anything like this picture."

Of Hunt he wrote enthusiastically in the account of the Water Colours Exhibition in *The Second Lecture on the Fine Arts*.

"If you want to see real nature now, real expression, real startling home-poetry, look at every one of Hunt's heads. Hogarth never painted anything better than these figures, taken singly. That man rushing away frightened from the beer-barrel is a noble head of terror; that Miss Jemima Crow, whose whole body is a grin regards you with an ogle that all the race of Richters could never hope to imitate. Look at yonder card-players; they have a penny pack of the devil's books, and one has just laid down the king of trumps! I defy you to look at him without laughing, or to examine the wondrous laughing face of his adversary without longing to hug the greasy rogue. Come hither, Mr. Maclise, and see what genuine comedy is: you who can paint better than all the Hunts and Leslies, and yet not near so well. If I were the Duke of Devonshire, I would have a couple of Hunts in every room in all my houses; if I had the blue-devils (and even their graces are, I suppose, occasionally so troubled), I would but cast my eyes upon these grand, good-humoured pictures and defy care. Who does not recollect *Before and after the Mutton-Pie*, the two pictures of that wondrous boy? Where Mr. Hunt finds his models I cannot tell; they are the very flower of the British youth—each of them is as good as *Sancho;* blessed is he that has his portfolio full of them."

It is not difficult to understand this great admiration of Hunt's work. Indeed, the explanation may be read in the following criticism of Stanfield:—

"All through this painter's life," Thackeray wrote, "his industry and his genius have been alike remarkable; and it is curious to note in his performances of the present time how the carefulness of the artist seems to increase with his skill, as if this conscientious man were bent each day upon improving or elaborating and polishing his works on approaching more nearly to nature. Does not such a progress tell of more than mere talent? Of honesty, of modesty, of faithful and cheerful labour, of constant love for truth? It seems to me that the pictures of some artists tell of these things, and that these are among the precious qualities which go to make a painter."

Thackeray had a fine instinct for high art. He despised the namby-pamby school, as we have seen, for he loathed sham art and sickly sentimentality in pictures; remember how he wrote of one of the late Mr. Ward's pictures as belonging "to the Muggletorian school of art—monstrous, livid, dreadful as the dream of a man in a scarlet fever." He did not believe horrors, however artistically portrayed and accurately drawn, to be true art. Somewhere, after remarking that Charles Landseer's *Monks of Rubrose* is not only good, but has "the further good quality of being pleasant," he added, "Some clever artists will do no harm in condescending so far to suit the general taste. For instance, take Mr. Poole's picture of *Solomon Eagle and the Plague of London.* It is exceedingly clever; but who would buy such a piece? Figures writhe over the picture blue and livid with the plague—some are dying in agony, some stupid with pain. You see the dead-cart in the distance; and in the midst stands naked Solomon, with bloodshot eyes and wild maniacal looks, preaching death, woe, and judgment. Where should such a piece hang? All is too gloomy for a hospital, and surely not cheerful enough for a dining-room. It is not a religious picture that would serve to decorate the walls of a church. A very dismal conventicle might perhaps be a suitable abode for it; but would it not be better to tempt the public with something more good-humoured?" And of the Royal Academy Exhibition of 1843 he recorded, "Every succeeding year shows a progress in the English school of painters. They paint from the *heart* more than of old, and less from the old heroic, absurd, incomprehensible, unattainable rules. They look at Nature very hard, and watch her with the best of their eyes and ability. They do not aim at such great subjects as heretofore, or at subjects which the world is pleased to call great—viz., tales from Hume or Gibbon of royal personages under various circumstances of battle, murder, and sudden death. Lemprière, too, is justly neglected; and Milton has quite given place to *Gil Blas* and *The Vicar of Wake-*

field. The heroic—and peace be with it!—has been deposed, and our artists in place cultivate the pathetic and the familiar. . . . The younger painters are content to exercise their art on subjects far less exalted: a gentle sentiment, an agreeable, quiet incident, a tea-table tragedy, or a bread-and-butter idyll, suffices for the most part their gentle powers. Not surely ought one to quarrel at all with this prevalent mode. It is at least natural, which the heroic was not. Bread and butter can be digested by every man; whereas Prometheus on his rock, or Orestes in his strait waistcoat, or Hector dragged behind Achilles' car, or Britannia, guarded by Religion and Neptune, welcoming General Tomkins in the Temple of Glory—the ancient heroic, allegorical subjects—can be supposed deeply to interest very few of the inhabitants of this city or kingdom. We have wisely given up pretending that we were interested in such, and confess a partiality for more simple and homely themes."

In art as in literature he believed, as, indeed, he wrote, that "there is a higher ingredient in beauty than mere form; a skilful hand is only the second artistic quality, worthless without the first, which is a great heart." In those words is the epitome of his criticisms. He admired the beautiful, loved the good, and worshipped the true, and he believed that the highest art was the exposition of the good, the beautiful, and the true.

CHAPTER XXVIII

THACKERAY, THE PHILOSOPHER

CHAPTER XXVIII

THACKERAY, THE PHILOSOPHER

OF the novelist it is enough to ask: is the story well written and interesting? but of the humourist and satirist we want more than an agreeable tale. We want to know what he teaches, and we demand that he shall instruct us what not to do as well as what to do. The novelist may content himself with amusing, but the humourist must direct his readers. With this general opinion Thackeray was thoroughly in accord. "The humorous writer," he said in a lecture, "professes to awaken and direct your love, your pity, your kindness, your scorn of untruth, pretension, imposture, your tenderness for the weak, the poor, the oppressed, the unhappy. To the best of his means and ability he comments on all the ordinary actions and passions of life almost."

It is now more than half a century since Thackeray was first labelled "cynic." Comparatively few writers have taken the trouble to combat seriously this impression; for the prevailing sentiment is that if a reader cannot see the deep tenderness that underlies all the writings, no arguments will have any weight with him. Now, though in the main this contention holds good, yet, in examining Thackeray's philosophy, it is necessary to take into account—so as to disprove them—the still popular, firm-seated, and absurd prejudices. Thackeray himself smarted under the injustice, and those who understand him can hear the ring of pain in his voice as he asks, in *On a Peal of Bells*, "Are authors affected by their own works? I don't know about other gentlemen, but if I make a joke myself I cry, if I write a pathetic scene I am laughing wildly all the time—at least, Tomkins thinks so. You know, I am such a cynic!" And one evening, when he had read to some young men *The Curate's Walk*, he exclaimed, "And they call the man who wrote that a *cynic!*"

Now the definition of cynic is one who does not believe in virtue, or who regards tender feeling as a fair object for ridicule. Thus the man who wrote such maxims as "*Il y a peu d' honnêtes femmes qui ne soient lassées de leur métier*," or "*L'honnêteté des femmes est souvent l'amour de leur réputation et de leur répos*," without deeply inquiring into the truth of his sayings may safely be called cynical; as may he who, on his death-bed, refused to see a priest, saying, "*Dieu me pardonnera; c'est son métier.*" But is the man a cynic who wrote continually in the following strain:—

"We advance in simplicity and honesty as we advance in civilisation; and it is my belief that we become better bred and less artificial, and tell more truth every day."

"What, indeed, does not that word 'cheerfulness' imply? It means a contented spirit; it means a pure heart; it means a kind and loving disposition; it means humility and charity; it means a generous appreciation of others, and a modest opinion of self."

"Who say the world is all cold? There is the sun and the shadows. And the heaven which ordains poverty or sickness sends pity and love and succour."

"Can we have too much of truth, and fun, and beauty, and kindness?"

Is a man a cynic who declares that he likes to hear and tell of kind things, and who is pleased that he finds pleasure in hearing his rivals praised, or who writes in a letter: "Behind them came dear, honest, kind Castlereagh, galloping alone; he pulled up on an errand of charity and kindness, consumption hospital, woman he knows to get in and so forth? There's a deal of good in the wicked world, isn't there?"

The man who is satirical at the pomp of the second funeral of Napoleon waxes tender at the thought of the mother spending a few of her hard-earned sous to buy a wreath for a little child's grave; and he who growls at cringing Nudgit smiles approval at the quiet independence of Goldsworthy.

But if it be cynical to believe that "wherever shines the sun, you are sure to find Folly basking in it; and Knavery is the shadow at Folly's heels"; if it be cynical to declare that grief for a departed relative will not last for ever, or that if the deceased had left you a fortune you would be in some degree reconciled to your loss after the first momentary pang of grief is over;—why, if these truisms be cynicisms, then, and then only, Thackeray was a cynic.

But though it is difficult to take seriously the charge of cynicism, the declaration that *Vanitas Vanitatum omnia Vanitas*, was the creed of the great novelist opens up the whole ground of his philosophy. It was against pride of purse, and birth, and place, against haughtiness, against those who meanly admire mean things, that he preached.

"I am sick of Court Circulars. I loathe *haut-ton*

intelligence," he wrote in the *Snob Papers*. "I believe such words as fashionable, exclusive, aristocratic, and the like, to be wicked, un-Christian epithets, that ought to be banished from honest vocabularies. A Court system that sends men of genius to the second table I hold to be a snobbish system. A society that sets up to be polite, and ignores art and letters, I hold to be a snobbish society. You, who despise your neighbour, are a snob; you, who forget your friends, meanly to follow after those of a higher degree, are a snob; you, who are ashamed of your poverty, and blush for your calling, are a snob; as are you who boast of your pedigree, or are proud of your wealth."

He was amused at the strivings of his contemporaries for fame, for his nature was inconsistent in so far as that, while to him life was real and earnest, he passed his existence in the attitude of a spectator, bewailing the faults and follies of mankind, and gently, almost tenderly, chiding them; and only roused from the kindliness of his nature when he met a man bullying a woman, or a strong man taking advantage of the weakness of a fellow-creature. Then he would up, buckle on his armour, and lash and lash again and again, with his thongs of satire and irony, until it became almost possible to see the writhings of the wretched creature, and to hear his cries of rage at the thrashing gradually turning into piteous appeals for mercy, when the author would relent, blame himself for undue severity, and endeavour to discover quickly good qualities in his victim. Read his philosophy in his poem *Vanitas Vanitatum*:—

"O Vanity of Vanities,
How wayward the decrees of Fate are;
How very weak the very wise,
How very small the very great are!

"What mean these stale moralities,
Sir Preacher, from your desk you mumble?
Why rail against the great and wise,
And tire us with your ceaseless grumble?

"Pray choose us out another text,
O man morose and narrow-minded!
Come, turn the page—I read the next,
And then the next, and still I find it.

"Read here how wealth was set aside,
And folly set in place exalted;
How princes footed in the dust
While lackeys in the saddle vaulted.

"Though thrice a thousand years are past
Since David's son, the sad and splendid,
The weary King Ecclesiast,
Upon his awful tablets penned it.

"Methinks the text is never stale,
And life is every day renewing
Fresh comments on the old, old tale
Of Folly, Fortune, Glory, Ruin."

And hear his summing-up of Napoleon:—

"He captured many thousand guns;
He wrote 'The Great' before his name;
And, dying, only left his sons
The recollection of his shame.

"Though more than half the world was his,
He died without a rood his own,
And borrowed from his enemies
Six feet of ground to lie upon.

"He fought a thousand glorious wars,
And more than half the world was his;
And somewhere now, in yonder stars,
Can tell, mayhap, *what greatness is*."

The world seemed to him a sad place — small wonder!—and he could not write of it cheerfully.

"A man with a reflective turn of mind, walking

through an exhibition of this sort'' [*Vanity Fair*], ''will not be oppressed, I take it, by his own or other people's hilarity,'' he declared. ''An episode of humour or kindness touches and amuses him here and there—a pretty child looking at a gingerbread stall; a pretty girl blushing whilst her lover talks to her and chooses her fairing; poor Tom Fool, yonder behind the waggon, mumbling his bone with the honest family which lives by his tumbling. But the general impression is one more melancholy than mirthful. When you come home, you sit down, in a sober, contemplative, not uncharitable, frame of mind, and apply yourself to your books or your business.''

The sadness that pervaded his life tinged his writings. In the book he thought his masterpiece, when he gave the man what he had desired for so many years, he could not refrain from exclaiming: ''Oh, *Vanitas Vanitatum!* Which of us is happy in the world? Which of us has his desire? or, having it, is satisfied?''

''My kind reader will please to remember that this history has *Vanity Fair* for a title, and that *Vanity Fair* is a very vain, wicked, foolish place, full of all sorts of humbugs and falseness and pretensions,'' he said elsewhere. ''People there are living and flourishing in the world . . . with no reverence except for prosperity, and no eye for anything beyond success — faithless, hopeless, charityless. Let us have at them, dear friends, with might and main.''

But to Thackeray all was not vanity. ''He could not have painted *Vanity Fair* as he has unless Eden had been in his inner eye,'' George Brinsley remarked. And indeed, Thackeray was the first to respect and to bow before such qualities as virtue, simplicity, honour, bravery, and unselfishness. In another ballad he gives us the brighter side of his philosophy, when he tells

> ". . . how fate may change and shift;
> The prize be sometimes with the fool,
> The race not always to the swift.
> The strong may yield, the good may fall,
> The great man be a vulgar clown,
> The knave be lifted over all,
> The kind cast pitilessly down."

But he preached,—

> "Come wealth or want, come good or ill,
> Let young and old accept their part,
> And bow before the Awful Will,
> And bear it with an honest heart.
> Who misses, or who wins the prize?
> Go, lose or conquer, as you can:
> But if you fail, or if you rise,
> Be each, pray God, a gentleman."

"Do your duty," he said, again and again; "do your duty with an honest heart." In that single word "Duty" is contained the teaching of his life, and the epitome of all his lectures and lay-sermons.

CHAPTER XXIX

THACKERAY, THE WRITER

CHAPTER XXIX

THACKERAY, THE WRITER

OF Thackeray's style there is not much to be said. He founded it upon the masters of the eighteenth century; and in this respect his books bear comparison with Addison and Fielding and Steele. I cannot remember that I have ever had to re-read a sentence in any of his writings to understand its meaning. "The great thing is to write no sentence without a meaning to it; that is what style really means," he told his eldest daughter. Long Latin words, too, were to be avoided as much as possible, he added; and he showed her a page of *The Newcomes* altogether re-written, with simpler words put in the place of longer ones. He was never guilty of enthusiastic writing, and this, Dr. John Brown has suggested, made him sacrifice something of the power of his original wording.

Yet careful revision never marred the exquisite simplicity of his style; and there are few finer pages in English Literature than those in which are described the parting of George Osborne with Amelia, the grief of old Osborne for his son, the Waterloo chapters, the death of Helen Pendennis, and the death of Colonel Newcome.

Is there anything more truly humourous than the conversation of the Political Snob, Captain Spitfire:—

"'Why wasn't the Princess Scragamoffsky at Lady Palmerston's party, Minns? Because *she can't show*—

and why can't she show? Shall I tell you, Minns, why she can't show? The Princess Scragamoffsky's back is flayed alive, Minns—I tell you it's raw, sir! On Tuesday last, at twelve o'clock, three drummers of the Præobajinski regiment arrived at Ashburnham House; and at half-past twelve, in the yellow drawing-room at the Russian Embassy, before the ambassadress and four ladies'-maids, the Greek Papa, and the Secretary of Embassy, Madame de Scragamoffsky received thirteen dozen. She was knouted, sir—knouted in the midst of England in Berkeley Square—for having said that the Grand-Duchess Olga's hair was red. And now, sir, will you tell me that Lord Palmerston ought to continue Minister?'

"MINNS: 'Good Ged!'

"Minns follows Spitfire about, and thinks him the greatest and wisest of human beings."

Or anything more poetical than the description of Esmond at his mother's grave:—

"Esmond came to this spot in one sunny evening of spring, and saw, amidst a thousand black crosses, casting their shadows across the grassy mounds, that particular one which marked his mother's resting-place. Many more of those poor creatures that lay there had adopted that same name, with which sorrow had rebaptized her, and which fondly seemed to hint their individual story of love and grief. He fancied her, in tears and darkness, kneeling at the foot of her cross, under which her cares were buried. Surely he knelt down, and said his own prayer there, not in sorrow so much as in awe (for even his memory had no recollection of her), and in pity for the pangs which the gentle soul in life had been made to suffer. To this cross she brought them; for this heavenly bridegroom she exchanged the husband who had wooed her, the traitor who had left her. A thousand such hillocks lay round about, the gentle daisies springing out of the grass over them, and each bearing its cross and requiescat. A nun, veiled in black, was kneeling hard by, at a sleeping sister's bedside (so fresh made that the spring had scarce had time to spin a coverlid for it); beyond the cemetery walls you had glimpses of life and the world, and the spires and gables of the city. A bird came down from a roof opposite, and lit first on a cross, and then on the grass below it, whence it flew away presently with a leaf in its mouth; then came a sound as of chanting, from the chapel of the sisters hard by; others had long since filled the place which poor Mary Magdalene once had there, were kneeling at the same stall, and hearing the same hymns and prayers in which her stricken heart had found consolation. Might she sleep in peace—might she sleep in peace; and we, too, when our struggles and pains are over! But the earth is the Lord's, as the heaven is; we are alike His creatures here and yonder. I took a little flower of the hillock and kissed it, and went my way, like the bird that had just lighted on the cross by me, back into the world again. Silent receptacle of death; tranquil depth of calm, out of reach of tempest and trouble! I felt as one who had been walking below the sea, and treading amidst the bones of shipwrecks."

So far I have said nothing of Thackeray's poetry. He would never have been a great poet—a Browning or a Tennyson; but that he had the true sense of poetry no one can deny. His rhymes were often appalling, his metre not always perfect; but he wrote that fine martial poem *The Chronicle of the Drum*, the beautiful and pathetic *Bouillabaisse*, and the sweet verses entitled *At the Church Gate*, as well as the delightful *Peg of Limavaddy*, *The White Squall*, *Piscator and Piscatrix*, *Lucy's Birthday*, *The Cane-bottom'd Chair*, *The Mahogany Tree*, and the especially Thackerayesque *Ballads of Pleaceman X*, from which I select *Jacob Omnium's Hoss* as the best. These must give him a considerable place among the ''lighter'' poets; and I think as time goes on his poems will increase in popularity, and that his reputation as a poet will be considerably strengthened.*

It is simply astonishing how many essays have been written upon the novels and poems of Thackeray. From the time of his death until the present day there has been a flood of printed matter. Much that has been written is valuable criticism, much, though, is simply undiscerning praise or blame.

Public opinion is not yet unanimous in according him his position in the literary ranks. The general reader, as a rule, prefers Dickens, and sometimes Bulwer, also, and would place Thackeray a considerable distance below Smollett; while the more highly cultured regard him as an equal of Fielding.

It is true that his works have never rivalled those of Dickens, or Bulwer, or even Lever, in mere popularity. Perhaps he had not the imagination of Dickens, or the learning of Bulwer, or the vivacity of Lever, but there

*It is somewhat significant that Thackeray is very strongly represented in Mr. Edmund Clarence Stedman's *Victorian Anthology*—by far the best selection in existence of English verse of this reign, though, owing to infringements of the Copyright Law, the book can only be obtained in the United States.

Mr. Stedman has taken no less than seven poems from Thackeray: *At the Church Gate*, *The Ballad of Bouillabaisse*, *The Age of Wisdom*, *The Sermons of Wether*, *The Pen and the Album*, *The Mahogany Tree*, and *The End of the Play*.

was always something more in his stories than in those of his contemporaries. His books were not mere fiction—he was the philosopher in fiction; and his novels were the cloak from under which he preached his sermons. Yet, being a great artist, he was able to write a philosophical work that should also be interesting as a story, even as Swift's most awful satire, which is read by many as a charming imaginative work, ranking very close to *Robinson Crusoe*.

Thackeray wrote of the world and its people as he saw them, and so disgusted many. The principal objections, maintained to this day, are that he never drew a good man or woman who was not insipid; that cynicism—an aggravated cynicism—is the keynote of his philosophy; and that he too frequently interrupted the narrative with his own reflections.

The question of his philosophy has been dealt with in the previous chapter. Whether or no he too often broke the thread of his always slender plot is to a great extent a matter for individual judgment. "Like the songs of the chorus, they bid us pause a moment over the wider laws and actions of human fate and human life," Mr. Andrew Lang has written in a charming article* of Thackeray's conversations with his readers. Only the first charge remains to be heard.

Read Mr. Hayward, in his paper on Thackeray†:—

"It is said that, having with great skill put together a creature of which the principal elements are indiscriminating affection, ill-requited devotion, ignorant partiality, a weak will, and a narrow intellect, he calls on us

**Letters to Dead Authors: W. M. Thackeray.*

†*Edinburgh Review*, January, 1847.

to worship his poor idol as the type of feminine excellence. This is true."

Listen to Mrs. Jameson declaring that *Pendennis* and *Esmond* "will never do":—

"No woman resents his Rebecca—inimitable Becky! No woman but feels and acknowledges with a shiver the completeness of that wonderful and finished artistic creation; but every woman resents the selfish, inane Amelia. . . . Laura in *Pendennis* is a yet more fatal mistake. She is drawn with every generous feeling, every good gift. We do not complain that she loves that poor creature Pendennis, for she loved him in her childhood. She grew up with that love in her heart; it came between her and the perception of his faults; it is a necessity indivisible from her nature. Hallowed through its constancy, therein alone would lie its best excuse, its beauty, and its truth. But Laura, faithless to that first affection; Laura waked up to the appreciation of a far more manly and noble nature, in love with Warrington, and then going back to Pendennis and marrying *him!* Such infirmity might be true of some women, but not of such a woman as Laura; we resent the inconsistency, the indelicacy of the portrait. And then Lady Castlewood, so evidently a favourite of the author, what shall we say of her? The virtuous woman, *par excellence*, who 'never sins and never forgives'; who never resents, nor relents, nor repents; the mother who is the rival of her daughter; the mother who for years is the confidante of a man's delirious passion for her own child, and then consoles him by marrying him herself! O Mr. Thackeray! this will never do! Such women may exist, but to hold them up as examples of excellence and fit objects of our best sympathies is a fault, and proves a low standard in ethics and in art."

"As usual, he is unjust to women—quite unjust," Charlotte Brontë wrote. "There is hardly any punishment he does not deserve for making Lady Castlewood peep through a keyhole, listen at a door, and be jealous of a boy and a milkmaid." And Miss Martineau thought that "the first drawback in his books, as in his manners, is the impression conveyed by both that he can never have known a good and sensible woman."

More recently Mr. Harrison has written in the same strain:—

"If we run over the characters in Thackeray, it is an effort of memory to recall the generous and fine natures. Thackeray has given us some lovable and affectionate men and women, but they all have qualities which lower them and tend to make them either tiresome or ridiculous. Henry Esmond is a high-minded, almost heroic gentleman, but he is glum, a regular kill-joy, and, as his author admitted, something of a prig. Colonel Newcome is a noble-hearted soldier; but he is too good for this world, and somewhat too innocent, too transparently a child of nature. Warrington, with all his sense and honesty, is rough; Pendennis is a bit of a puppy; Clive Newcome is not much of a hero; and as for Dobbin, he is almost intended to be a butt.

"A more serious defect is a dearth in Thackeray of women to love and honour. Shakespeare has given us a gallery of noble women; Fielding has drawn the adorable Sophia Western; Scott has his Jeanie Deans. But though Thackeray has given us over and over again living pictures of women of power, intellect, wit, charm, they are all marred by atrocious selfishness, cruelty, ambition, like Becky Sharp, Beatrix Esmond, and Lady Kew; or else they have some weakness, silliness, or narrowness, which prevents us from at once loving and respecting them. Amelia is rather a poor thing, and decidedly silly; we do not really admire Laura Pendennis; the Little Sister is somewhat colourless; Ethel Newcome runs great risk of being a spoilt beauty; and about Lady Castlewood, with all her love and devotion, there hangs a certain sinister and unnatural taint which the world cannot forgive, and perhaps ought not to forgive.''*

Now to hear the defence:—

''My object is not to make a perfect character, or

*It is so easy to see things as we wish them to be. Mr. Harrison cannot find a good character in Thackeray's works; Mrs. Potts, an ardent supporter of the "Shakespeare was Bacon" theory, can scarcely find a good woman in the plays. Read a note in her editions of *Promus* (London. 1883):—

"From the entries which refer to women we see that Bacon formed very unfavourable views regarding them—views which unhappy passages in his own life probably tended to confirm. *The Shakespeare plays seem to exhibit the same unfavorable sentiments of their author.* There are a hundred and thirty female personages in the plays, and the characters of these seem to be easily divisible into six classes:—

"1. Furies or viragos, such as Tamova, Queen Margaret, Goneril, Regan, and even Lady Macbeth in the dark side of her character.

"2. Shrews and sharp-tongued women, as Katharine, Constance, and many others, when they are represented as angry.

"3. Gossiping and untrustworthy women, as most of the maids, hostesses, etc., and as Percy insinuates that he considers his wife to be.

"4. Fickle, faithless, and artful—a disposition which seems assumed throughout the plays to be the normal condition of womanhood.

"5. Thoroughly immoral, as Cleopatra, Phrynia, Timandra, Bianca.

"6. Gentle, simple, and colourless, as Hero, Olivia, Ophelia, Cordelia, etc.

"Noteworthy exceptions, which exhibit more exalted and finer pictures of good and noble women, are the characters of Isabella, Volumnias, and of Katharine of Aragon; but these are not sufficient to do away with the impression that *on the whole the author of the plays had but a poor opinion of women; that love he regarded as a youthful passion, marriage as a doubtful happiness.*"

anything like it,'' he wrote to his mother about *Vanity Fair*. ''Don't you see how odious all the people are in the book (with the exception of Dobbin)?''

''*You* would have the heroine of your novel so beautiful that she should charm the captain (or hero, whoever he may be) with her appearance; surprise and confound the bishop with her learning; outride the squire, and get the brush, and, when he fell from his horse, whip out a lancet and bleed him; rescue from fever and death the poor cottager's family whom the doctor had given up; make twenty-one at the butts with the rifle, when the poor captain only scored eighteen; give him twenty in fifty at billiards and beat him; and draw tears from the professional Italian people by her exquisite performance (of voice and violoncello) in the evening—I say, if a novelist would be popular with ladies—the great novel-readers of the world—this is the sort of heroine who would carry him through half a dozen editions.'' Thus he wrote in a *Roundabout Paper*. He knew that the general reader *wants* sentiment, not truth; but he would only give them truth. They have not the courage—or is it discernment they lack?—to see things as they are, and they only see them and ask for them to be described in books as they wish them to be. This, to Thackeray's clear intellect, did not seem honest.

''Since the author of *Tom Jones* was buried, no writer of fiction among us has been permitted to depict to his utmost power a MAN,'' he said, in the preface to *Pendennis*. ''We must drape him, and give him a certain conventional simper. Society will not tolerate the Natural in our Art. Many ladies have remonstrated and subscribers left me because, in the course of the story, I described a young man resisting and affected by temptation. My object was to say that he had the passions to feel, and the manliness and generosity to overcome them. You will not hear—it is best not to know it—what moves in the real world, what passes in society, in the clubs, colleges, news-rooms,—what is the life and talk of your sons. A little more frankness than is customary has been attempted in this story, with no bad desire on the writer's part, it is hoped, and with no ill consequence to any reader. If truth is not always pleasant, at any rate truth is best, from whatever chair—from those whence grave writers or thinkers argue as from that at which the story-teller sits as he concludes his labour and bids his kind reader farewell."

"Our friend is not Amadis or Sir Charles Grandison," he wrote of *Philip Firmin;* "and I don't set him up for a moment as a person to be revered or imitated, but try to draw him faithfully, and as Nature made him."

Thackeray's characters are always human: there is no utterly unredeemed scoundrel in his writings, except perhaps Sir Francis Clavering, who is so weak and pitiable that sorrow rather than detestation is demanded, and Dr. Firmin, who is convinced of his own honest intentions, and whose moral standpoint is so perverted that he really cannot realise his own immoralities. Perhaps, though, Tufton Hunt is the worst in the whole gallery, for even the Marquis of Steyne, debauched old man as he is, is not quite without feeling, since he can sympathize with Major Pendennis on reading the news of Pen's illness.

Thackeray, then, portrayed the world as he saw it. But he could appreciate good men and women, and describe them too. If he has not joined pure goodness to pure intellect, if he has not allied the strength of

Becky's intellect with the goodness of Amelia, it is perhaps not because he could not do so, or was incapable of appreciating or imagining this amalgamation, but because he had never met it in the world.

Is not Helen Pendennis a good woman, a good wife, a good mother? Is not Laura clever and good? and surely Ethel Newcome is not a fool? and Theo and Kitty Lambert other than good and true women should be? It is strange that women can forgive him Becky Sharp, and can tolerate even Blanche Amory, but cannot pardon him Amelia Sedley!

There are others who, on broader grounds, objected to his works.

Matthew Arnold did not greatly admire him, and never disguised the fact that his private opinion of him, as well as of Tennyson and the other great writers of the early Victorian era, differed widely from the general verdict. "Thackeray is not, I think, a great writer," he observed; though he was bound to admit that "at any rate, his style is that of one." But then, Mr. Arnold could never be brought to recognise Addison as a writer of the first rank, because of "the commonplace of his ideas." He preferred such a writer as Burke ("our greatest English prose-writer" he called him), who expressed "new and profound ideas in a perfectly sound and classical style." Burke, too, was a master-stylist; but surely Mr. Arnold might have seen much to delight him in Thackeray and in Addison.

Mr. Ruskin prefers Dickens to Thackeray. For the latter, at one time, he conceived something approaching dislike. But then, I think Mr. Ruskin has always underrated the merits of the fictionists. Read the outbreak in *Fors Clavigera*:—

"Of the four great English tale-tellers whose dynasties have set or risen within my own memory—Miss Edgeworth, Scott, Dickens, and Thackeray—I find myself greatly at pause in conjecturing, however dimly, what essential good has been effected by them, though they all had the best intentions. Of the essential mischief done by them there is, unhappily, no doubt whatever. Miss Edgeworth made her morality so impertinent, that, since her time, it has only been with fear and trembling that any good novelist has ventured to show the slightest bias in favour of the Ten Commandments. Scott made his romance so ridiculous, that, since his day, one can't help fancying helmets were always pasteboard, and horses were always hobby. Dickens made everybody laugh, or cry, so that they could not go about their business till they had got their faces in wrinkles; and Thackeray settled like a meat-fly on whatever one had for dinner, and made one sick of it."

In conclusion it must be admitted that among a certain small section of the younger writers of the day (who correspond in England to the School of French décadents, and include several men of brilliant but rather one-sided ability) there is a strong tendency to depreciate Thackeray's genius.

On the other hand, it is pleasant to read the fine appreciation by that exquisite master of literary style and criticism—the late Robert Louis Stevenson:—

"Whether because he was himself a gentleman in a very high degree, or because his methods were in a very high degree suited to this class of work, or from the common operation of both causes, a gentleman came from his pen by the gift of Nature," he writes in *Some*

Gentlemen in Fiction. "He could draw him as a character-part, full of pettiness, tainted with vulgarity, and yet still a gentleman, in the inimitable Major Pendennis. He could draw him as the full-blown hero in Colonel Esmond. He could draw him—the next thing to the work of God—human and true and noble and frail, in Colonel Newcome. If the art of being a gentleman were forgotten, like the art of staining glass, it might be learned anew from that one character. It is learned there, I dare to say, daily. Mr. Andrew Lang, in a graceful attitude of melancholy, denies the influence of books. I think he forgets his philosophy, for surely there go two elements to the determination of conduct: heredity and experience—that which is given to us at birth, that which is added and cancelled in the course of life; and what experience is more formative, what step of life is more efficient, than to know and weep for Colonel Newcome? And surely he forgets himself, for I call to mind other pages, beautiful pages, from which it may be gathered that the language of *The Newcomes* sings still in his memory, and its gospel is sometimes not forgotten. I call it a gospel; it is the best I know. Error and suffering and failure and death, those calamities that our contemporaries paint upon so vast a scale—they are all depicted here, but in a more true proportion. We may return, before this picture, to the simple and ancient faith. We may be sure (although we know not why) that we give our lives, like coral insects, to build up insensibly, in the twilight of the seas of time, the reef of righteousness. And we may be sure (although we see not how) it is a thing worth doing."

How many novelists are there who have such a gallery of characters as can be collected from Thackeray's stories? what admirable character drawing! what marvellous insight into men and women! If *we* met the originals in everyday life, if we saw them, and talked with them, and observed them, we should not notice their virtues and vices so. To describe people as truly, as minutely, as humanly, and as humanely too, as he has done, requires the unfettered genius of a broad-minded man. Some one has said that to provide an author for *The Egoist* God had first to create a gentleman, and then give him genius; could there be a better basis upon which to build a criticism of Thackeray's work?

A writer is as great as his finest work—Thackeray takes his place in Literature as the author of *Esmond*, *Vanity Fair*, *Pendennis*, *Barry Lyndon*, *The Newcomes*, *Rebecca and Rowena*, and *The Roundabout Papers*—and I believe his name will stand to future ages as that of the most representative Englishman of Letters of our age, and as that of the greatest master of fiction since Henry Fielding.

APPENDICES

A. THE DIGNITY OF LITERATURE

B. CAPERS AND ANCHOVIES

C. MR. WASHINGTON

D. PREFACE TO MESSRS. APPLETON'S EDITION OF HIS MINOR WORKS.

APPENDIX A

THE DIGNITY OF LITERATURE*

REFORM CLUB, January 8, 1850.

TO THE EDITOR OF THE "MORNING CHRONICLE."

SIR,—In a leading article of your journal of Thursday, the 3rd instant, you commented upon literary pensions and the *status* of literary men in this country, and illustrated your argument by extracts from the story of *Pendennis*, at present in course of publication. You have received my writings with so much kindness, that, if you have occasion to disapprove of them or the author, I can't question your right to blame me, or doubt for a moment the friendliness and honesty of my critic; and however I might dispute the justice of your verdict in my case, I had proposed to submit to it in silence, being, indeed, very quiet in my conscience with regard to the charge made against me. But another newspaper of high character and repute takes occasion to question the principles advocated in your article of Thursday, arguing in favour of pensions for literary persons, as you argued against them; and the only point upon which the *Examiner* and the *Chronicle* appear to agree unluckily regards myself, who am offered up to general reprehension in two leading articles by the two writers: by the latter for "fostering a baneful prejudice" against literary men; by the former for "stooping to flatter" this prejudice in the

*The *Morning Chronicle*, January 12, 1850.

public mind, and condescending to caricature (as is too often my habit) my literary fellow-labourers in order to pay court to "the non-literary class." The charges of the *Examiner* against a man who has never, to his knowledge, been ashamed of his profession, or (except for its dullness) of any single line from his pen—grave as they are—are, I hope, not proven. "To stoop to flatter" any class is a novel accusation brought against my writings; and as for my scheme "to pay court to the non-literary class by disparaging my literary fellow-labourers," it is a design which would exhibit a degree, not only of baseness, but of folly, upon my part, of which I trust I am not capable. The editor of the *Examiner* may, perhaps, occasionally write, like other authors, in a hurry, and not be aware of the conclusions to which some of his sentences may lead. If I stoop to flatter anybody's prejudice for some interested motives of my own, I am no more nor less than a rogue and a cheat; which deductions from the *Examiner's* premises I will not stoop to contradict, because the premises themselves are simply absurd. I deny that the considerable body of our countrymen described by the *Examiner* as "the non-literary class" has the least gratification in witnessing the degradation or disparagement of literary men. Why accuse "the non-literary class" of being so ungrateful? If the writings of an author give a reader pleasure or profit, surely the latter will have a favourable opinion of the person who so benefits him. What intelligent man, of what political views, would not receive with respect and welcome that writer of the *Examiner* of whom your paper once said that "he made all England laugh and think"? Who would deny to that brilliant wit, that polished satirist, his just tribute of respect and admiration? Does any man who has written a book worth reading—any poet, novelist, man of science—lose reputation by his character for genius or for learning? Does he not, on the contrary, get friends, sympathy, applause—money, perhaps? all good and pleasant things in themselves, and not ungenerously awarded, as they are honestly won. That generous faith in men of letters, that kindly regard in which the whole reading nation holds them, appear to me to be so clearly shown in our country every day, that to question them would be as absurd as, permit me to say for my part, it would be ungrateful. What is it that fills mechanics' institutes in the great provincial towns when literary men are invited to attend their festivals? Has not every literary man of mark his friends and his circle, his hundreds, or his tens of thousands, of readers? And has not every one had from these constant and affecting testimonials of the esteem in which they hold him? It is of course one writer's lot, from the nature of his subject or of his genius, to command the sympathies or awaken the curiosity of many more readers than shall choose to listen to another author; but surely all get their hearing. The literary profession is not held in disrepute; nobody wants to disparage it; no man loses his social rank, whatever it may be, by practising it. On the contrary, the pen gives a place in the world to men who had none before—a fair place, fairly achieved by their genius, as any other degree of eminence is by any other kind of merit. Literary men need not, as it seems to me, be in the least querulous about their position any more, or want the pity of anybody. The money-prizes which the chief among them get are not so high as those which fall to men of other callings—to bishops, or to judges, or to opera-singers and actors; nor have they received stars and garters as yet, or peerages and governorships of islands, such as fall to the lot of military officers. The rewards of the profession are not to be measured by the money standard: for one man spends a life of learning and labour on a book which does not pay the printer's bill, and another gets a little fortune by a few light volumes. But, putting the money out of the question, I believe that the social estimation of the man of letters is as good as it deserves to be, and as good as that of any other professional man. With respect to the question in debate between you and the *Examiner* as to the propriety of public rewards and honours for literary men, I don't see why men of letters should not very cheerfully coincide with Mr. *Examiner* in accepting all the honours, places, and prizes which they can get. The amount of such as will be awarded to them will not, we may be pretty sure, impoverish the country much; and if it is the custom of the State to reward by money, or titles of honour, or stars and garters of any sort, individuals who do the country service, and if individuals are gratified at having "Sir" or "My lord" appended to their names, or stars and ribands hooked on their coats and waistcoats, as men most undoubtedly are, and as their wives, families, and relations are, there can be no reason why men of letters should not have the chance, as well as men of the robe or the sword; or why, if honour and money are good for one profession, they should not be good for another. No man in other callings thinks himself degraded by receiving a reward from his Government; nor, surely, need the literary man be more squeamish about pensions, and ribands, and titles, than the ambassador, or general, or judge. Every

European State but ours rewards its men of letters; the American Government gives them their full share of its small patronage; and if Americans, why not Englishmen?* If Pitt Crawley is disappointed at not getting a riband on retiring from his diplomatic post at Pumpernickel, if General O'Dowd is pleased to be called Sir Hector O'Dowd, K.C.B., and his wife at being denominated my Lady O'Dowd, are literary men to be the only persons exempt from vanity, and is it to be a sin in them to covet honour? And now, with regard to the charge against myself of fostering baneful prejudices against our calling—to which I no more plead guilty than I should think Fielding would have done if he had been accused of a design to bring the Church into contempt by describing Parson Trulliber—permit me to say that before you deliver sentence it would be as well if you had waited to hear the whole of the argument. Who knows what is coming in the future numbers of the work which has incurred your displeasure and the *Examiner's?* and whether you, in accusing me of prejudice, and the

*Mr. Trollope has written that Thackeray "held strong ideas that much was due by the Queen's ministers to men of letters, and no doubt had his feeling of slighted merit because no part of the debt was paid to him." On this I would gladly have joined issue with Mr. Trollope. Thackeray certainly saw no good reason why literary men should not be awarded pensions, ribands, and titles, like other men of other professions; "but," he wrote in his essay on *The Chances of the Literary Profession*, "there is not the least call to be holding up literary men as martyrs. Even that prevailing sentiment which regrets that means should not be provided for giving them leisure, for enabling them to perfect great works in retirement, that they should waste away their strength upon fugitive literature, etc., I hold to be often uncalled for and dangerous. I believe, if most men of letters were to be pensioned, I am sorry to say I believe they wouldn't work at all; and of others, that the labour which is to answer the calls of the day is the one quite best suited to their genius. Suppose Sir Robert Peel were to write to you, and, enclosing a cheque for twenty thousand pounds, instruct you to pension any fifty deserving authors so that they might have leisure to retire and write "great" works, on whom would you fix?"

Examiner (alas!) of swindling and flattering the public, have not been premature? Time and the hour may solve this mystery, for which the candid reader is referred "to our next." That I have a prejudice against running into debt, and drunkenness, and disorderly life, and against quackery and falsehood in my profession, I own; and that I like to have a laugh at those pretenders in it who write confidential news about fashion and politics for provincial *gobemouches;* but I am not aware of feeling any malice in describing this weakness, or of doing anything wrong in exposing the former vices. Have they never existed amongst literary men? Have their talents never been urged as a plea for improvidence, and their very faults adduced as a consequence of their genius? The only moral that I, as a writer, wished to hint in the descriptions against which you protest, was, that it was the duty of a literary man, as well as any other, to practise regularity and sobriety, to love his family, and to pay his tradesmen. Nor is the picture I have drawn "a caricature which I condescend to," any more than it is a wilful and insidious design on my part to flatter "the non-literary class." If it be a caricature, it is the result of a natural perversity of vision, not of an artful desire to mislead; but my attempt was to tell the truth, and I meant to tell it not unkindly. I have seen the bookseller whom Bludyer robbed of his books; I have carried money, and from a noble brother man of letters, to some one not unlike Shandon in prison, and have watched the beautiful devotion of his wife in that dreary place. Why are these things not to be described, if they illustrate, as they appear to me to do, that strange and awful struggle of good and wrong which takes place in our hearts and in the world? It may be that I worked out my moral ill, or it may be possible that the critic of the *Examiner* fails in apprehension. My efforts as an artist come perfectly within his province as a censor; but when Mr. *Examiner* says of a gentleman that he is "stooping to flatter a public prejudice"—which public prejudice does not exist—I submit that he makes a charge which is as absurd as it is unjust, and am thankful that it repels itself. And, instead of accusing the public of persecuting and disparaging us as a class, it seems to me that men of letters had best silently assume that they are as good as any other gentlemen, nor raise piteous controversies upon a question which all people of sense must take to be settled. If I sit at your table, I suppose that I am my neighbour's equal, as that he is mine. If I began straightway with a protest of "Sir, I am a literary man, but I would have you to know I am as good as you," which of us is it that questions the dignity of the literary profession—my neighbour, who would like to eat his soup in quiet, or the man of letters who commences the argument? And I hope that a comic writer, because he describes one author as improvident and another as a parasite, may not only be guiltless of a desire to vilify his profession, but may really have its honour at heart. If there are no spendthrifts or parasites amongst us, the satire becomes unjust; but if such exist, or have existed, they are as good subjects for comedy as men of other callings. I never heard that the Bar felt itself aggrieved because *Punch* chose to describe Mr. Dunup's notorious state of insolvency; or that the picture of Stiggins in *Pickwick* was intended as an insult to all Dissenters; or that all the attorneys in the empire were indignant at the famous history of the firm of "Quirk, Gammon & Snap." Are we to be passed over because we are faultless, or because we cannot afford to be laughed at? And if every character in a story is to represent a class, not an individual—if every bad figure is to have its obliged contrast of a good one, and a balance of vice and virtue is to be struck—novels, I think, would become impossible, as they would be intolerably stupid and unnatural, and there would be a lamentable end of writers and readers of such compositions.

Believe me, Sir, to be your very faithful servant,

W. M. THACKERAY.

APPENDIX B

"CAPERS AND ANCHOVIES"*

To the Editor of the "Morning Chronicle."

Sir,—I hope no Irish gentleman will be insulted by my recalling a story, venerable for its antiquity, of the Irish officer who, having stated that he had seen anchovies growing in profusion upon the rocks of Malta, called out and shot an Englishman who doubted his statement. As the unhappy Saxon fell, writhing with his wound, the Irishman's second remarked, "Look, Sir Lucius, you have made him cut capers." "Bedad, it's capers I mane!" the gallant and impetuous O'Trigger remarked; and instantly apologised in the handsomest terms for his error. It was capers he had seen, and not anchovies, growing on the rocks; the blunder was his, but the bullet was in the Englishman's leg, who went away grumbling because the other had not thought of the truth before.

Sir, three Irish newspapers and an Irish member of Parliament in his place in the Rotunda have delivered their fire into me through a similar error. Every post brings me letters containing extracts from Irish papers sent to me by friends; and one of them, who is most active on my behalf, informs me that there is a body of Irish gentlemen who are bent upon cudgelling me, and who are very likely waiting at my door, whilst I write

*The *Morning Chronicle*, April 12, 1850.

from the club, where, of course, I have denied myself. It is these, while it is yet time, whom I wish to prevent; and as many of them will probably read your journal to-morrow morning, you may probably be the means of saving my bones, valuable to me and my family, and which I prefer, before any apology for breaking them. The blunder of which I am the victim is at once absurd and painful, and I am sorry to have recourse to the press for explanation.

Ten years ago I wrote a satirical story in *Fraser's Magazine*, called *Catherine*, and founded upon the history of the murderess Catherine Hayes. The tale was intended to ridicule a taste then prevalent for making novel heroes of Newgate malefactors. Every single personage in my story was a rascal, and hanged, or put to a violent death; and the history became so atrocious that it created a general dissatisfaction, and was pronounced to be horridly immoral. When the public went on reading the work which I had intended to ridicule, *Catherine* was, in a word, a failure, and is dead, with all its heroes.

In the last number of the story of *Pendennis* (which was written when I was absent from this country, and not in the least thinking about the opera here), I wrote a sentence to the purport that the greatest criminals and murderers — Bluebeard, George Barnwell, Catherine Hayes—had some spark of human feeling, and found some friends, meaning thereby to encourage minor criminals not to despair. And my only thought in producing the last of these instances was about Mrs. Hayes, who died at Tyburn, and subsequently perished in my novel—and not in the least about an amiable and beautiful young lady now acting at Her Majesty's Theatre.

I quite forgot her existence. I was pointing my moral, such as it was, with quite a different person, and never for a single instant, I declare upon my word of honour, remembering the young lady, and not knowing anything regarding her engagement at the Haymarket.

From this unlucky sentence in *Pendennis* my tribulations begin, and my capers are held up as the most wicked anchovies to indignant Ireland. *Vindex* writes to the *Freeman's Journal*, saying that I have an intention to insult the Irish nation in the person of an accomplished and innocent young lady, whom I class with murderers and cut-throats—whereby I damn myself to everlasting infamy. The *Freeman's Journal*, in language intelligible always, if not remarkable for grammatical or other propriety, says I am "the Big Blubberman," "the hugest humbug ever thrust on the public"; that I am guilty of unmanly grossness and cowardly assault; and that I wrote to ruin Miss Hayes, but did not succeed. The *Freeman* adds, in a concluding paragraph, that there may have been some person happening to bear a name coincident with that of the *Freeman's* accomplished countrywoman; and that if I have "this very simple and complete defence to make, I shall hasten to offer it." I don't take in the *Freeman's Journal*—I am not likely to be very anxious about reading it; but the *Freeman* never gives me any notice of the attack which I am to hasten to defend, and, calling me coward and ruffian, leaves me. It is the anchovy-caper question settled in the approved manner.

The *Mail*, assuming that I intended insult and injury, remarks on the incriminated sentence thus: "Its brutality is so far neutralised by its absurdity as to render it utterly harmless." No. 2.

No. 3. The *Packet*, speaking on the judgment of both of its contemporaries, says admirably:—"*This prompt and chivalrous espousal of a lady's cause is just what we would have expected from our brethren of the Irish press, and will be, no doubt, a source of gratification to Miss Hayes.* But . . . we think it only fair to state that he has not been guilty of the 'incredibly gross act' of associating our pure and amiable Catherine with the murderess and tyrants about whom he has written so nonsensically"—and then follows the revelation of the mystery about the real Catherine, the writer remarking that I am neither a fool nor a madman, and that I would not outrage Miss Hayes, lest some Saxon should kick me.

Sir, if some pictures of the Irish, drawn by foreign hands, are caricatures, what are they compared to the pictures of the Irish drawn by themselves? Would any man—could any man out of Ireland—invent such an argument as the last? It stands thus—

1. I have not intended to injure, nor have I in the least injured, Miss Hayes.

2. The people who have abused me for injuring her have acted with chivalrous promptitude, and, no doubt, have greatly gratified Miss Hayes. Poor young lady! She is to be gratified by seeing a man belaboured who never thought of her or meant her a wrong.

3. But if I *had* injured Miss Hayes, many Saxon boot-toes would have taught me decency—that is, capers not being anchovies, gentlemen would have acted with much chivalry in shooting me; and if capers *had* been anchovies, I should richly have merited a kicking. Comfortable dilemma!

I should not have noticed this charge except in Ireland, believing that it must be painful to the young lady whose name has been most innocently and unfortunately brought forward; but I see the case has already passed the Channel, and that there is no help for all parties but publicity. I declare upon my honour then to Miss Hayes that I am grieved to have been the means of annoying her, if I have done so; and I need not tell any gentleman—what gentleman would question me?—that I never for a moment could mean an insult to innocence, and genius, and beauty.

I am, Sir, your very faithful servant,

W. M. THACKERAY.

GARRICK CLUB, *April* 11, 1850.

APPENDIX C

"MR. WASHINGTON"*

November 22, 1853.

TO THE EDITOR OF THE "TIMES."

SIR,—Allow me a word of explanation in answer to a strange charge which has been brought against me in the United States, and which your New York correspondent has made public in this country.

In the first number of a periodical story which I am now publishing appears a sentence in which I should never have thought of finding any harm until it has been discovered by some critics over the water. The fatal words are these:—

"When pigtails grew on the backs of the British gentry, and their wives wore cushions on their heads, over which they tied their own hair, and disguised it with powder and pomatum; when ministers went in their stars and orders to the House of Commons, and the orators of the opposition attacked nightly the noble lord in the blue riband; when Mr. Washington was heading the American rebels with a courage, it must be confessed, worthy of a better cause;—there came to London, out of a northern county, Mr., etc."

This paragraph has been interpreted in America as an insult to Washington and the whole Union; and from the sadness and gravity with which your correspondent

*The *Times*, November 23, 1853.

quotes certain of my words, it is evident he, too, thinks they have an insolent and malicious meaning.

Having published the American critic's comment, permit the author of a faulty sentence to say what he did mean, and to add the obvious moral of the apologue which has been so oddly construed. I am speaking of a young apprentice coming to London between the years 1770 and '80, and want to depict a few figures of the last century. (The illustrated head-letter of the chapter was intended to represent Hogarth's "Industrious Apprentice.") I fancy the old society, with its hoops and powder—Barré or Fox thundering at Lord North asleep on the Treasury bench—the news-readers in the coffee-room talking over the paper, and owning that this Mr. Washington who was leading the rebels was a very courageous soldier, and worthy of a better cause than fighting against King George. The images are at least natural and pretty consecutive. 1776—the people of London in '76—the Lord and House of Commons in '76—Lord North—Washington—what the people thought about Washington—I am thinking about '76. Where, in the name of common sense, is the insult to 1853? The satire, if satire there be, applies to us at home, who called Washington "Mr. Washington," as we called Frederick the Great "the Protestant Hero," or Napoleon "the Corsican Tyrant" or "General Bonaparte." Need I say that our officers were instructed (until they were taught better manners) to call Washington "Mr. Washington"? and that the Americans were called rebels during the whole of that contest? Rebels!—of course they were rebels; and I should like to know what native American would not have been a rebel in that cause?

As irony is dangerous, and has hurt the feelings of kind friends whom I would not wish to offend, let me say, in perfect faith and gravity, that I think the cause for which Washington fought entirely just and right, and the champion the very noblest, purest, bravest, best, of God's men.

I am, Sir, your very faithful servant,

W. M. THACKERAY.

APPENDIX D

PREFACE TO MESSRS. APPLETON & CO.'S EDITION OF THACKERAY'S MINOR WORKS

On coming into this country, I found that the projectors of this series of little books had preceded my arrival by publishing a number of early works, which have appeared under various pseudonyms during the last fifteen years. I was not the master to choose what stories of mine should appear or not: these miscellanies were all advertised, or in course of publication; nor have I had the good fortune to be able to draw a pen, or alter a blunder of author or printer, except in the case of the accompanying volumes, which contain contributions to *Punch*, whence I have been enabled to make something like a selection. In the *Letters of Mr. Brown*, and the succeeding short essays and descriptive pieces, something graver and less burlesque was attempted than in other pieces which I here publish. My friend *The Fat Contributor* accompanied Mr. Titmarsh in his *Journey from Cornhill to Cairo.* The prize novels contain imitations of the writings of some contemporaries who still live and flourish in the novelist's calling. I myself had scarcely entered on it when these burlesque tales were begun, and I stopped further parody from a sense that this merry task of making fun of the novelists should be left to younger hands than my own; and, in a little book published some four years since in England, by my friends

Messrs. Hannay and Shirley Brooks, I saw a caricature of myself and writings to the full as ludicrous and faithful as the prize novels of Mr. Punch. Nor was there, had I desired it, any possibility of preventing the reappearance of these performances. Other publishers, besides the Messrs. Appleton, were ready to bring my hidden works to the light. Very many of the other books printed I have not seen since their appearance twelve years ago; and it was with no small feelings of curiosity (remembering under what sad circumstances the tale had been left unfinished) that I bought the incomplete *Shabby Genteel Story* in a railway-car on my first journey from Boston hither, from a rosy-cheeked little peripatetic book-merchant, who called out *Thackeray's Works* in such a kind, gay voice as gave me a feeling of friendship and welcome.

There is an opportunity of being either satiric or sentimental. The careless papers written at an early period, and never seen since the printer's boy carried them away, are brought back and laid at the father's door; and he cannot, if he would, forget or disown his own children.

Why were some of the little brats brought out of their obscurity? I own to a feeling of anything but pleasure in reviewing some of these misshapen juvenile creatures, which the publisher has disinterred and resuscitated. There are two performances especially (among the critical and biographical works of the erudite Mr. Yellowplush) which I am very sorry to see reproduced; and I ask pardon of the author of *The Caxtons* for a lampoon, which I know he himself has forgiven, and which I wish I could recall.

I had never seen that eminent writer but once in public when this satire was penned, and wonder at the recklessness of the young man who could fancy such personality was harmless jocularity, and never calculate that it might give pain. The best experiences of my life have been gained since that time of youth and gaiety and careless laughter. I allude to them, perhaps, because I would not have any kind and friendly American reader judge of me by the wild performances of early years. Such a retrospect as the sight of these old acquaintances perforce occasioned cannot, if it would, be gay. The old scenes return, the remembrance of the bygone times, the chamber in which the stories were written, the faces that shone round the table.

Some biographers in this country have been pleased to depict that homely apartment after a very strange and romantic fashion; and an author in the direst struggles of poverty, waited upon by a family domestic in all the splendour of his menial decorations, has been circumstantially described to the reader's amusement as well as to the writer's own. I may be permitted to assure the former that the splendour and the want were alike fanciful, and that the meals were not only sufficient, but honestly paid for.

That extreme liberality with which American publishers have printed the works of English authors has had at least this beneficial result for us—that our names and writings are known by multitudes using our common mother tongue, who never had heard of us or our books but for the speculators who have sent them all over this continent.

It is of course not unnatural for the English writer to hope that some day he may share a portion of the profits which his works bring at present to the persons who vend them in this country; and I am bound gratefully to say myself that since my arrival here I have met with several publishing houses who are willing to acknowledge our little claim to participate in the advantages arising out of our books; and the present writer, having long since ascertained that a portion of a loaf is more satisfactory than no bread at all, gratefully accepts and acknowledges several slices which the book-purveyors in this city have proffered to him of their own free-will.

If we are not paid in full and in specie as yet, English writers surely ought to be thankful for the very great kindness and friendliness with which the American public receives them; and if in hope some day that measures may pass here to legalise our right to profit a little by the commodities which we invent and in which we deal, I, for one, can cheerfully say that the good-will towards us from publishers and public is undoubted, and wait for still better times with perfect confidence and good-humour.

If I have to complain of any special hardship, it is not that our favourite works are reproduced, and our children introduced to the American public—children whom we have educated with care, and in whom we take a little paternal pride—but that ancient magazines are ransacked, and shabby old articles dragged out which we had gladly left in the wardrobes where they have lain hidden many years. There is no control, however, over a man's thoughts—once uttered and printed, back they may come upon us any sudden day; and in this collection which Messrs. Appleton are publishing I find two or three such early productions of my own that I gladly would take back, but that they have long since gone out of the paternal guardianship.

If not printed in this series, they would have appeared from other presses, having not the slightest need of the author's own imprimatur; and I cannot sufficiently condole with a literary gentleman of this city, who (in his voyages of professional adventure) came upon an early performance of mine, which shall be nameless, carried the news of the discovery to a publisher of books, and had actually done me the favour to sell my book to that liberal man; when behold, Messrs. Appleton announced the book in the press, and my *confrère* had to refund the prize-money which had been paid to him. And if he is a little chagrined at finding other intrepid voyagers beforehand with him in taking possession of my island, and the American flag already floating there, he will understand the feelings of the harmless, but kindly-treated, aboriginal, who makes every sign of peace, who smokes the pipe of submission, and meekly acquiesces in his own annexation.

It is said that those only who win should laugh: I think in this case my readers will not grudge the losing side its share of harmless good-humour. If I have contributed to theirs, or provided them with means of amusement, I am glad to think my books have found favour with the American public, as I am proud to own the great and cordial welcome with which they have received me.

W. M. THACKERAY.

NEW YORK, *December*, 1852.

THE BIBLIOGRAPHY
OF
WILLIAM MAKEPEACE THACKERAY, 1829—1899

NOTE

I HAVE endeavoured in the following pages to compile a bibliographical list of Thackeray's writings and drawings which shall be as complete as possible.

I have arranged the Works published in book-form in chronological order, while the contributions to periodicals have been inserted under the headings of the periodicals themselves, alphabetically arranged.

In every case, where nothing to the contrary is stated, the illustrations are by the author.

To the late Mr. R. H. Shepherd's *Bibliography*, and to Mr. C. P. Johnson's *Early Writings of W. M. Thackeray*, I am much indebted, and gladly acknowledge the assistance which I have derived from these volumes.

L. M.

PART I

VOLUMES

1836

"Flore et Zéphyr. Ballet mythologique, par Théophile Wagstaffe." [Eight plates lithographed by E. Morton from sketches by Thackeray.] London: J. Mitchell. Paris: Rittner & Goupil.

Reprinted in the Biographical Edition of the Collected Works, 1898.

1837

"King Glumpus. An Interlude in One Act." [With three illustrations.] For private circulation only. London.

The illustrations were reproduced in *The Autographic Mirror*, vol. ii. (1865). A fac-simile reprint was issued in 1898 by Mr. W. T. Spencer, 27, New Oxford Street, London, W. C.

1839

"Stubbs's Calendar; or, The Fatal Boots. With Twelve Illustrations by George Cruikshank." London: Charles Tilt. [Comic Almanack for 1839.]

Reprinted as "The Fatal Boots," in "Miscellanies," vol. i. (1856) and in Collected Works.

"The Exquisites. A Farce. In Two Acts.

"Whate'er they did was done with so much ease,
In them alone 'twas natural to please:
Their notions all accompanied with grace,
And Paradise was open'd in their face.—DRYDEN."

[With four illustrations.] For private circulation only. London: 1839.

This has been attributed to Thackeray.

1840

"Barber Cox, and the Cutting of his Comb. With Twelve Illustrations by George Cruikshank." London: Charles Tilt. [Comic Almanack for 1840.]

Reprinted as "Cox's Diary," in "Miscellanies," vol. i. (1855), and in Collected Works.

"An Essay on the Genius of George Cruikskank. With Numerous Illustrations of His Work. From the *Westminster Review*, No. 66." London: Henry Hooper.

Again reprinted in 1884, with a prefatory note on Thackeray as an artist and art-critic, by W. E. Church; also in Collected Works.

"The Paris Sketch-Book. By Mr. Titmarsh. With Numerous drawings by the Author on copper and wood." In two volumes. London: John Macrone.

With a Preface dated: London, July 1, 1840.

Vol. I.: An Invasion of France; A Caution to Travellers;* The Fêtes of July; On the French School of Painting; The Painter's Bargain;* Cartouche; On Some French Fashionable Novels;* A Gambler's Death;* Napoleon and his System;* The Story of Mary Ancel; Beatrice Merger.*

Vol. II.: Caricatures and Lithography in Paris; * Little Poinsinet; The Devil's Wager; Madame Sand and the New Apocalypse; The Case of Peytel;* Imitations of Beranger;* French Dramas and Melodramas;* Meditations at Versailles.*

Reprinted in Collected Works when the "Imitations of Beranger" are omitted, and placed in the "Ballads."

1841

"Comic Tales and Sketches. Edited and Illustrated by Mr. Michael Angelo Titmarsh." In two volumes. London: Hugh Cunningham.

The Preface is dated: Paris, April 1, 1841.

Vol. I.: The Yellowplush Papers.

Vol. II.: Some Passages in the Life of Major Gahagan; The Professor; The Bedford-Row Conspiracy; The Fatal Boots.

The Illustrations to "The Fatal Boots" were by Cruikshank.

"The Second Funeral of Napoleon, in Three Letters to Miss Smith of London, and The Chronicle of the Drum. By Mr. M. A. Titmarsh." [With a frontispiece and a vignette]. London: Hugh Cunningham.

"The Second Funeral of Napoleon" was reprinted in *The*

*Published for the first time.

Cornhill Magazine, vol. xiii., pages 48—50, and afterwards in Collected Works.

"The Chronicle of the Drum" was reprinted in "Miscellanies," vol. i. (1855), and in Collected Works.

1843

"The Irish Sketch-Book. By Mr. M. A. Titmarsh. With Engravings on Wood drawn by the Author." In two volumes. London: Chapman & Hall.

The Dedication, to Charles Lever, signed W. M. Thackeray, is dated: London, April 27, 1843. Reprinted in Collected Works.

1846

"Notes of a Journey from Cornhill to Grand Cairo, by way of Lisbon, Athens, Constantinople, and Jerusalem. By Mr. M. A. Titmarsh." [With numerous illustrations.] London: Chapman & Hall.

The Dedication, to Captain Lewis, is dated: London, December 24, 1845. Reprinted in Collected Works.

1847

"Mrs. Perkyns's Ball. By Mr. M. A. Titmarsh." [With numerous coloured illustrations.] London: Chapman & Hall.

Reprinted in "Christmas Books," 1857; in Collected Works, and in fac-simile by Messrs. Smith, Elder & Co., 1898.

1848

"Our Street. By Mr. M. A. Titmarsh." [With coloured illustrations.] London: Chapman & Hall.

Reprinted in "Christmas Books," 1857, and in Collected Works.

"The Book of Snobs. By W. M. Thackeray." [With numerous illustrations.] London: *Punch* Office.

Reprinted from *Punch*. Chapters xvii., xviii., xix., xx., xxi., xxii., xxiii., were omitted.

"On re-perusing these papers, I have found them so stupid, so personal, so snobbish, in a word, that I have withdrawn them from this collection."—*Author's Note.*

Reprinted in Collected Works. The suppressed chapters reprinted in a supplementary volume of Collected Works, vol. xxvi. (1886.)

"Vanity Fair. A Novel without a Hero. By William Makepeace Thackeray. With Illustrations on steel and wood by the Author." London: Bradbury & Evans.

Issued originally in twenty monthly parts in yellow wrappers as *Vanity Fair; Pen and Pencil Sketches of English Society. By*

W. M. Thackeray. No. 1 is dated January 1847; Nos. 19 and 20 (double number), July 1848. The Preface is dated: London, June 28, 1848. The illustration on the wrapper has not been reproduced, and a plate in No. 11 (p. 336) was immediately suppressed.

Reprinted in Collected Works.

1849

"The History of Samuel Titmarsh and the Great Hoggarty Diamond. By W. M. Thackeray." [With illustrations.] London: Bradbury & Evans. The Preface is dated: Kensington, January 25, 1849.

Reprinted from *Fraser's Magazine.* Subsequently printed again in "Miscellanies," vol. iv. (1857), and in Collected Works.

"Doctor Birch and His Young Friends. By Mr. M. A. Titmarsh." [With coloured illustrations.] London: Chapman & Hall.

Reprinted in "Christmas Books" (1857), and in Collected Works.

1849—1850

"The History of Pendennis. His Fortunes and Misfortunes, his Friends, and his greatest Enemy. By William Makepeace Thackeray. With Illustrations on steel and wood by the Author." In two volumes. London: Bradbury & Evans.

Issued originally in twenty-four monthly parts in yellow wrappers. No. 1 is dated November 1848; No. 11, September 1849; No. 12, January 1850; Nos. 23 and 24 (double number), December 1850. The Preface is dated: Kensington, November 26, 1850. The illustration on the wrapper was not reproduced.

Reprinted in Collected Works.

1850

"Rebecca and Rowena; A Romance upon Romance. By Mr. M. A. Titmarsh. With Illustrations by Richard Doyle." London: Chapman & Hall. The Preface is dated: Kensington, December 20, 1849.

Reprinted in "Miscellanies," vol. iii. (1856), and in Collected Works.

"Sketches after English Landscape Painters. By Louis Marvy. With Short Notices by W. M. Thackeray." London: David Bogue.

"The Kickleburys on the Rhine. By Mr. M. A. Titmarsh." [With illustrations.] London: Smith, Elder & Co.

A second edition was published in 1851, "With Preface, being an Essay on Thunder and Small Beer."

Reprinted in Collected Works.

1852

"The History of Henry Esmond, Esq., a Colonel in the Service of Her Majesty Queen Anne. Written by Himself." In three volumes. London: Printed for Smith, Elder & Co., over against St. Peter's Church in Cornhill, 1852.

The half-title is: "Esmond; A Story of Queen Anne's Reign. By W. M. Thackeray."

Reprinted in Collected Works.

1853

"The English Humourists of the Eighteenth Century. A Series of Lectures delivered in England, Scotland, and the United States of America. By W. M. Thackeray." London: Smith, Elder & Co. The Notes were written by Mr. George Hodder.

Reprinted in Collected Works.

1855

"The Rose and the Ring; or, The History of Prince Giglio and Prince Bulbo. A Fireside Pantomime for Great and Small Children. By Mr. M. A. Titmarsh." [With illustrations.] London: Smith, Elder & Co. The Preface is dated: December 1854.

Reprinted in Collected Works.

1854—1855

"The Newcomes. Memoirs of a Most Respectable Family. Edited by Arthur Pendennis, Esq. With Illustrations on steel and wood by Richard Doyle." In two volumes. London: Bradbury & Evans.

Issued originally in twenty-four monthly numbers in yellow wrappers. No. 1 is dated October 1853; Nos. 23 and 24 (double number), August 1855. The illustration on the cover has not been reproduced.

Reprinted in Collected Works.

1855—1857

"Miscellanies: prose and verse. By W. M. Thackeray." In four volumes. London: Bradbury & Evans.

Vol. I. (1855): Ballads; The Book of Snobs; The Tremendous Adventures of Major Gahagan; The Fatal Boots; Cox's Diary.

Vol. II. (1856): The Yellowplush Papers; Jeames's Diary; Sketches and Travels in London; The Prize Novelists; Character Sketches.

Vol. III. (1856): Barry Lyndon; A Legend of the Rhine; Rebecca and Rowena; A Little Dinner at Timmins's; The Bedford-Row Conspiracy.

Vol. IV. (1857): The Fitz-Boodle Papers; Men's Wives; A Shabby Genteel Story; The Great Hoggarty Diamond.

Another edition: Tauchnitz collection of British Authors, vols. 171, 197, 345, 353, 354, 369, 379, 408. 8 vols. Leipzig: 1849—1857.
Another edition: Appleton's Edition of W. M. Thackeray's Minor Works. New York, 1852—1854. With an original Preface by the Author.

1857

"Christmas Books. Mrs. Perkyns's Ball. Our Street. Dr. Birch. With Illustrations by the Author." London: Chapman & Hall.

A Reprint.

1858—1859

"The Virginians: A Tale of the Last Century. By W. M. Thackeray. With Illustrations on steel and wood by the Author." In two volumes. London: Bradbury & Evans.

Issued originally in twenty-four monthly parts in yellow wrappers. No. 1 is dated November 1857; Nos. 23 and 24 (double number), October 1859.

Reprinted in Collected Works.

1861.

"The Four Georges. By W. M. Thackeray. With Illustrations." London: Smith, Elder & Co.

Reprinted from *The Cornhill Magazine*, and printed again in Collected Works.

"Lovel the Widower. By W. M. Thackeray. With Illustrations." London: Smith, Elder & Co.

This story was adapted from "The Wolves and the Lamb," a play written by Thackeray, which has been printed in Collected Works.

Reprinted from *The Cornhill Magazine*, and printed again in Collected Works.

1862

"The Adventures of Philip on his Way through the World; shewing who robbed him, who helped him, and who passed him by. By W. M. Thackeray. In three volumes." London: Smith, Elder & Co.

Reprinted from *The Cornhill Magazine*. The illustrations by the author and by Frederick Walker were not reproduced in this edition. Printed again in Collected Works.

1863

"Roundabout Papers. Reprinted from *The Cornhill Magazine*. With Illustrations. By W. M. Thackeray." London: Smith, Elder & Co.

Printed again in Collected Works.

1867

"Denis Duval. By W. M. Thackeray." London: Smith, Elder & Co.

Reprinted from *The Cornhill Magazine*, and printed again in Collected Works.

"Early and Late Papers. Hitherto Uncollected. By William Makepeace Thackeray." [With a Note by J. T. Fields.] Boston: Ticknor & Fields.

Memorials of Gormandizing; Men and Coats; Bluebeard's Ghost; Dickens in France; John Leech's Pictures of Life and Character; Little Travels and Roadside Sketches; On Men and Pictures; Picture Gossip; The Anonymous in Periodical Literature; Goethe; A Leaf out of a Sketch-Book; The Last Sketch; "Strange to say, on Club Paper," Autour de mon Chapeau; On a Peal of Bells; On Some Carp at Sans Souci; Desseins; On a Pear Tree; On a Medal of George the Fourth; On Alexandrines; The Notch on the Axe; De Finibus.

1875

"Thackerayana; notes and anecdotes illustrated by nearly six hundred sketches by W. M. Thackeray, depicting humourous incidents in his school-life, and favourite scenes and characters in the books of his everyday reading." London. John Camden Hotten.

[Compiled by Joseph Grego (?).]

1876

"The Orphan of Pimlico, and other Sketches, Fragments, and Drawings. By W. M. Thackeray. With some Notes by Anne Isabella Thackeray." London: Smith, Elder & Co.

1878

"Etchings by the late William Makepeace Thackeray while at Cambridge, illustrative of University Life, etc. Now first published from the original plates." London: H. Sotheran & Co.

1880 (?)

"The Students' Quarter; or, Paris Five-and-Thirty Years Since: By the late W. M. Thackeray. Not included in his collected writings. With original coloured illustrations." London: John Camden Hotten.

Contributions to "The Corsair," "Cartouche," "A Ramble in the Picture-Galleries."

1869—1886

The Collected Works of W. M. Thackeray. In twenty-six volumes. London: Smith, Elder & Co.

Vols. I.—II.: "Vanity Fair." In two volumes. With forty-one steel plates, and a hundred and forty-nine wood engravings by the Author.

Vols. III.—IV.: "Pendennis." In two volumes. With forty-eight steel plates and a hundred and twenty-nine wood engravings by the Author.

Vols. V.—VI.: "The Newcomes." In two volumes. With forty-eight steel plates by Richard Doyle, and a hundred and twenty-four wood engravings.

Vols. VII.: "Esmond." With eight full-page illustrations by George du Maurier, and sixty-seven wood engravings.

Vols. VIII.—IX.: "The Virginians." In two volumes. With forty-eight steel plates, and ninety-seven wood engravings by the Author.

Vols. X.—XI.: "The Adventures of Philip." To which is prefixed: "A Shabby Genteel Story." In two volumes. With twenty full-page illustrations and fifty-five wood engravings by the Author and Frederick Walker.

Vol. XII.: "The Great Hoggarty Diamond;" "A Little Dinner at Timmins's;" and "Notes of a Journey from Cornhill to Grand Cairo." With eleven steel plates and sixty-one wood engravings by the Author.

Vol. XIII.: "Christmas Books." With illustrations by the Author and Richard Doyle. "Mrs. Perkyns's Ball;" "Dr. Birch;" "Our Street;" "The Kickleburys on the Rhine;" "Rebecca and Rowena."

Vol. XIV.: "The Book of Snobs;" and "Sketches and Travels in London." With a hundred and twenty-six woodcut illustrations by the Author.

Vol. XV.: "Burlesques." With eighty-seven woodcut illustrations by the Author and George Cruikshank. "Novels by Eminent Hands;" "Jeames's Diary;" "Adventures of Major Gahagan;" "A Legend of the Rhine;" "The History of the Next French Revolution."

Vol. XVI.: "Paris Sketch-Book;" "Little Travels and Roadside Sketches." With twelve steel plates and forty-eight wood engravings by the Author, T. R. Macquoid, and J. P. Atkinson.

Vol. XVII.: "The Yellowplush Papers;" "The Fitzboodle Papers;" "Cox's Diary;" "Character Sketches." With seventeen steel plates, and fifty-five wood engravings by the Author and George Cruikshank.

Vol. XVIII.: "The Irish Sketch-Book;" "Critical Reviews." With eleven full-page illustrations and a hundred and fourteen wood engravings by the Author, George Cruikshank, John Leech, and M. Fitzgerald.

Vol. XIX.: "The Memoirs of Barry Lyndon;" "The Fatal Boots." With sixteen full-page illustrations and thirty-seven wood engravings by J. E. Millais, B.A., George Cruikshank, and W. Ralston.

Vol. XX.: "Catherine, A Story;" "Men's Wives;" "The Bedford Row Conspiracy." With twelve full-page illustrations and thirty-five wood engravings by the Author, Luke Fildes, A.R.A., and R. B. Wallace.

Vol. XXI.: "Ballads;" "The Rose and the Ring." With eight full-page illustrations, and a hundred and thirteen wood engravings by the Author, Mrs. Butler (Miss Elizabeth Thompson), George du Maurier, John Collier, H. Furniss, G. G. Kilburne, M. Fitzgerald, and P. J. Atkinson.

Vol. XXII.: "Roundabout Papers. To which is added 'The Second Funeral of Napoleon.'" With eleven full-page illustrations and fifty-four wood engravings by the Author, Charles Keene, and M. Fitzgerald.

Vol. XXIII.: "The Four Georges;" and "The English Humourists of the Eighteenth Century." With twenty full-page illustrations, four steel portraits, and twenty wood engravings by the Author, Frank Dicksee, Linley Sambourne, F. Barnard, Frederick Walker, and G. A. Sala.

Vol. XXIV.: "Lovel the Widower;" "The Wolves and the Lamb;" "Denis Duval." With two steel plates, ten full-page illustrations, and fourteen wood engravings by the Author and Frederick Walker. To which is added an Essay on the Writings of W. M. Thackeray, by Leslie Stephens.

"The Wolves and the Lamb" was now printed for the first time.

Vol. XXV.: "Miscellaneous Essays, Sketches, and Reviews." With illustrations by the Author.

Containing the "Charity and Humour" lecture, published for the first time in England, though in New York, Messrs. Harper Brothers had printed it in "The English Humourists," 1853.

Vol. XXVI.: "Contributions to *Punch*" (not previously reprinted). With a hundred and thirty-two illustrations by the Author.

[*Messrs. Smith, Elder & Co. have published several editions of Collected Works, including an Edition de Luxe* 1878—1886 (*4to*).]

1887

"Sultan Stork, and other Stories and Sketches. By William Makepeace Thackeray (1829—1844.) Now first collected. To which is added The Bibliography of Thackeray, revised and considerably enlarged." London; George Redway.

With an introduction by the Editor [R. H. Shepherd ?].

Sultan Stork; Little Spitz; Dickens in France; An Exhibition Gossip; Letters on the Fine Arts; The Partie Fine; Arabella, or the Moral of the Partie Fine; Carlyle's French Revolution; Elizabeth Brownrigge; Contributions to *The Snob;* Contributions to *The National Standard;* "Daddy, I'm Hungry"—a Scene in an Irish Coach-maker's Family.

"A Collection of Letters of W. M. Thackeray, 1847—1855. With portraits and reproductions of letters and drawings." [With an introduction by Mrs. Brookfield.] London: Smith, Elder & Co.

Issued originally in *Scribner's Magazine*, 1887.

1891

"Reading a Poem. By William Makepeace Thackeray." London: The Chiswick Press.

Privately printed for C. P. Johnson, and issued to Members of the Sette of Odd Volumes.

1894

"Loose Sketches; An Eastern Adventure, etc." By W. M. Thackeray. With a frontispiece by John Leech. London: F. T. Sabin.

Reading a Poem; A St. Philip's Day at Paris; Shrove Tuesday in Paris, etc.

1898—1899

"The Biographical Edition of W. M. Thackeray's Complete Works. . . . Each volume includes a memoir in the form of an introduction by Mrs. Richmond Ritchie. In Thirteen Volumes." London: Smith, Elder & Co.

Vol. I.: "Vanity Fair." With twenty full-page illustrations, eleven woodcuts, a facsimile letter, and a new portrait.

Vol. II.: "Pendennis." With twenty full-page illustrations and ten woodcuts.

Vol. III.: "Yellowplush Papers," etc. With twenty-four full-page reproductions of steel plates by George Cruikshank, eleven woodcuts, and a portrait of the author by Maclise.

Vol. IV.: "The Memoirs of Barry Lyndon;" "The Fitzboodle Papers," etc. With sixteen full-page illustrations by J. E. Millais, R.A., Luke Fildes, A.R.A., and the Author, and fourteen woodcuts.

Vol. V.: "Sketch-Books:"—"The Paris Sketch-Book," "The Irish Sketch-Book," "Notes of a Journey from Cornhill to Grand Cairo," etc. With sixteen full-page illustrations, thirty-nine woodcuts, and a portrait of the author by Maclise.

Vol. VI.: "Contributions to *Punch*," etc. With twenty full-page illustrations, twenty-six woodcuts, and an engraving of the author from a portrait by Samuel Lawrence.

Vol. VII.: "The History of Henry Esmond;" and "the Lectures." With twenty full-page illustrations by George du Maurier, F. Barnard, and Frank Dicksee, R.A., and twelve woodcuts.

Vol. VIII.: "The Newcomes." With twenty full-page illustrations and eleven woodcuts by Richard Doyle.

Vol. IX.: "Christmas Books," etc. With ninety-seven full-page illustrations, one hundred and twenty-two woodcuts, and a facsimile letter.

Vol. X.: "The Virginians." With twenty full-page illustrations, six woodcuts, and a photogravure of a new portrait.

Vol. XI.: "The Adventures of Philip;" and "A Shabby Genteel Story." With twenty-four full-page illustrations by Frederick Walker, A.R.A., and W. M. Thackeray, six woodcuts, a facsimile of MS., and two facsimile letters.

Vol. XII.: "Lovel the Widower;" "Roundabout Papers;" "Denis Duval," etc. With twenty full-page and eleven text illustrations by Frederick Walker, A.R. A., Charles Keene, and the Author, and two pages of MS. in facsimile.

Vol. XIII.: "Ballads and Miscellanies." With thirty-five full-page illustrations by the author, George Cruikshank and John Leech, thirty-five woodcuts, three portraits of Thackeray's ancestors, and a photogravure from a drawing by Chinnery of Thackeray at the age of three with his father and mother. Also a "Life of Thackeray," by Leslie Stephen (reprinted from the *Dictionary of National Biography*), and a Bibliography.

PART II

CONTRIBUTIONS TO PERIODICALS, ETC.

Ainsworth's Magazine

1842. "Sultan Stork; being the One Thousand and Second Night. By Major G. O'G. Gahagan, H.E.I.C.S. Part the First: The Magic Powder. Part the Second: The Enchanted Princess." With two illustrations by George Cruikshank. (Vol. i., pp. 33–38, 233–37.)

Reprinted in "Sultan Stork."

"An Exhibition Gossip. By Michael Angelo Titmarsh." (Vol. i., pp. 319–22.)

Reprinted in "Sultan Stork."

Anti-Corn Law Circular

1839. "Poles Offering Corn." A drawing. (No. 8, July 23). "The Choice of a Loaf." A drawing. (No. 18, December 10.)

Autographic Mirror

1864. "The History of Dionysius Diddler." Nine drawings. (Vol. i., pp. 6, 15, 28, 39, 40, 60, 68, 76.)

Reprinted in Collected Works, vol. xxvi. (1886.)

"The Gamblers." (Vol. i., p. 27.)

1865. A Sketch of Thackeray by Himself and two letters—facsimile. (Vol. ii., p. 139.)

"The Three Sailors." Facsimile of original MS. (Vol. ii., p. 156.)

Printed in *Sand and Canvas*, 1849; as "Little Billie" in Collected Works.

1865. Illustrations to King Glumpus: King Glumpus, Lady Popkins, Lord Lollypop. (Vol. ii., p. 212.)

"A German Student." A drawing. (Vol. ii., p. 228.)

Bentley's Miscellany

1837. "The Professor. By Goliah Gahagan." (Vol. ii., pp. 277–88.)
Reprinted in "Comic Tales and Sketches," vol. ii., and Collected Works. vol. xxv. (1885.)

The Britannia

1841. "Loose Sketches. By Mr. Michael Angelo Titmarsh." "Reading a Poem." In Two Parts. (*May* 1.)
Privately reprinted by Mr. C. P. Johnson, 1891.

British and Foreign Review

1839. "Lord Brougham's Speeches." (Vol. viii., pp. 490–539.)

The Constitutional

"Paris Correspondence." Mr. C. J. Johnson gives the following list of Thackeray's letters:—

1836. September 27, 29; October 5, 8, 11, 13, 14, 18, 21, 22, 29, 31; November 5, 9, 14, 16, 18, 22, 26; December 1, 8, 14, 19, 20, 22, 26, 31.

1837. January 2, 4, 6, 7, 10, 13, 14, 18, 19, 21, 24, 28, 31; February 3, 8, 18.

The Cornhill Magazine

1860. "A Letter from the Editor to a friend and contributor." Dated November 1, 1859, and signed W. M. Thackeray.

*"Roundabout Papers, No. 1. On a Lazy Little Boy." (Vol. i., pp. 124–28.)

"Nil Nisi Bonum." (Vol. i., pp. 129–34.)
Reprinted in Collected Works.

*"Roundabout Papers, No. 2. On Two Children in Black." (Vol. i., pp. 380–4.)

"The Last Sketch." (Vol. i., pp. 485–87.)
Reprinted in Collected Works.

*"Roundabout Papers, No. 3. On Ribbons." (Vol. i., pp. 631–40.)

*"Roundabout Papers, No. 4. On Some Late Great Victories." (Vol. i., pp. 755–60.)

*Reprinted in book-form in 1863—"Roundabout Papers," and subsequently reprinted in Collected Works.

THE CORNHILL MAGAZINE (*continued*)

"Lovel the Widower." (Vol. i., pp. 44–60, 233–47, 330–45, 385–402, 583–97, 652–68.)
Reprinted in book-form, 1861.

"Vanitas Vanitatum. By W. M. Thackeray." (Vol. ii., pp. 59, 60.)
Reprinted in Collected Works.

*"Roundabout Papers, No. 5. Thorns in the Cushion." (Vol. ii., pp. 122–8.)

*"Roundabout Papers, No. 6. On Screens in Dining-rooms." (Vol. ii., pp. 252–6.)

*"Roundabout Papers, No. 7. Tunbridge Toys." (Vol. ii., pp. 380–84.)

"The Four Georges: Sketches of Manners, Morals, Court and Town Life." Illustrated. (Vol. ii., pp. 1–20, 175–91, 257–77, 385–406.)
Reprinted in book-form, 1861.

*"Roundabout Papers, No. 8. De Juventute." (Vol. ii., pp. 501–12.)

*"A Roundabout Journey: Notes of a Week's Holiday." (Vol. ii., pp. 623–40.)

*"Roundabout Papers, No. 9. On a Joke I once heard from the late Thomas Hood." (Vol. ii., pp. 752–60.)

1861. *"Roundabout Papers, No. 10. Roundabout the Christmas Tree." (Vol. iii., pp. 250–56.)

*"Roundabout Papers, No. 11. On a Chalk Mark on the Door." (Vol. iii., pp. 504–12.)

*"Roundabout Papers, No. 12. On Being Found Out.' (Vol. iii., pp. 636–40.)

*"Roundabout Papers, No. 13. On a Hundred Years Hence." (Vol. iii., pp. 755–60.)

*"Roundabout Papers, No. 14. Small Beer Chronicle." (Vol. iv., pp. 122–8.)

*Reprinted in book-form in 1863—"Roundabout Papers;" and subsequently reprinted in Collected Works.

THE CORNHILL MAGAZINE (*continued.*)

*"Roundabout Papers, No. 15. Ogres." (Vol. iv., pp. 251–6.)

*"Roundabout Papers, No. 16. On Two Roundabout Papers which I Intended to write." (Vol. iv., 377–84.)

*"Roundabout Papers, No. 17. A Mississippi Bible." (Vol. iv., 754–60.)

1862. *"Roundabout Papers, No. 18. On Lett's Diary." (Vol. v., pp. 122–8.)

*"Roundabout Papers, No. 19. On Half a Loaf. A Letter to Messrs. Broadway, Battery & Co., of New York, Bankers." (Vol. v., pp. 250–56.)

A Valedictory Address of the Editor to Contributors and Correspondents, dated March 18.

*"Roundabout Papers, Nos. 20–22. The Notch on the Axe. A Story *à la mode.* In Three Parts." (Vol. v., pp. 508–12, 634–40, 754–60.)

"The Adventures of Philip on his way through the World; shewing who Robbed him, who Helped him, and who Passed him by." [With illustrations by the Author and by Frederick Walker.] (Vol. iii., pp. 1–24, 166–89, 270–93, 385–408, 556–83, 641–65; vol. iv., pp. 1–24, 129–52, 257–80, 385–408, 513–36, 641–64; vol. v., pp. 1–24, 129–52, 257–80, 385–408, 513–36, 641–64; vol. vi., pp. 120–44, 217–40.)

Reprinted in book-form, 1862.

*"Roundabout Papers, No. 23. De Finibus." (Vol. vi., pp. 282–8.)

*"Roundabout Papers, No. 24. On a Peal of Bells." (Vol. vi., pp. 425–32.)

*"Roundabout Papers, No. 25. On a Pear Tree." (Vol. vi., pp. 715–20.)

*"Roundabout Papers, No. 26. Dessein's. (Vol. vi., pp. 771–9.)

1863. *"Roundabout Papers, No. 27. On Some Carp at Sans Souci." (Vol. vii., pp. 126–31.)

*Reprinted in book-form in 1863—"Roundabout Papers"; and subsequently reprinted in Collected Works.

THE CORNHILL MAGAZINE (*continued*).

*"Roundabout Papers, No. 28. Autour de mon Chapeau." (Vol. vii., pp. 260–67.)

*"On Alexandrines. A Letter to some Country Cousins." (Vol. vii., pp. 546–52.)

*"On a Medal of George the Fourth." (Vol. viii., pp. 250–56.)

*"Strange to say, on Club Paper." (Vol. viii., pp. 636–40.)

1864. "Denis Duval. By W. M. Thackeray." With Illustrations. (Vol. ix., pp. 257–91, 385–409, 513–36, 641–65.)

Reprinted in book-form, 1867.

1866. "The Second Funeral of Napoleon." [Reprinted, with a prefatory note.] (Vol. xiii., pp. 48–80.)

Reprinted in Collected Works.

The Corsair

1839. "Off to France" (*August* 24).

Reprinted as "An Invasion of France" in "The Paris Sketch-Book" (1840).

"Madame Sands and Spiridion" (*September* 14, 21).

Reprinted as "Madame Sands and the New Apocalypse" in "The Paris Sketch-Book" (1840).

1839. "Captain Rook and Mr. Pigeon" (*September* 28).

Reprinted in "Heads of the People" (1840).

1840. "A Week of Fêtes (*October* 5).

Reprinted as "The Fêtes of July" in *Fraser's Magazine*, and subsequently in "The Paris Sketch-Book," 1840.

"A French Jack Shepherd" (*October* 19).

Reprinted as "Cartouche" in *Fraser's Magazine*, vol. xx., and subsequently in "The Paris Sketch-Book," 1840.

"More Aspects of Paris Life" (*October* 26, *December* 28).

"A Ramble in the Picture-Galleries" (*January* 18).

Reprinted as "A Letter on the French School of Painting" in *Fraser's Magazine*, vol. xx., and subsequently in "The Paris Sketch-Book" (1840).

[*All these articles, with the exception of "Captain Rook and Mr. Pigeon," were reprinted in "The Students' Quarter,"* 1880 (?).]

*Reprinted in book-form in 1863—"Roundabout Papers"; and subsequently reprinted in Collected Works.

The Edinburgh Review

1855. "A Notice of N. P. Willis's 'Dashes at Life.'" (Vol. lxxxii., pp. 470–80.)

Fraser's Magazine

1832. (?)"Elizabeth Brownrigge." (Vol. 6, pp. 67–88, 131–48.)

Reprinted in "Sultan Stork," 1887.

1834. "The Frazer Papers for May. The King of Brentford. (*Il était un Roi d' Yvetot*, Beranger.)" (Vol. 9, pp. 617–18.)

Reprinted in "The Early Writings of W. M. Thackeray" (1888).

Rewritten for George Cruikshank's *Omnibus*, No. 8 (1841).

1837. "Fashnable Fax and Polite Annygoats. By Charles Yellowplush, Esq." (Vol. 16, pp. 644–49.)

Reprinted in Collected Works, vol. xxv. (1885).

"A Word on the Annuals." (Vol. 16, pp. 757–63.)

1838. "On a Batch of Novels for Christmas, 1837." (Vol. 17, pp. 79–103.)

"Half-a-crown's worth of Cheap Knowledge." (Vol. 17, pp. 279–90.)

"Strictures on Pictures. A Letter from Michael Angelo Titmarsh, Esq." With an illustration. (Vol. 17, pp. 758–64.)

Reprinted in Collected Works, vol. xxv. (1885).

"Passages from the Diary of the late Dolly Duster, with Elucidations, Notes, etc., by various Editors" (*October, November*).

"Yellowplush Papers":—

"Miss Shum's Husband." (Vol. 17, pp. 39—49.)

"Dimond cut Dimond." (Vol. 17, 243–50.)

"Skimmings from the Diary of George IV." (Vol. 17, pp. 353–59.)

"Foring Parts." (Vol. 17, 404–8).

"Mr. Deuceace at Paris." (Vol. 17, pp. 616–27, 734–41.)

FRASER'S MAGAZINE (*continued*)

"The End of Mr. Deuceace's History." (Vol. 18, pp. 57–71.)

"Mr. Yellowplush's Ajeu." (Vol. 18, pp. 195–200.)

Reprinted in "Comic Tales and Sketches," vol. i., 1841, "Miscellanies," vol. i., 1856, and subsequently in Collected Works.

1839. (?)"Paris Pastimes for the Month of May." (Vol. 19, 710–16.)

"A Second Lecture on the Fine Arts. By Michael Angelo Titmarsh, Esq." (Vol. 19, pp. 743–50.)

Reprinted in Collected Works, vol. xxv. (1885.)

(?)"Paris Revels of the Twelfth of May." (Vol. 20, pp. 212–23.)

"The Fêtes of July." (Vol. 20, pp. 348–59.)

Reprinted in "The Paris Sketch-Book."

1839. "The French Plutarch: No. I., Cartouche; No. II., Poinsinet." (Vol. 20, pp. 447–59.)

Reprinted in "The Paris Sketch-Book."

"On the French School of Painting. A Letter from Michael Angelo Titmarsh to Mr. McGilp of London." (Vol. 20, pp. 679–88.)

Reprinted in "The Paris Sketch-Book."

"The Great Cossack Epic of Demetrius Rigmarolovicz. Translated by a Lady." (Vol. 20, pp. 715-27.)

Reprinted as "St. Sophia of Kioff" in "Miscellanies," vol. i., (1855) and Collected Works.

1839 *to* 1840. "Catherine. A Story. By Ikey Solomons, Esq., Junr." With Four Illustrations. (Vol. 19, pp. 604–17, 694–709; vol. 20, pp. 98–112, 224–32, 531–48.)

Reprinted in Collected Works.

1840. "Epistles to the Literati, No. XIII. Ch——s Y——ll——w Pl——sh, Esq., to Sir Edward Bulwer Lytton, Bart. John Thomas Smith, Esq., to C——s Y——h, Esq." (Vol. 21, pp. 71—80.)

Reprinted in "Miscellanies," vol. ii. (1856), and in Collected Works.

FRASER'S MAGAZINE (*continued*)

"A Pictorial Rhapsody. By M. A. Titmarsh. With an introductory Letter to Mr. Yorke." (Vol. 21, pp. 720–32.)

Reprinted in Collected Works, vol. xxv. (1885).

"A Picture Rhapsody Concluded, and followed by a remarkable statement of facts by Mrs. Barbara." (Vol. 22, pp. 112–26.)

Reprinted in Collected Works, vol. xxv. (1885).

"Going to see a man hanged. By W. M. T." (Vol. 22, pp. 150–58.)

Reprinted in "Miscellanies," vol. ii. (1856), and in Collected Works.

"A Shabby-Genteel Story." (Vol. 21, pp. 677–89; vol. 22, pp. 90–101, 226–37, 399–414.)

Reprinted in "Miscellanies," vol. iv. (1857), and in Collected Works.

1841. "Memorials of Gormandising. In a Letter to Oliver Yorke. By M. A. Titmarsh." (Vol. 23, pp. 710–25.)

Reprinted in "Early and Late Papers," 1867, and in Collected Works, vol. xxv. (1885).

"On Men and Pictures. Apropos of a Walk in the Louvre." (Vol. 24, pp. 98–111.)

Reprinted in "Early and Late Papers," 1867, and in Collected Works, vol. xxv. (1885).

"Men and Coats." (Vol. 24, pp. 208–17.)

Reprinted in "Early and Late Papers," 1867, and in Collected Works, vol. xxv. (1885).

"The History of Samuel Titmarsh and the Great Hoggarty Diamond. Edited and Illustrated by Sam's Cousin, Michael Angelo." (Vol. 24, pp. 324–43, 389–99, 594–611, 717–34.)

Reprinted in book-form, 1849, in "Miscellanies," vol. iv. (1857), and in Collected Works.

1842. "Dickens in France. With two Illustrations." (Vol. 25, pp. 342–52.)

Reprinted in "Early and Late Papers," 1867, and in "Sultan Stork," 1887.

"Fitz-Boodle's Confessions." (Vol. 25, pp. 707–21.)

FRASER'S MAGAZINE (*continued*)

"Professions. By George Fitz-Boodle. Being Appeals to the Unemployed Younger Sons of the Nobility." (Vol. 26, pp. 43–60.)

1842 *to* 1843. "Fitz-Boodle's Confessions":—

"Miss Löwe." (Vol. 26, pp. 395–405.)

"Dorothea." (Vol. 27, 76–84.)

"Ottelia." (Vol. 27, 214–24.)

"Men's Wives. I.—Mr. and Mrs. Frank Berry." (Vol. 27, pp. 349–61.)

"Men's Wives. II.—The Ravenswing." (Vol. 27, pp. 465–75, 597–608, 723–33; Vol. 28, pp. 188–205, 321–37.)

Men's Wives. III.—Denis Haggarty's Wife." (Vol. 28, pp. 494–504.)

"Men's Wives. IV.—The ——'s Wife." (Vol. 28, pp. 581–92.)

The "Confessions" and "Professions" (the third "Profession" omitted), "Mr. and Mrs. Frank Berry," and "The Ravenswing," were reprinted in "Miscellanies," vol. iv. (1857). These and "Denis Haggarty's Wife" were reprinted in the Collected Works, and "Miss Löwe" was included in the supplementary vol. xxv. (1885). "The ——'s Wife" has never been reprinted.

1843. "Jerome Paturot. With Consideration on Novels in General. In a Letter from M. A. Titmarsh." (Vol. 28, pp. 349–62.)

Reprinted in Collected Works, vol. xxv. (1885).

"Bluebeard's Ghost. By M. A. Titmarsh." (Vol. 28, pp. 413–25.)

Reprinted in Collected Works, vol. xxv. (1885).

"Grant in Paris. By Fitz-Boodle." (Vol. 28, pp. 702–12.)

Reprinted in Collected Works, vol. xxv. (1885).

1844. "A Box of Novels. By M. A. T." (Vol. 29, pp. 153–69.)

Reprinted in Collected Works, vol. xxv. (1885).

FRASER'S MAGAZINE (*continued*)

"Titmarsh's Carmen Lilliense." (Vol. 29, pp. 361–3.)

Reprinted in "Miscellanies," vol. i. (1855), and in Collected Works.

"May Gambols, or Titmarsh in the Picture Galleries." (Vol. 29, pp. 700–16.)

Reprinted in Collected Works, vol. xxv. (1885).

"The Luck of Barry Lyndon. A Romance of the Last Century. By Fitz-Boodle." (Vol. 29, pp. 35–51, 187–202, 318–30, 391–410, 548–63, 723–38; vol. 30, pp. 93–108, 227–42, 353–64, 584–97, 666–83.)

Reprinted in "Miscellanies," vol. iii. (1856), and in Collected Works.

1844 *to* 1845. "Little Travels and Roadside Sketches. By Titmarsh. From Richmond in Surrey to Brussels in Belgium. Ghent, Bruges, Waterloo." (Vol. 29, pp. 517–28; vol. 30, pp. 465–71; vol. 31, pp. 94–96.)

Reprinted in "Early and Late Papers" (1867), and in Collected Works.

1845. "Picture Gossip. In a Letter from Michael Angelo Titmarsh." (Vol. 31, pp. 713–24.)

Reprinted in "Early and Late Papers" (1867), and in Collected Works, vol. xxv. (1885).

"Barmecide Banquets with Joseph Brejion and Anne Miller. George Savage Fitz-Boodle, Esq., to the Rev. Lionel Gaster." (Vol. 32, pp. 584–93.)

Reprinted in Collected Works, vol. xxv. (1885).

"About a Christmas Book. In a letter from M. A. T. to Oliver Yorke." (Vol. 32, pp. 744–48.)

1846. "Ronsard to His Mistress." (Vol. 33, p. 120.)

Reprinted in "Miscellanies," vol. i. (1855), and in Collected Works.

"A Brother of the Press on the History of a Literary Man, Laman Blanchard, and the chances of the Literary Profession. In a Letter to the Rev. Francis Sylvester at Rome from Michael Angelo Titmarsh." (Vol. 33, pp. 332–42.)

Reprinted in Collected Works, vol. xxv. (1885).

"On Some Illustrated Children's Books. By Michael Angelo Titmarsh." (Vol. 33, pp. 495–502.)

FRASER'S MAGAZINE (*continued*)

"Proposals for a Continuation of Ivanhoe. In a Letter to M. Alexandre Dumas from M. Michael Angelo Titmarsh." (Vol. 34, pp. 237–45, 359–67.)

Rewritten and republished as "Rebecca and Rowena."

1847. "A Grumble about the Christmas Books. By Michael Angelo Titmarsh." (Vol. 35, pp. 111–26.)

1853. "Mr. Thackeray in the United States. John Small to the Editor of *Fraser's Magazine*." (Vol. 47, pp. 100–3.)

Reprinted in Collected Works, vol. xxv. (1885).

George Cruikshank's Omnibus

1841. "Little Spitz. A Lenten Anecdote from the German of Professor Spass. By Michael Angelo Titmarsh." (No. 6, pp. 167–72.)

Reprinted in "Sultan Stork," 1887.

1841. "The King of Brentford's Testament. By Michael Angelo Titmarsh." (No. 8, pp. 244–6.)

Reprinted in "Miscellanies," vol. i. (1855), and in Collected Works.

George Cruikshank's Table Book

1845. "A Legend of the Rhine. By Michael Angelo Titmarsh. With fourteen illustrations by George Cruikshank." (Pages 119, 144, 167, 193, 224, 241, 267.)

Reprinted in "Miscellanies," vol. iii. (1856), and in Collected Works.

The Gownsman

1829. "I'd be a Tadpole." Signed "Θ." (*November 12.*)

Reprinted in "The Early Writings of W. M. Thackeray," 1888.

"From Anacreon." Signed "Θ." (*December 3.*)

Reprinted in "The Early Writings of W. M. Thackeray" (1888).

The Idler

1856. "The Idler. By Essel." (No. 3, pp. 172–3.)

Reprinted in Collected Works, vol. xxv.

The Keepsake

1840. "An Interesting Event. By Mr. Titmarsh." (Pages 207–15.)

1851. "Voltigeur." (Pages 238–50.)

1853. "The Pen and the Album. By W. M. Thackeray." (Pages 48–50.)

Reprinted in Miscellanies," vol. i. (1855), and in Collected Works.

1854. "Lucy's Birthday." (Page 18.)

Reprinted in "Miscellanies," vol. i. (1855), and in Collected Works.

The Morning Chronicle

1844. "Review of A New Spirit of the Age. By R. H. Horne" (*April* 2).

Reprinted in Collected Works, vol. xxv. (1885).

1850. "The Dignity of Literature. To the Editor" (*January* 12).

Reprinted in Collected Works, vol. xxv. (1885).

"Capers and Anchovies. To the Editor" (*April* 12).

The Nation

1843. "Daddy, I'm Hungry—A Scene in a Coachmaker's Family. With an illustration" (*May* 13).

Reprinted in Sir Charles Gavan Duffy's "Young Ireland," and in "Sultan Stork" (1887).

The National Standard

1833. "Louis Philippe." With an illustration (*May* 4).

Reprinted in "Sultan Stork" (1887).

"Mr. Braham, 'Sonnet by W. Wordsworth.'" With an illustration (*May* 11).

Reprinted in "Sultan Stork" (1887).

"N.M. Rothschild, Esq." With an illustration (*May* 18).

Reprinted in "Sultan Stork" (1887).

"A. Bunn." With an illustration (*June* 1).

Reprinted in "Sultan Stork" (1887).

THE NATIONAL STANDARD (*continued*)

"Love in Fetters; a Tottenham Court Road Ditty." With an illustration (*June* 8).
Reprinted in "Sultan Stork" (1887).

"Foreign Correspondence." With four illustrations (*June* 29, *July* 6, 13, 20).
Reprinted in "Sultan Stork" (1887).

"The Devil's Wager." With an illustration (*August* 10, 24).
Reprinted in "The Paris Sketch-Book."

"Original Papers: A Tale of Wonder" (*October* 12).
Reprinted in "The Early Writings of W. M. Thackeray" (1888).

(?)"Original Papers: the History of Crakatuk" (*November* 30, *December* 7).

1834. "Father Gahagan's Exhortation" (*January* 18).

"Review of Etude sur Mirabeau. Par Victor Hugo." Signed "Θ." (*February* 1).

The New Monthly Magazine

1838. "The Story of Mary Ancel." (Vol. 54, pp. 185-97).
Reprinted in "The Paris Sketch-Book."

1838 *to* 1839. "Some Passages in the Life of Major Gahagan." (Vol. 52, pp. 174–82; vol. 54, pp. 543–52; vol. 55, pp. 266–81.)
Reprinted in "Comic Tales and Sketches," vol. ii., and in Collected Works.

1840. "The Bedford Row Conspiracy." (Vol. 58, pp. 99–111, 416–25, 547–57.)
Reprinted in "Miscellanies," vol. iii. (1856), and in Collected Works.

1844. "The Partie Fine. By Launcelot Wagstaff, Esq." (Vol. 71, pp. 22–28.)
Reprinted in "Sultan Stork" (1887).

"Arabella; or the Moral of 'The Partie Fine.' By Titmarsh." (Vol. 71, pp. 169–72.)
Reprinted in "Sultan Stork" (1887).

THE NEW MONTHLY MAGAZINE (*continued*)

"Greenwich—Whitebait. By Mr. Wagstaff." (Vol. 71, pp. 416–21.)

Reprinted in Collected Works, vol. xxv. (1885).

1845. "The Chest of Cigars. By Launcelot Wagstaff, Esq." (Vol. 74, pp. 381–5.)

"Bob Robinson's First Love. By Launcelot Wagstaff, Esq." (Vol. 74, pp. 519–25.)

The Pictorial Times

1843. "Letters on the Fine Arts":—

No. I.—"The Art Unions" (*March* 18).

No. II.—"The Objections against Art Unions" (*April* 1).

No. III.—"The Objections against Art Unions" (*April* 8).

No. IV.—"The Water-Colours Exhibition" (*May* 6).

No. V.—"The Royal Academy" (*May* 13).

No. VI.—"The Royal Academy." Second Notice (*May* 27).

Reprinted in "Sultan Stork" (1887).

Punch

1842. "The Legend of Jawbrahim-Heraudu." With four illustrations. (Vol. ii., pp. 254-6.)

"Miss Tickletoby's Lectures on English History." With twenty-two illustrations. (Vol. iii., pp. 8–9, 12–13, 28–30, 58–9, 70–2, 84–5, 91–2, 116–7, 121–2, 131–3, 142–3.)

Reprinted in Collected Works, vol. xxvi. (1886).

"Mr. Spec's Remonstrance." With two illustrations. (Vol. iv., pp. 69–70.)

Reprinted in Collected Works, vol. xxvi. (1886).

"A Turkish Letter concerning the Divertissement 'Les Houris.'" With two illustrations. (Vol. iv., p. 199.)

"Second Turkish Letter." With one illustration. (Vol. iv., p. 209.)

PUNCH (*continued*)

1843. "Singular Letter from the Regent of Spain." (Vol. v., pp. 267–8.)
Reprinted in Collected Works, vol. xxvi. (1886).

"Sherry Perhaps." "Rum, I hope." "Tracts, by Jove." (Vol. v., p. 268.)

"The Flying Duke." With two illustrations. (Vol. v., p. 207.)
Reprinted in Collected Works, vol. xxvi. (1886).

1844. "The History of the Next French Revolution. From a forthcoming History of Europe." With fourteen illustrations. (Vol. vi., pp. 90–1, 98–9, 113–4, 117, 127–8, 137–9, 147–8, 157, 167–8.)
Reprinted in Collected Works.

"Wanderings of Our Fat Contributor." With three illustrations. (Vol. vii., pp. 61–2.)
Reprinted in Collected Works, vol. xxvi. (1886).

"Travelling Notes. By Our Fat Contributor." With thirteen illustrations. (Vol. vii., pp. 66–7, 83–4, 237, 256–7, 265–6.)
Reprinted in Collected Works.

1845. "Punch in the East. From Our Fat Contributor." With ten illustrations. (Vol. viii., pp. 31–2, 35–6, 45, 61, 75.)
Reprinted in Collected Works, vol. xxvi. (1886).

A drawing accompanying Gilbert à Beckett's "Debate on the Navy." (Vol. viii., p. 266.)

"The Ascot Cup Day." A sketch. (Vol. ix., p. 3.)

A drawing accompanying Gilbert à Beckett's "The Footman." (Vol. ix., p. 40.)

A drawing accompanying the article "The Gomersal Museum." (Vol. ix., p. 41.)

A drawing accompanying Percival Leigh's "The Lowly Bard to his Lady Love." (Vol. ix., p. 56.)

"A Lucky Speculator—Jeames of Buckley Square. A Helegey." (Vol. ix., p. 59.)
Reprinted in "Miscellanies," vol. ii. (1856), and in Collected Works.

PUNCH (*continued*)

"The Pimlico Pavilion. By the Mulligan (of Kilballymulligan)." (Vol. ix., p. 66.)

Reprinted in "Miscellanies," vol. i. (1855), and in Collected Works.

"A Letter from Jeames of Buckley Square." (Vol. ix., p. 76.)

Reprinted in "Miscellanies," vol. ii. (1856), and in Collected Works.

"Meditations on Solitude. By Our Stout Commissioner." With an illustration. (Vol. ix., p. 123.)

"Beulah Spa. By *Punch's* Commissioner." With two illustrations. (Vol. ix., p. 137–8.)

"The Georges." (Vol. ix., p. 159.)

Reprinted in Collected Works, vol. xxvi. (1886).

"Brighton. By *Punch's* Commissioner." With three illustrations. (Vol. ix., p. 158.)

Reprinted in Collected Works, vol. xxvi. (1886).

"A Brighton Night Entertainment. By *Punch's* Commissioner." With four illustrations. (Vol. ix., p. 168.)

Reprinted in Collected Works, vol. xxvi. (1886).

"Meditations over Brighton. By *Punch's* Commissioner." With an illustration. (Vol. ix., p. 187.)

Reprinted in Collected Works, vol. xxvi. (1886).

"A Doe in the City. By Frederick Haltamont de Montmorency." With an illustration. (Vol. ix., p. 191.)

Reprinted in Collected Works.

"Jeames on Time Bargings." With an illustration. (Vol. ix., p. 195.)

Reprinted in Collected Works.

1845 *to* 1846. "Jeames's Diary." With twenty illustrations. (Vol. ix., pp. 207–8, 210, 227, 233, 242–3, 251; vol. x., 10–11, 13, 30–1, 35, 54–5, 72–3.)

Reprinted in "Miscellanies," vol. ii. (1856), and in Collected Works.

"The Snobs of England. By one of themselves." With illustrations.

"Prefatory Remarks." (Vol. x., p. 101. With two illustrations.)

PUNCH (*continued*)

Chap.

I.—"The Snob Socially Considered." (Vol. x., pp. 111–2. With an illustration.)

II.—"The Snob Royal." (Vol. x., p. 115. With an illustration.)

III.—"The Influence of the Aristocracy on Snobs." Vol. x., pp. 125–6. With two illustrations.)

IV.—"The Court Circular, and its influence on Snobs." (Vol. x., pp. 137–8. With two illustrations.)

V.—"What Snobs Admire." (Vol. x., p. 147. With two illustrations.)

VI.—VII.—"On Some Respectable Snobs." (Vol. x., pp. 157–8, 167. With two illustrations.)

VIII.—"Great City Snobs." (Vol. x., pp. 177–8. With two illustrations.)

IX.—"On Some Military Snobs." (Vol. x., p. 197. With an illustration.)

X.—"Military Snobs." (Vol. x., p. 207. With two illustrations.)

XI.—"On Clerical Snobs." (Vol. x., p. 217. With an illustration.)

XII.—"On Clerical Snobs and Snobbishness." (Vol. x., pp. 227–8. With an illustration.)

XIII.—"On Clerical Snobs." (Vol. x., pp. 238–9. With two illustrations.)

XIV.—XV.—"On University Snobs." (Vol. x., pp. 250–1, 261. With three illustrations.)

XVI.—XVII.—"On Literary Snobs." (Vol. x., pp. 271, 281. With three illustrations.)

XVIII.—"On Some Political Snobs." (Vol. xi., p. 4.)

XIX.—"On Whig Snobs." (Vol. xi., p. 19. With two illustrations.)

XX.—"On Conservative or Country Party Snobs." (Vol. xi., p. 23.)

XXI.—"Are there any Whig Snobs?" (Vol. xi., p. 39. With an illustration.)

XXII.—"On the Snob Civilian." (Vol. xi., p. 43.)

XXIII.—"On Radical Snobs." (Vol. xi., p. 59. With an illustration.)

XXIV.—"A Little More about Irish Snobs." (Vol. xi., p. 63.)

XXV.—"Party-Giving Snobs." (Vol. xi., pp. 81–2. With an illustration.)

PUNCH (*continued*)

Chap.

XXVI.—"Dining-Out Snobs." (Vol. xi., pp. 91–2. With an illustration.)

XXVII.—"Dinner-Going Snobs further considered." (Vol. xi., pp. 95–6. With two illustrations.)

XXVIII.—"Some Continental Snobs." (Vol. xi., pp. 105–6. With an illustration.)

XXIX.—"Continental Snobbery Continued." (Vol. xi., p. 115. With three illustrations.)

XXX.—"English Snobs on the Continent." (Vol. xi., p. 125. With an illustration.)

XXXI.—"On Some Country Snobs." (Vol. xi., p. 141. With an illustration.

XXXII.—"A Visit to Some Country Snobs." (Vol. xi., pp. 148–9. With an illustration.)

XXXIII.—"On Some Country Snobs." (Vol. xi., pp. 157–8. With three illustrations.)

XXXIV.—"A Visit to Some Country Snobs." (Vol. xi., p. 167. With an illustration.)

XXXV.—"On Some Country Snobs." (Vol. xi., pp. 177–8. With two illustrations.)

XXXVI.—"A Visit to Some Country Snobs." (Vol. xi., p. 187. With an illustration.)

XXXVII.—"On Some Country Snobs." (Vol. xi., pp. 197–8. With two illustrations.)

XXXVIII.—"A Visit to some Country Snobs." (Vol. xi., p. 214. With an illustration.)

XXXIX.—"Snobbium Gatherum." (Vol. xi., pp. 225–6. With an illustration.)

XL.—XLIII.—"Snobs and Marriage." (Vol. xi., pp. 229, 247–8, 251–2, 261–2. With four illustrations.)

XLIV.—LI.—"Club Snobs." (Vol. xii., pp. 7, 11–12, 23–4, 34–5, 43–4, 53, 73, 81–2. With fifteen illustrations.)

"Chapter the Last." (Vol. xii., pp. 85–6. With an illustration.)

Reprinted in book-form, 1846; in "Miscellanies," vol. i. (1855); and in Collected Works.

1846. "Titmarsh *v.* Tait. A Letter to Mr. Punch." With an illustration. (Vol. x., p. 124.)

Reprinted in Collected Works, vol. xxvi. (1886).

PUNCH (*continued*)

"The Royal Academy." With six illustrations. (Vol. x., p. 214.)
Reprinted in Collected Works, vol. xxvi. (1886).

"Jeames on the Gauge Question." With an illustration. (Vol. x., p. 223.)
Reprinted in Collected Works.

"Mr. Jeames Again." With an illustration. (Vol. x., p. 267.)
Reprinted in Collected Works.

"A Plea for Plush." Signed "Modest Merit." With an illustration. (Vol. xi., p. 46.)
Reprinted in Collected Works, vol. xxvi. (1886).

"One Who can minister to a mind diseased?" A drawing. (Vol. xi., p. 50.)
Reprinted in Collected Works, vol. xxvi. (1886).

"A Tea-Table Tragedy." A drawing. (Vol. xi., p. 63.)
Reprinted in Collected Works, vol. xxvi. (1886).

"The Heavies; Captain Ragg and Cornet Famish." A drawing. (Vol. xi., p. 72.)

"Half an hour before dinner." A drawing. (Vol. xi., p. 92.)
Reprinted in Collected Works, vol. xxvi.

"The Heavies; Captain Ragg dictating to Cornet Famish." A drawing. (Vol. xi., p. 103.)
Reprinted in Collected Works, vol. xxvi. (1886).

"What's come to the Clubs?" Signed "Alured Mogyns de Mogyns." With three illustrations. (Vol. xi., p. 123.)

"A Scene in St. James's Park." A drawing. (Vol. xi., p. 180.)
Reprinted in Collected Works, vol. xxvi. (1886).

1847. "An Eastern Adventure of the Fat Contributor." With an illustration. *Punch's Pocketbook for* 1847. Pages 148–56.)
Reprinted in Collected Works.

PUNCH (*continued*)

"The Mahogany Tree." (Vol. xii., p. 13.)

Reprinted in "Miscellanies," vol. i. (1855), and in Collected Works.

*"Horrid Tragedy in Private Life." A drawing. (Vol. xii., p. 59.)

"Mr. Jeames's Sentiments on the Cambridge Election." (Vol. xii., p. 102.)

"Love Songs Made Easy. 'What makes my heart to thrill and glow?' By Fitzroy Clarence." With an illustration. (Vol. xii., p. 101.)

Reprinted in "Miscellanies," vol. i. (1855), and in Collected Works.

"Literature at a Stand." A drawing. (Vol. xii., p. 113.)

Reprinted in Collected Works, vol. xxvi. (1886).

"Love Songs by the Fat Contributor. The Domestic Love Song. 'The Cane-Bottomed Chair.'" With two illustrations. (Vol. xii., p. 125.)

Reprinted in "Miscellanies," vol. i. (1855), and in Collected Works.

"Love Songs by the Fat Contributor. The Ghazuh, or Oriental Love Song. The Rocks. The Merry Bard. The Caique." With two illustrations. (Vol. xii., p. 227.)

Reprinted in "Miscellanies," vol. i. (1855), and in Collected Works.

* This was a drawing, says the *History of Punch*, representing a room in which two ladies, or a lady and a servant, are in the state of the greatest alarm. What the meaning of it all is there is nothing whatever to indicate (unless it be that something has fallen on the taller lady's dress), and on its appearance the 'Man in the Moon' offered a reward of £500 and a free pardon to any one who would publish an explanation. The reward was never claimed, and Thackeray's contribution remains one of Punch's Prize Puzzles, unsolved, and apparently unsolvable."

Mrs. Ritchie, however, has since explained it: "The room was my father's study, and where his two little girls were found by him" dressed up in various table-cloths and curtains. One was enacting a queen, and was ordering the rival sovereign off to instant execution; when he came home unexpectedly, and drew them then and there.

PUNCH (*continued*)

1847. *Punch's* Prize Novelists:—

I.—"George de Barnwell. By Sir E. L. B. L. BB. LL. BBB. LLL." With three illustrations. (Vol. xii., pp. 136–7, 146–7, 155.)

II.—"Codlingsby. By B. de Shrewsbury, Esq." With four illustrations. (Vol. xii., pp. 166, 198–9, 213–4, 223.)

III.—"Lords and Liveries. By the authoress of 'Dukes and Dejeuners,' 'Hearts and Diamonds,' Marchionesses and Millions,' etc., etc." With four illustrations. (Vol. xii., pp. 237–8, 247, 257–8.)

IV.—"Barbazure. By G. P. R. Jeames, Esq., etc." With five illustrations." (Vol. xiii., pp. 2, 12–13, 21–2.)

V.—"Phil Fogarty. A Tale of the Fighting Onety-Oneth. By Harry Rollicker." With five illustrations. (Vol. xiii., pp. 49–50, 56–7, 67–8.)

VI.—"Crinoline. By Je—mes Pl—sh, Esq." With six illustrations. (Vol. xiii., pp. 72–3, 82–3, 97–8.)

VII.—"The Stars and Stripes. By the author of 'The Last of the Mulligans,' 'Pilot,' etc." With two illustrations. (Vol. xiii., pp. 117–8, 137.)

Nos. I.—V. Reprinted in "Miscellanies," vol. ii. (1856), and in Collected Works.

"Professor Byle's Opinion of the Westminster Hall Exhibition." With six illustrations. Signed "Growley Byles." (Vol. xiii., pp. 8–9.)

Reprinted in Collected Works, vol. xxvi. (1886).

"Brighton in 1847. By the F. C." With two illustrations. (Vol. xiii., pp. 157–8.)

Reprinted in Collected Works, vol. xxvi.

"*Punch* and the Influenza." With four illustrations. (Vol. xiii., p. 238.)

Reprinted in Collected Works, vol. xxvi. (1886).

PUNCH (*continued*)

1847 to 1848. "Travels in London. By Spec."

*"Introductory." With an illustration. (Vol. xiii., p. 193.)

* "The Curate's Walk. With an illustration. (Vol. xiii., p. 201.)

* "A Walk with the Curate." With two illustrations. (Vol. xiii., pp. 211–2.)

* "A Dinner in the City." With five illustrations. (Vol. xiii., pp. 233–4, 247–8, 251.)

* "A Night's Pleasure." With ten illustrations. (Vol. xiv., pp. 11, 19, 29, 35–6, 61–2, 65–6.)

† A Club in an Uproar." With two illustrations. (Vol. xiv., pp. 95–6.)

† "A Roundabout Ride." With an illustration. (Vol. xiv., p. 119.)

1848. "Mr. Smith and Mr. Moses." With an illustration. (Vol. xiv., p. 127.)

Reprinted in Collected Works, vol. xxvi. (1886).

"The Persecution of British Footmen. By Mr. Jeames." With three illustrations. (Vol. xiv., pp. 131, 143–4.)

Reprinted in Collected Works, vol. xxvi. (1886).

"Irish Gems." With an illustration. (Vol. xiv., p. 153.)

Reprinted in Collected Works, vol. xxvi. (1886).

"The Battle of Limerick." (Vol. xiv., p. 195.)

Reprinted in "Miscellanies," vol. i. (1855), and in Collected Works.

"On the New Forward Movement. A Letter from an old friend, Mr. Snob, to Mr. Joseph Hume." With an illustration. (Vol. xiv., p. 20.)

"Mr. Snob's Remonstrance with Mr. Smith." With an illustration. (Vol. xiv., p. 217.)

Reprinted in Collected Works, vol. xxvi. (1886).

* Reprinted in "Miscellanies," vol. ii. (1856), and in Collected Works, vol. xxvi. (1886).

† Reprinted in Collected Works, vol. xxvi. (1886).

PUNCH (*continued*)

"A Little Dinner at Timmins's." With eight illustrations. (Vol. xiv., pp. 219, 220 and 223, 247, 258–9; vol. xv., pp. 5, 13, 33–4, 43.)

Reprinted in "Miscellanies," vol. iii. (1856), and in Collected Works.

"Letters to a Nobleman visiting Ireland." With two illustrations. (Vol. xv., pp. 95–6, 107.)

1848. "Authors' Miseries." (Vol. xv., pp. 105, 115, 127, 144, 154, 198, 240.)

Reprinted in Collected Works, vol. xxvi. (1886).

"Science at Cambridge." With an illustration. (Vol. xv., p. 201.)

Reprinted in Collected Works, vol. xxvi. (1886).

"A Bow Street Ballad. By a Gentleman of the Force. Pleaceman X 54." With an illustration. (Vol. xv., p. 229.)

Reprinted in Collected Works.

"Death of the Earl of Robinson. (In the manner of a popular necrographer)." With an illustration. (Vol. xv., p. 231.)

"Bow Street Ballads. No. II.—Jacob Omnium's Hoss. A New Pollice Court Chaunt." With an illustration. (Vol. xv., p. 251.)

Reprinted in "Miscellanies," vol. i. (1855), and in Collected Works.

"The Great Squattleborough Soirée." With an illustration. (Vol. xv., pp. 253–4.)

Reprinted in Collected Works, vol. xxvi. (1886).

"The Three Christmas Waits." (Vol. xv., p. 265.)

Reprinted in "Miscellanies," vol. i. (1855), and in Collected Works.

1849. "Child's Parties; and a Remonstrance concerning them." With two illustrations. (Vol. xvi., pp. 13–14, 35–6.)

Reprinted in "Miscellanies," vol. ii. (1856), and in Collected Works.

"Paris Revisited. By an Old Paris Man." With an illustration. (Vol. xvi., pp. 55–6.)

Reprinted in Collected Works, vol. xxvi. (1886).

PUNCH (*continued*)

"The Froddylent Butler." (Vol. xvi., p. 62.)

Reprinted in Collected Works, vol. xxvi. (1886).

"The Ballad of Bouillabaisse. From the Contributor at Paris." (Vol. xvi., p. 67.)

Reprinted in "Miscellanies," vol. i. (1855), and in Collected Works.

"Two or three theatres at Paris." With an illustration by Richard Doyle. (Vol. xvi., p. 75.)

Reprinted in Collected Works, vol. xxvi. (1886).

"On Some Dinners at Paris." With an illustration by Richard Doyle. (Vol. xvi., pp. 92–3.)

Reprinted in Collected Works, vol. xxvi. (1886).

"Mr. Brown's Letters to a Young Man about town":—

"First Letter." With an illustration. (Vol. xvi., p. 115.)

"On Tailoring—and Toilettes in general." With an illustration. (Vol. xvi., p. 125.)

"The Influence of Lovely Woman upon Society." With an illustration. (Vol. xvi., pp. 135–6.)

"Some more Words about the Ladies." With an illustration. (Vol. xvi., pp. 145–6.)

"On Friendship." With two illustrations. (Vol. xvi., pp. 165–6, 184–5.)

"Mr. Brown the elder takes Mr. Brown the younger to a Club." With two illustrations. (Vol. xvi., pp. 187–8, 197–8, 207–8.)

"A Word about Balls in Season." With an illustration. (Vol. xvi., pp. 229–30.)

"A Word about Dinners." With an illustration. (Vol. xvi., pp. 239–40.)

"On Some Customs of the Dinner Table." With an illustration. (Vol. xvi., 249–50.)

"Great and Little Dinners." With an illustration. (Vol. xvii., pp. 1–2.)

"On Love, Marriage, Men, and Women." With three illustrations. (Vol. xvii., 13–14, 23, 43.)

PUNCH (*continued*)

"Out of Town." With two illustrations. (Vol. xvii., pp. 53, 66, 69.)

Reprinted in "Miscellanies," vol. ii. (1856), and in Collected Works.

1849 *to* 1850. "The Proser. Essays and Discourses by Dr. Solomon Pacifico."

I.—* "On a Lady in an Opera-Box." With an illustration. (Vol. xviii., pp. 151–2.)

II.—* "On the Pleasures of being a Fogy." With an illustration. (Vol. xvii., p. 173.)

III.—* "On the Benefits of being a Fogy." With an illustration. (Vol. xvii., pp. 197–8.)

IV.—* "On a good-looking young Lady." With an illustration. (Vol. xvii., pp. 223–4.)

V.—* "On an interesting French Exile." With an illustration. (Vol. xvii., pp. 234–5.)

VI.—† "On an American Traveller." With an illustration. (Vol. xviii., pp. 7–8.)

VII.—† "On the Press and the Public." With an illustration. (Vol. xviii., p. 59.)

"Ballads of Pleaceman X":—

"The Ballad of Eliza Davis." With an illustration. (Vol. xvii., p. 53.)

"The Lamentable Ballad of the Founding of Shoreditch." With an illustration. (Vol. xvii., p. 73.)

"Lines of a Late Hospicious Event. By a Gentleman of the Foot Guards (Blue)." (Vol. xvii., p. 189.)

"The Wofle New Ballad of Jane Roney and Mary Brown." (Vol. xvii., p. 209.)

"Damages, Two Hundred Pounds." (Vol. xviii., p. 88.)

Reprinted in "Miscellanies," vol. i. (1855), and in Collected Works.

* Reprinted in "Miscellanies," vol. ii. (1856), and in Collected Works.

† Reprinted in Collected Works, vol. xxvi. (1886).

PUNCH (*continued*)

1850. "Hobson's Choice; or, The Perplexities of a Gentleman in search of a Man-Servant." (Vol. xviii., pp. 32–3.)

Reprinted in Collected Works, vol. xxvi. (1886).

"Thoughts on a New Comedy. Being a Letter from J——s Plush to a friend." (Vol. xviii., pp. 49–50.)

Reprinted in Collected Works, vol. xxvi. (1886).

"The Sights of London." Signed "Goliah Muff." With an illustration. (Vol. xviii., p. 132.)

Reprinted in Collected Works, vol. xxvi. (1886).

"Mr. Malony's Account of the Ball." (Vol. xix., p. 53.)

Reprinted in "Miscellanies," vol. i. (1855), and in Collected Works.

"The Lion Huntress of Belgravia. Being Lady Nimrod's Journal of the Past Season." (Vol. xix., pp. 89, 90, 91.)

Reprinted in Collected Works, vol. xxvi. (1886).

1851. "Yankee Volunteers." (Vol. xx., p. 2.)

Reprinted in Collected Works.

"The Excitement in Belgravia." (Vol. xx., p. 8.)

"Why Can't they leave us alone in the Holidays?" Signed "Under Petty." With an illustration. (Vol. xx., p. 23.)

Reprinted in Collected Works, vol. xxvi. (1886).

"A Woeful Ballad of the Protestant Conspiracy to take the Pope's Life. By a Gentleman who has been on the spot." (Vol. xx., p. 113.)

"A Strange Man just discovered in Germany." With an illustration. (Vol. xx., p. 151.)

Reprinted in Collected Works, vol. xxvi. (1886).

"Mr. Malony's Account of the Crystal Palace." (Vol. xx., p. 171.)

Reprinted in "Miscellanies," vol. i. (1855), and in Collected Works.

PUNCH (*continued*)

"What I remarked at the Exhibition." (Vol. xx., p. 189.)

Reprinted in Collected Works, vol. xxvi. (1886).

"M. Gobemouche's Authentic Account of the Grand Exhibition." (Vol. xx., p. 198.)

Reprinted in Collected Works, vol. xxvi. (1886).

"The Charles the Second Ball." With an illustration. (Vol. xx., p. 221.)

Reprinted in Collected Works, vol. xxvi. (1886).

"Panorama of the Ingleez—An Inglese Family." With an illustration. (Vol. xxi., pp. 138, 147–8.)

Reprinted in Collected Works, vol. xxvi. (1886).

1852. "Poor Puggy." With an illustration. (Vol. xxi., p. 167.)

"Portraits from the Lake Exhibition." With three illustrations. (Vol. xxi., pp. 190–1.)

Reprinted in Collected Works, vol. xxvi. (1886).

1853. "The Organ Boy's Appeal." (Vol. xxv., p. 141.)

1854. "Important from the Seat of War. Letters from the East by our own Bashi-Bazouk." With seven illustrations. (Vol. xxvi., pp. 257–8, 267–8. Vol. xxvii., pp. 1–2, 11–12, 21–2, 31–2, 41.)

Reprinted in Collected Works.

"Mr. Punch to an Eminent Personage." With two illustrations. (Vol. xxvii., pp. 110–11.)

"A Second Letter to an Eminent Personage." With one illustration. (Vol. xxvii., pp. 113–14.)

The Quarterly Review

1854. "Pictures of Life and Character. By John Leech." (Vol. xcvi., pp. 75—86.)

Reprinted in "Early and Late Papers" (1867), and in Collected Works.

The Snob

1829. (?) "Our Snob's Birth, Parentage, and Education" (*April* 23).

Reprinted in "Sultan Stork" (1887).

THE SNOB (*continued*)

"Extract from a Letter from one in Cambridge to one in town." Signed "T. T." (*April* 23).

Reprinted in "The Early Writings of W. M. Thackeray" (1888).

"Timbuctoo" (*April* 30).

Reprinted in "The Early Writings of W. M. Thackeray" (1888), and in Collected Works, vol. xxv. (1885).

"To Guinevere." Signed "A Literary Snob" (*May* 14).

Reprinted in "The Early Writings of W. M. Thackeray" (1888).

"Mr. Ramsbottom in Cambridge" (*May* 21).

Reprinted in "Sultan Stork" (1887).

"A Statement of Fax relative to the Late Murder. By D. J. Ramsbottom" (*June* 4).

Reprinted in "Sultan Stork" (1887).

(?) "To the Free and Independent Snobs of Cambridge" (*June* 11).

(?) "The End of all Things" (*June* 18).

The Times

1837. Review of "Carlyle's French Revolution" (*August* 3).

Reprinted in "Sultan Stork" (1887), and in the Biographical Edition of the Collected Works (1899).

1838. Review of "The Duchess of Marlborough's Private Correspondence" (*January* 6).

Review of "Eros and Anteros, or, Love. By Lady Charlotte Bury. A Diary relative to George IV. and Queen Caroline" (*January* 11).

Review of "The Memoirs of Holt, the Irish Rebel" (*January* 31).

Review of "The Poetical Works of Dr. Southey" (*April* 17).

1840. Review of "Henry Fielding's Works" (*September* 2).

1851. "May Day Ode" (*April* 30).

Reprinted in "Miscellanies," vol. i. (1885), and in Collected Works.

THE TIMES (*continued*)

1853. "Mr. Washington. A Letter to the Editor" (*November* 23).

1863. "Cruikshank's Gallery" (*May* 15).

The Victoria Regia

1861. "A Leaf out of a Sketch-Book." With two illustrations. (Pages 118–25.)

Reprinted in "Early and Late Papers" (1867), and in Collected Works, vol. xxv. (1885).

The Westminster Review

1840. "The Humourist. A Collection of Entertaining Tales, Anecdotes, Epigrams, Bon-mots, etc." J. Robins & Co., London, 1819, etc. Signed "Θ." (Vol. 34, pp. 1—60.)

Reissued in book-form under the title of "The Genius of George Cruikshank" (1840).

PART III

MISCELLANEA

"Men of Character. By Douglas Jerrold." In three volumes. London: Henry Colburn, 1838. Twelve illustrations by Thackeray.

"Sketches. By Spec. No. 1.—Britannia protecting the Drama." H. Cunningham, 1840.

Privately reprinted for Mr. Charles Plumtree Johnson, by the Autotype Company (1885).

"Heads of the People. Drawn by Kenny Meadows. With Original Essays by Distinguished Writers." London: Robert Tyas.

1840. "Captain Rook and Mr. Pigeon. By William Thackeray." (Pages 305–20.)

Reprinted from *The Corsair.*

1841. "The Fashionable Authoress. By William Thackeray." (Pages 73—84.)

"The Artist. By Michael Angelo Titmarsh." (Pages 161–74.)

Reprinted as "Character Sketches," in "Miscellanies," vol. ii. (1856), and in Collected Works.

"Sand and Canvas; a Narrative of Adventures in Egypt, with a Sojourn among the Artists in Rome. By Samuel Bevan." London: Charles Gilpin, 1849.

"The Three Sailors (with Reminiscences of Michael Angelo Titmarsh at Rome)."

Facsimile in The Autographic Mirror (vol. ii., p. 60), Reprinted in Collected Works as "Little Billie."

"Life and Works of Goethe. By G. H. Lewes." London: David Nutt, 1855.

"Reminiscences of Weimar and Goethe. A Letter to Mr. Lewes from Thackeray."

Dated: London, 28th April, 1855. (Vol. ii., pp. 442–6.)

Reprinted in Collected Works, vol. xxv. (1885).

"Address to the Electors of Oxford." Dated: The Mitre, 9th July, 1857. Signed: W. M. Thackeray.

"The Princess Alexandra Gift-Book," 1868. The Anglers. By the late W. M. Thackeray" (pp. 22–3).

PART IV

VOLUMES CONTAINING LETTERS OR BIOGRAPHICAL INFORMATION

Sir Walter Besant: "Fifty Years Ago."
Dr. John Brown: "Horæ Subsecivæ."
Dr. John Brown: "Thackeray, his literary career."
Elizabeth Barrett Browning: "Letters."
Robert Browning: "Life and Letters."

Jane Carlyle: "Letters and Memorials."
Sir Henry Cole: "Fifty Years of Public Life."
Sara Coleridge: "Letters."
S. D. Collingwood: "Life of Lewis Carroll."
G. and E. Compton: "Memoir of Henry Compton."
C. A. Cooper: "An Editor's Retrospect."
Sidney Cornish: "Short Notes of the Parish of Ottery St. Mary, Devon."
Eyre Crowe: "With Thackeray in America."
Sir Joseph Crowe: "Reminiscences."

Charles Dickens: "Letters."
Sir E. M. Grant Duff: "Notes from a Diary, 1851—1872."
Sir E. M. Grant Duff: "Notes from a Diary, 1873—1881."
Sir C. Gavan Duffy: "Conversations with Carlyle."

Maria Edgeworth: "Life and Letters."
T. H. S. Escott: "Platform, Press, and Politics."
J. T. Fields: "Biographical Notes."
J. T. Fields: "Yesterdays with Authors."
Edward Fitzgerald: "Letters."
Edward Fitzgerald: "Letters to Fanny Kemble."

W. Fitzpatrick: "Life of Charles Lever."
John Francis and the *Athenæum*.
W. P. Frith: "Reminiscences."

Mrs. Gaskell: "The Life and Letters of Charlotte Brontë."
[Joseph Grego]: "Thackerayana."
Henry Greville: "Memoirs."

T. G. Hake; "Memories of Eighty Years."
J. Hannay: "A Brief Memoir of Mr. Thackeray."
J. Hannay: "Characters and Criticisms."
A. Hayward: "Correspondence."
G. Hodder: "Memories of My Time."
Dean Hole: "Memories."
J. Hollingshead: "My Lifetime."

J. L. Jeaffreson: "Book of Recollections."
B. Jerrold: "The Best of all Good Company."
B. Jerrold: "Life of George Cruikshank."
C. P. Johnson: "The Early Writings of W. M. Thackeray."
C. P. Johnson: "Hints to Collectors of Original Editions of the Works of W. M. Thackeray."

Fanny Kemble: "Records of Later Life."
Fanny Kemble: "Further Records."
Charles Knight: "Passages from a Working Life."

G. S. Layard: "Life and Letters of Charles Keene."
J. K. Laughton: "Life of Henry Reeve."
A. G. L'Estrange: "Life of M. R. Mitford."
F. Locker-Lampson: "My Confidences."
W. H. Longfellow: "Life and Letters."
Lord Lytton: "The Life of Lord Lytton."

C. Mackay: "Forty Years Recollections of Life, Literature, and Public Affairs."
J. Macready: "Reminiscences."
F. G. Marks: "Life and Letters of Frederick Walker."
Sir Theodore Martin: "Memoir of W. S. Aytoun."

Charles Matthews: "Life."
Harriet Martineau: "Autobiography."
J. F. Maurice, "Life of F. D. Maurice."
Athol Mayhew: "A Jorum of *Punch*."
Hermann Merivale and Frank Marzials: "Thackeray."
M. R. Mitford: "Recollections of a Literary Life."
J. F. Molloy: "The Most Gorgeous Lady Blessington."
J. L. Motley: "Correspondence."
F. Max Müller: "Literary Recollections."

Macvey Napier: "Selections from his Correspondence."

Mrs. Oliphant: "William Blackwood and His Sons."
J. R. Planché: "Memoirs."
James Payn: "Some Literary Recollections."
A. Peddie: "Recollections of Dr. John Brown."
T. E. Pemberton: "Memoirs of E. A. Sothern."
Sir F. Pollock: "Personal Remembrances."

A. T. Ritchie: "Chapters from Some Unwritten Memoirs."
W. B. Reed: "Haud Immemor."
Sir T. W. Reed: "The Life of Lord Houghton."
W. H. Riding: "Thackeray's London."

G. A. Sala: "His Life and Opinions."
R. H. Shepherd: "Memoir of Thomas Carlyle."
Clement Shorter: "Charlotte Brontë and Her Circle."
Archdeacon Sinclair: "Sketches of old Times and Distant Places."
John Skelton: "Table Talk."
M. H. Spielmann: "History of *Punch*."
Leslie Stephen: "The Life of Sir J. FitzJames Stephen."
R. H. Stoddard: "Anecdote Biographies."

H. Taine: "Notes on England."
Sir H. Taylor: "Letters."
Theodore Taylor: "Thackeray, the Man of Letters and the Humourist."

Hallam, Lord Tennyson: "The Life of Alfred, Lord Tennyson."

G. W. Thornbury: "The Life of J. M. W. Turner."

Sir O. G. Trevelyan: "The Life of Lord Macaulay."

Anthony Trollope: "Thackeray."

T. A. Trollope: "What I remember."

Martin Tupper: "My Life as an Author."

H. Vizetelly: "Looking Back through Seventy Years."

H. Waddington: "Life of Clough."

Lester Wallack: "Memories."

W. G. Wills: "Life and Letters."

H. Wilmot & E. Streatfield: "Charterhouse, old and new."

E. Yates: "Mr. Thackeray, Mr. Yates, and the Garrick Club."

E. Yates: "His Recollections and Experiences."

Biographical Magazine Articles, etc.

J. F. Boyes: "The Schooldays of Thackeray" (*Cornhill*, 1865).

G. S. Davis: "Thackeray at Charterhouse" (*Greyfriars*, 1892, No. 4).

D. D.: "Some Few Thackerayana" (*National Review*, 1889).

John Irvine: "A Study for Colonel Newcome" (*Nineteenth Century* [Oct.], 1893).

Raymond Blathwayt: "Work and Play at Charterhouse" (*Cassell's* [Aug.], 1893).

Russell Sturgis: "Thackeray as a draughtsman" (*Scribner's*, 1880).

Dutton Cook: "Thackeray and the theatre" (*Longmans*, 1884).

Mrs. Ritchie: "The First Number of the *Cornhill*" (*Cornhill* [July], 1896).

Dr. Merriman: Thackeray (*St. Mary Abbotts Parish Magazine* [Sept.], 1889).

R. Bedingfield: "Recollections of Thackeray" (*Cassell's*, 1870—1871).

J. E. Cooke: "A History of Thackeray" (*Appleton*, 1879).

F. St. John Thackeray: "Reminiscences of William Makepeace Thackeray" (*Temple Bar*, 1893).

Henrietta Cockran: (*Temple Bar*, 1887).

H. Merivale: "About two Great Novelists" (*Temple Bar*, 1888).

Bayard Taylor: "William Makepeace Thackeray" (*Atlantic Monthly*, 1864).

C. P. Johnson: "The Works of William Makepiece Thackeray contemplated or commenced, but not completed" (Walford's *Antiquarian*, vol. 8).

W. H. Pollock: "William Makepeace Thackeray" (*Encyclopædia Britannica*).

R. T. Ritchie: "William Makepeace Thackeray" (*Chamber's Encyclopædia*).

Leslie Stephen: "William Makepeace Thackeray" (*Dictionary of National Biography*).

Leslie Stephen: "The Writings of William Makepeace Thackeray" (*Collected Works*, Vol. xxiv.).

PRINTED BY R. R. DONNELLEY
AND SONS COMPANY AT THE
LAKESIDE PRESS, CHICAGO, ILL.